The Panther Project Vol.2
Engine and Turret

By **THE RESEARCH SQUAD**

LEE LLOYD
BRIAN BALKWILL
ALASDAIR JOHNSTON

THE RESEARCH SQUAD

The Panther Project Vol. 2
Engine and Turret

Text and Layout:
Lee Lloyd
Editing:
Lee Lloyd, Brian Balkwill & Alasdair Johnston
Logistics and Multimedia:
Brian Balkwill
Photography:
Brian Balkwill, Alasdair Johnston & Lee Lloyd
Translations:
Liejon Schoot

Acknowledgments:

- The authors express their deepest thanks to Kevin Wheatcroft and his staff for their complete and unreserved access granted to us for the production of this book.
- Special thanks are given to Brian Rutter, senior engineer at The Wheatcroft Collection, who was an amazing source of information on all things technical and historical.

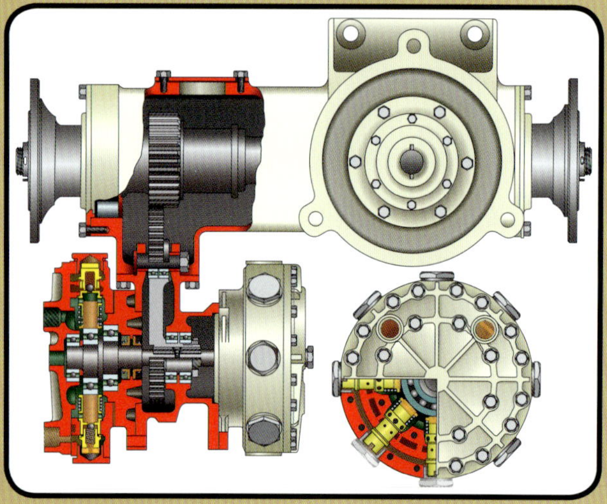

ISBN 978-0-9935646-4-2

Further information regarding THE RESEARCH SQUAD can be found at:

www.wheatcroftcollection.com
www.theresearchsquad.com

The Wheatcroft Collection would like to thank and acknowledge those people and companies who have provided both technical information and manufacturing facilities used throughout this restoration project:

William Cook Defence (now Astrum)
Mr. Nathan Johnson - Engine Mountings, Armour Plate and Heavy Engineering

Lahoma Engineers Ltd
Mr. John Sismey - Cranks and Main Bearings
Manning Road Industrial Estate

Cross & Sansam Ltd
Mr. David Sansom - Pattern Equipment, Small Machining and Castings

Crosthwaite & Gardiner Ltd
Mr. Oliver Crosthwaite - Carburettor Parts
Hogge Farm

Heritage Motor Works Ltd
Mr. Terry Roberts - Internal Fittings

THE RESEARCH SQUAD invites interested parties to get in touch with respect to information available for publication that relates to The Wheatcroft Collection. Full credit will be given for all materials used.

AFV modeller publications

AFV Modeller Limited,
Old Stables, East Moor, Stannington,
Morpeth, Northumberland, NE61 6ES

www.mengafvmodeller.com

Pz.Kpfw V Ausf.A
(Fgst.Nr. 158134)

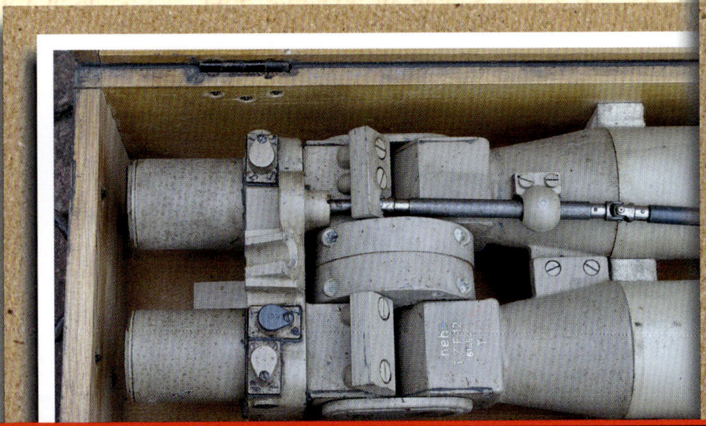

Introduction

by Brian Balkwill

During a recent discussion with Brian and Alan Rutter, the collections restorers, we were all stunned to realised that the work on the Panther had been in progress for nearly seventeen years. While there have been periods of downtime on the project, the main reason is the ethos at the collection: It does not matter how long it takes, as long as it's done right.

This ethos drives the entire process from the minute the vehicle first arrives. Every single component is stripped – down to the last nut and bolt, and evaluated as to whether it can be restored back to original working condition. Where it cannot be used an availability hierarchy comes into play: first prize will be an 'as new' unused wartime spare, second will be a useable item from a different vehicle, or used stock, and a last resort is to manufacture a new item from scratch. On some occasions, none of these options are available, as there is no template from which to even manufacture a missing item – in this case the collection has often waited years for such items to be discovered and acquired.

It was while thinking about this that I remembered Theseus's paradox - a thought experiment that raises the question of whether an object that has had all of its components replaced remains fundamentally the same object. (The paradox is most notably recorded by Plutarch in Life of Theseus from the late first century. Plutarch asked whether a ship – the Theseus - that had been restored by replacing every single wooden part remained the same ship.)

When looking at a project such as the Panther where do you draw the philosophical line as to when it is no longer the original vehicle? The day it leaves the factory, after its first repairs in the field, its first or second new turret after combat damage? And does this affect decisions on what to restore/replace on the vehicle?

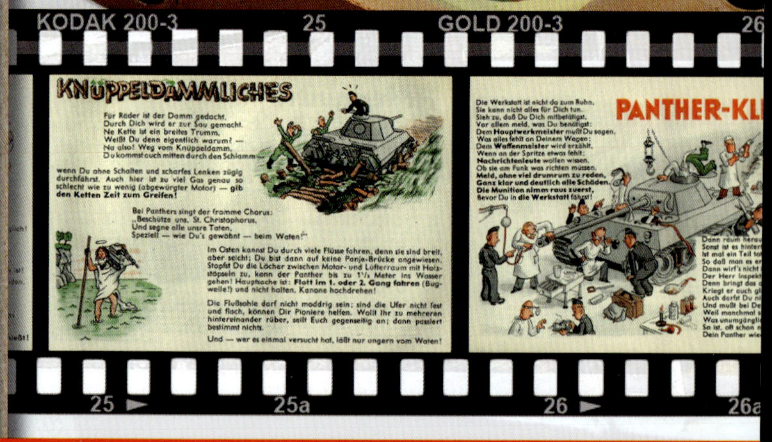

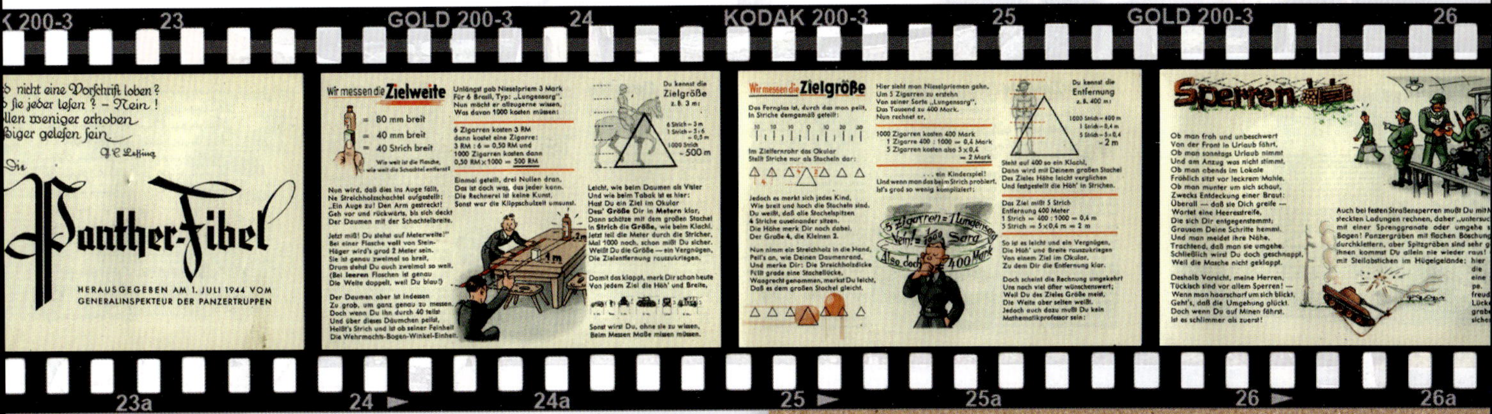

Considering this, as the finished vehicle has to be in perfect running order, this also means that some critical components are better replaced from the outset (torsion bars, track links, perishable pipes and gaskets etc.). As there is no way of knowing what wear and abuse such items have been through, taking a chance they will hold up after restoration makes no sense. A good example of this are the engine valves – having one of these fail and cause catastrophic damage in one of the few running Maybach HL230 P30 left in the world is not worth the risk.

Again, this takes us back to the paradox above – is replacing seventy year old valves diluting the 'originality' of the vehicle? Both ourselves and collection agree that it does not – had the vehicle been in constant service for the last seventy years, virtually every component would have been replaced multiple times from spares, scavenged parts, or newly manufactured - in much the same way as the collection is carrying out the restoration.

What is beyond doubt is that every effort has been made to use as much original content as possible, so as to restore to the same condition this Panther as it was the day it originally left the factory.

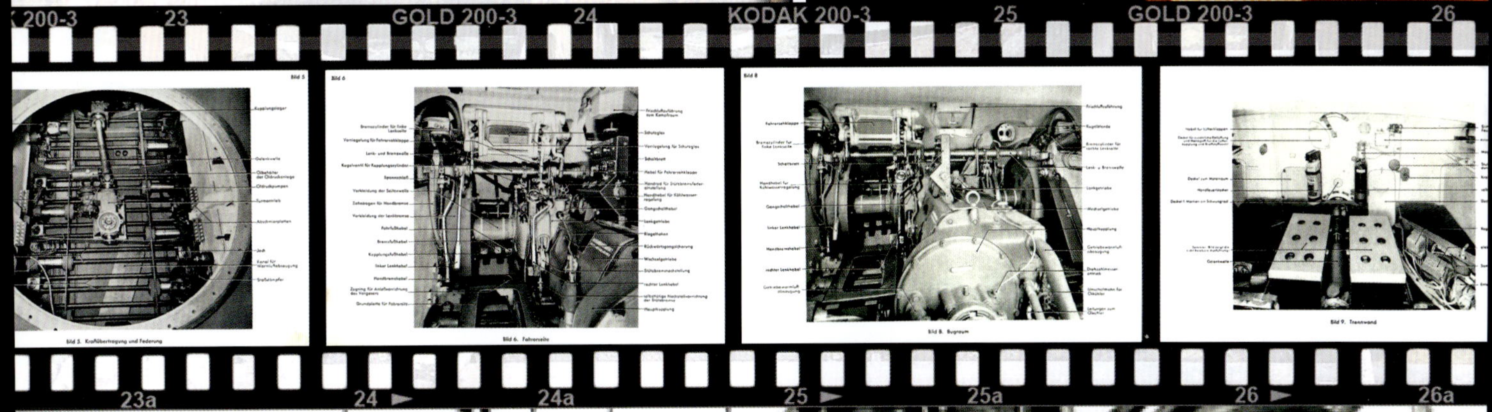

Panther Fgst.Nr. 158134: A Further History

In November 1943 **Panzerkampfwagen V Panther Ausf. A Fgst.Nr. 158134** rolled off the production line of the **DEMAG** facilities at Berlin-Falkensee. As such, it was one of only fifty such units that **DEMAG** manufactured before they switched to production of Bergepanther vehicles. Of these fifty, the bulk were sent to the Eastern front (courtesy of Martin Block [1]), with the remaining few being sent to Italy and France. The Wheatcroft Panther was one of latter.

Location

In our first volume we had minimal information as to the history of the vehicle prior to the purchase in France. This situation has changed substantially after two images came to light in 2011 in the photo timeline of Vincent Leclerc [2]. The images were taken by Vincent's grandfather and scanned from an album belonging to his aunt, photo **A** & **B**. When researchers Alexis Boban, Patrick Peccatte and Fred Blais came across them during a project, they conducted interviews and established that they were dated as being taken **9th March 1945**, on the Chemin du Vieux-Moulin in an area of the town of Briouze known as Le Val de Breuil. A third image similar to the first was also uncovered, page **9**, photo **C**, and several of the women posing in the image were found to be resident in Briouze. At this point the information from witnesses stipulated that the vehicle was disabled during bombings of **16-17th**

A

© Vincent Leclerc

August 1944 whilst parked in an orchard off Chemin de Vieux du Moulin. We know all three images are of the same tank, and in the same location, given the angle and distance of the tank off the road, the rotated turret angle, the angle of the barrel, and the removed engine deck cover appearing in the same position in the second and third images. What was very unusual in the rear-view image, was what looked like a snorkel cover on the rear engine deck, thought to have been phased out some time before this tank was produced.

B

© Vincent Leclerc

However it was not until 2013 that Kent Wiik [3] was able to match damage to the front glacis zimmerit, seen in the first of Vincents images, to underlying scarring on the glacis plate visible in an image of the tank at the collection prior to any restoration work being commenced. It was at that this point we now knew we had both matching wartime images and a wartime physical location of the Wheatcroft panther.

However there are several anomalies that have since come to light that may cast doubt on both the exact location within Briouze, and the date and location of the Panther's demise.

Panther Fgst.Nr. 158134: A Further History

Anomalies - Briouze

The first inconsistency is that the rear-view image of the tank shows it is positioned near a metalled road. In photo **D**, taken in 1948, we see an image of Chemin du Vieux-Moulin. This road was not metalled in 1944 and indeed only became so in the 1960's. Second, if we then posit that the images were taken on the main Argentan road, there is no position in that stretch where the details behind the tank (no trees or buildings) correlate with the two side images nor the details in the distance of the rear-view image. However there is a small hamlet just outside western Briouze named Le Val *du* Breuil, on a road which **was** metalled in 1944, where the surrounding flora and lack of features behind the tank do tend to match the images we observe, see **1**, page **10**, photo **E**.

We are still conducting further research by reaching out to locals and historians to see if we can confirm our suppositions.

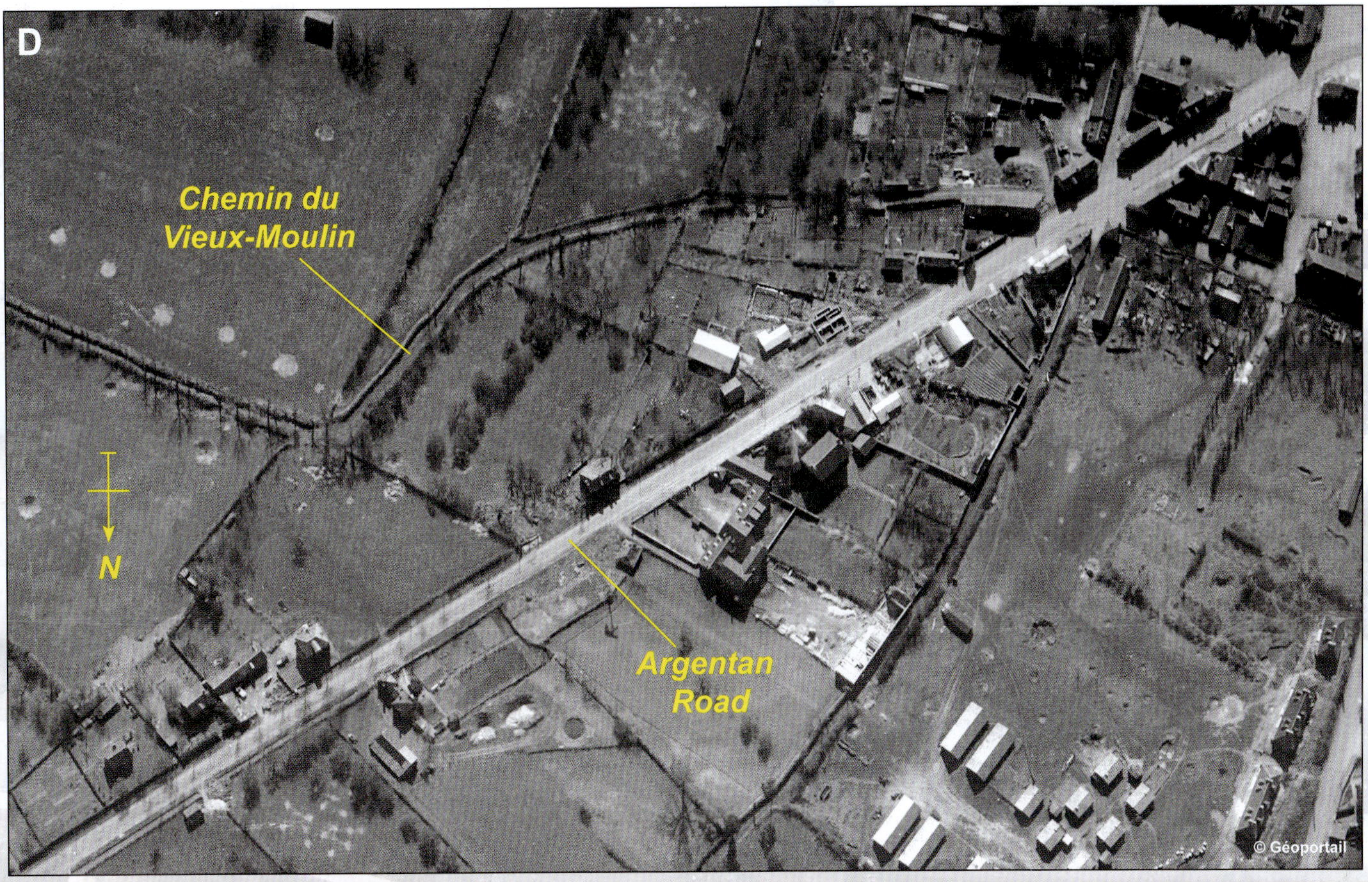

Panther Fgst.Nr. 158134: A Further History

The Library of Congress image

In 2015 we were shown a new image of the vehicle which had been emailed to the collection by Roddy MacDougall [4]. This was clearly identifiable as the same vehicle (unique logo on turret, identical damage to stowage bin, snorkel cover on rear deck etc.), but was now shown in a completely different location. Very significantly, on the rear of the image, were markings added by the US Army censor stating this image had been released for publication in October 1944, photo **F**. We immediately got in touch with Darren Neely [5] who had found the image at the Library of Congress. He told us that the image was located in General Patton's papers in a folder named **1944-France/Falaise Pocket**, which appeared to be a set of random images that had been collated by an adjutant.

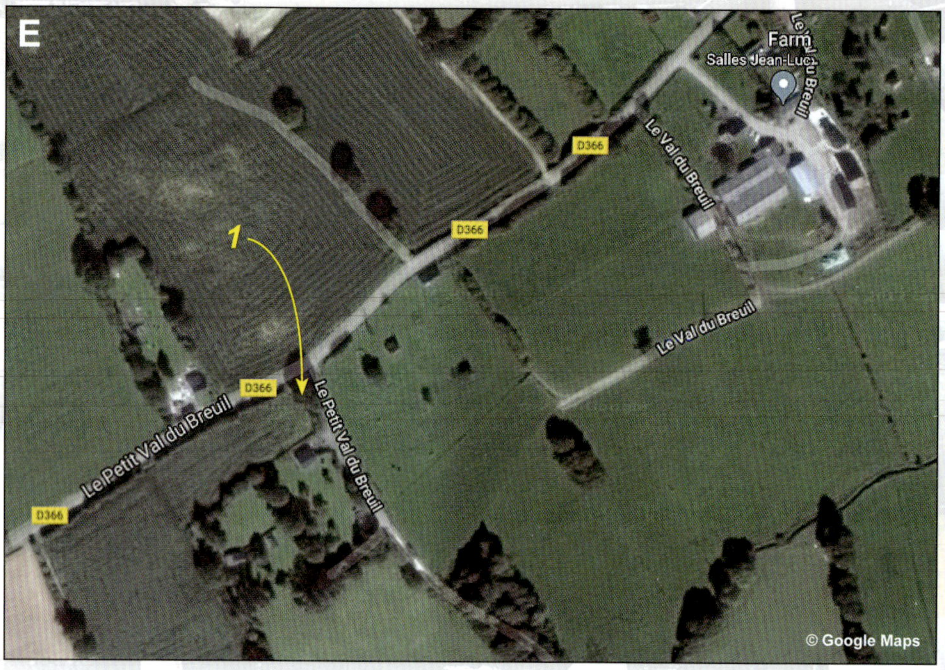

What is clear from the topography in the image is that this was not Briouze (confirmed by Alexis Boban and Fred Blais, the latter whom was a resident of Briouze [6]). The majority of Briouze sits on a slight plateau above the surrounding plains, and there is only a 3m variation in altitude across the entire plateau. Also the location is clearly under Allied control, as seen by the US Jeep. This means that this image shows the possible location of where the tank was first disabled, prior to a move to the second location in Briouze. This move could only have been done either by Allied engineers or locals. This would also suggest that the Panther was not knocked out by Allied bombing on **16-17th August** at Briouze. At this point Darren suggested we get in touch with author and historian Frédéric Deprun, an expert on the 2nd Panzer Division, as the Panther had become a strong contender now for belonging to this unit.

Unit ID

I contacted Frédéric Deprun and we started sharing information [7]. Frédéric has been conducting research and interviews for two upcoming volumes on the 2nd PD in Normandy, and during the course of this, was able to identify the vehicle unit and some of its history as related to him. He was also able to confirm that companies within **Panzer Regiment 3** were known for having personalised turret emblems, which made them fairly unique in this respect.

"The I02 turret number is a Stab vehicle of the **I. Abt. of Pz.Rgt. 3** [8]. It was renumbered 231 and assigned to **2.Kompanie** (**2.PzD.**) before the Mortain battle. The reason behind the white number is certainly due to the connection with the **I./Pz.Rgt. 24** (Major Meyer, 116.PzD.). During Operation Lüttich near Mortain, just before the attack on Mesnil-Adelée on the **7th August 1944**, one Kampfgruppe was created (KG Meyer merged into KG Schake) using 20 Panther tanks from **116.PzD.** (white numbers on turret sides) and was attached to **2.PzD**. The Panther was probably donated temporarily to Major Kuno Meyer where this Pz.Bef.Wg. Panther likely commanded one of the three Panther-zug during the attack."

From Paul Hocking and Martin Block [9] came the following:

*In theory the Panther turret numbers of the **Stabskp. I./Pz.Rgt. 3** and the **2.Kp.** should have been:*

I01,	I02,	I03			(Nachrichtenzug)
I04,	I05,	I06,	I07,	I08	(Aufklärungszug)
200,	201				(Kompanietrupp)
211,	212,	213,	214,	215	(1. Zug)
221,	222,	223,	224,	225	(2. Zug)
231,	232,	233,	234,	235	(3. Zug)

Panther Fgst.Nr. 158134: A Further History

"At the time of the Allied landings in Normandy the **I./Pz.Rgt. 3** [10] was commanded by Major von Lehsten. The Abteilungs-Adjutant was Hauptmann Graf Spannocchi and the Abteilungs-Ordonanz-Offizier was Leutnant von Oppel. The commander of the **2. Kompanie** was Hauptmann Kleine. On **1st June 1944** the **Stabskp. I./Pz.Rgt. 3** was listed having 3 only Pz.Bef.Wg. V left, i.e. all 5 Pz. V of the Aufkl.Zug had disappeared. Possibly the platoon had been disbanded and split up between the other 4 companies. The **2.Kp.** had 13 tanks left. Unfortunately the organisational history of the unit for the **1st August 1944** does not survive."

Personnel

It was information on personnel that Frédéric obtained from interviews with veterans which gave us a whole new line of enquiry. He had discovered that the tank was assigned to either Leutnant Strobl or Leutnant Spannocchi after the death of Hauptmann Kleine. In addition, he had several times been told of an Oberleutnant nicknamed **'Der Schreiber' (The Writer)**, which would tie in with the personalised Inkpot and Quill emblem found on the vehicle.

When researching the Spannocchi family we found that Emil Graf Spannocchi had been assigned to **2.PzD**, and quite fortuitously, discovered he had a surviving nephew living at the family home in Austria. When we contacted Dr. Hieronymus Spannocchi it transpired it was his father Lelio (brother to Emil) we should have been looking at [11]. We can see from his documents, **G**, **H** & **I**, that Lelio was Oberleutnant and Regimentsadjutant of **Panzerregiment 3** throughout the battle of Normandy and the Ardennes Offensive.

Of most importance to our research however was an anecdote Dr. Spannocchi related to us. Lelio was unusual in that he wrote a letter to his wife every day of his service, and Dr. Spannocchi is certain therefore that the nickname **'Der Schreiber'** was given to his father by his troops, and is the reason for the emblem on the turret.

G

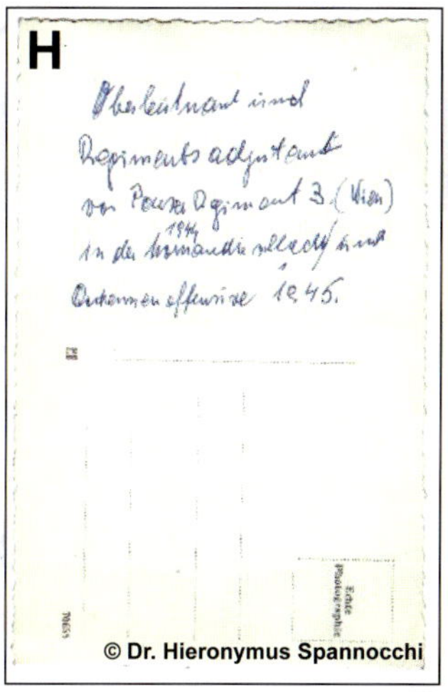
H

Oberleutnant und
Regimentsadjutant
von Panzer Regiment 3 (Wien)
1944
in der Normandie schlacht und
Ardennenoffensive 1945.

Conclusion

At time of print we are working on the premise that the vehicle was originally assigned to **Panzer Regiment 3**, later seconded to take part in Operation Lüttich, and was commanded for part or all of this period by Oberleutnant Lelio Spannocchi. From that point we have no further information on its movements until it shows up disabled in the Patton image, and again disabled in the images from Briouze. A working theory as to how/why it moved between the two locations came from Frédéric. He suggested this was the result of a civil tow to move the vehicle to a scrapyard either at Argentan or Saint-Lambert.

We are still hoping to find more information on all of the above, and have offered a small reward to anyone who can identify the location of the Patton Image.

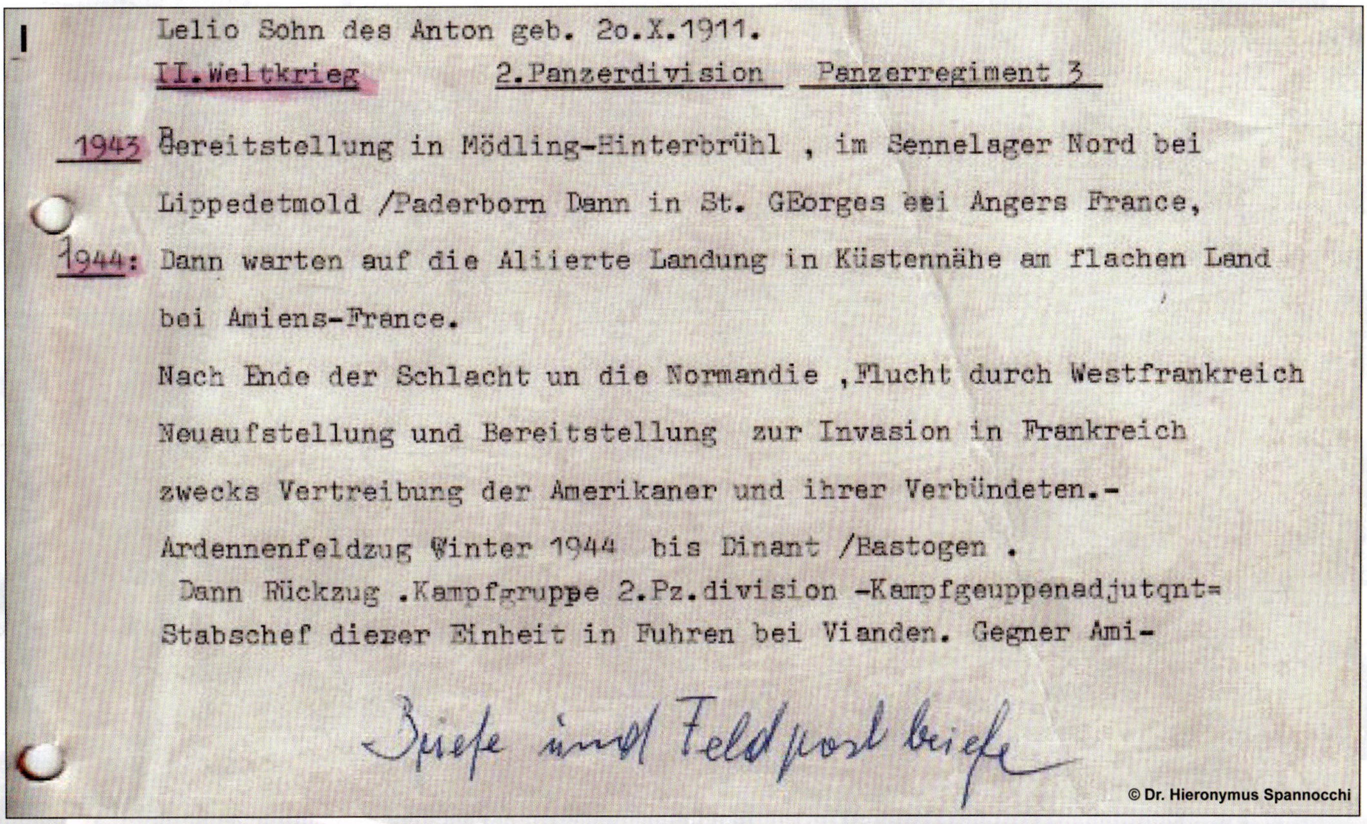
I

Lelio Sohn des Anton geb. 2o.X.1911.
II.Weltkrieg 2.Panzerdivision Panzerregiment 3

1943 Bereitstellung in Mödling-Hinterbrühl , im Sennelager Nord bei
Lippedetmold /Paderborn Dann in St. GEorges bei Angers France,
1944: Dann warten auf die Aliierte Landung in Küstennähe am flachen Land
bei Amiens-France.
Nach Ende der Schlacht un die Normandie ,Flucht durch Westfrankreich
Neuaufstellung und Bereitstellung zur Invasion in Frankreich
zwecks Vertreibung der Amerikaner und ihrer Verbündeten.-
Ardennenfeldzug Winter 1944 bis Dinant /Bastogen .
Dann Rückzug .Kampfgruppe 2.Pz.division -Kampfgeuppenadjutqnt=
Stabschef dieser Einheit in Fuhren bei Vianden. Gegner Ami-

Briefe und Feldpost briefe

Pre-Restoration - Arrival

As is often the case on a long running project, such as the restoration of this Panther, information is received at infrequent or at unexpected times. Literally about three weeks before we were due to go to print with this current volume we were given a number of paper copies of a few images, some of which are seen on page **12** of this book, of the Panther where those photographs were taken right at the time **The Wheatcroft Collection** received the tank. We were also told that there was an accompanying CD on which there were a lot more photographs to be seen!

Desiring to see those new photographs, because we knew there would be a wealth of original details to be uncovered, **Mrs. Alex Wheatcroft** searched **The Wheatcroft Collection** archive for that information. Alex then presented to us a CD with a large number of images that had been taken just as the vehicle was undergoing the initial strip down. Three pages of the best of those images are presented here. Some very interesting details were to be seen, not least of which was original zimmerit still on the lower hull sides, a complete engine and gearbox and even some remaining electrical wiring.

Pre-Restoration - Arrival

Over the years, as we have visited Kevin Wheatcroft's restoration facilities to document the latest work completed on vehicles being worked on or to record a new acquisition to the collection, we have been lucky enough at times to be able to photograph a number of items that are in the pre-restoration stage. By that we mean those items of equipment that may be in a state of extreme disrepair that with a lot of love and attention can be restored to their former glory of a working component within a military vehicle.

Of prime interest to us has been the restoration of the engine of this particular Panther, a **Maybach HL 230 P30**, that was actually in the Panther when acquired by Kevin (see The Panther Project: Volume One page **80**) [12]). Oft times we only get to see elements being restored once the restoration is actually under way so the photographs presented here represent a few of the times we were actually able to capture images prior to any such work being commenced. Of course, with respect to the engine, we have been able to comprehensively document the restoration progress that has taken place due to the length of time needed to perform such work. As such a major aspect of this book has been to record the work undertaken on the engine over the past few years.

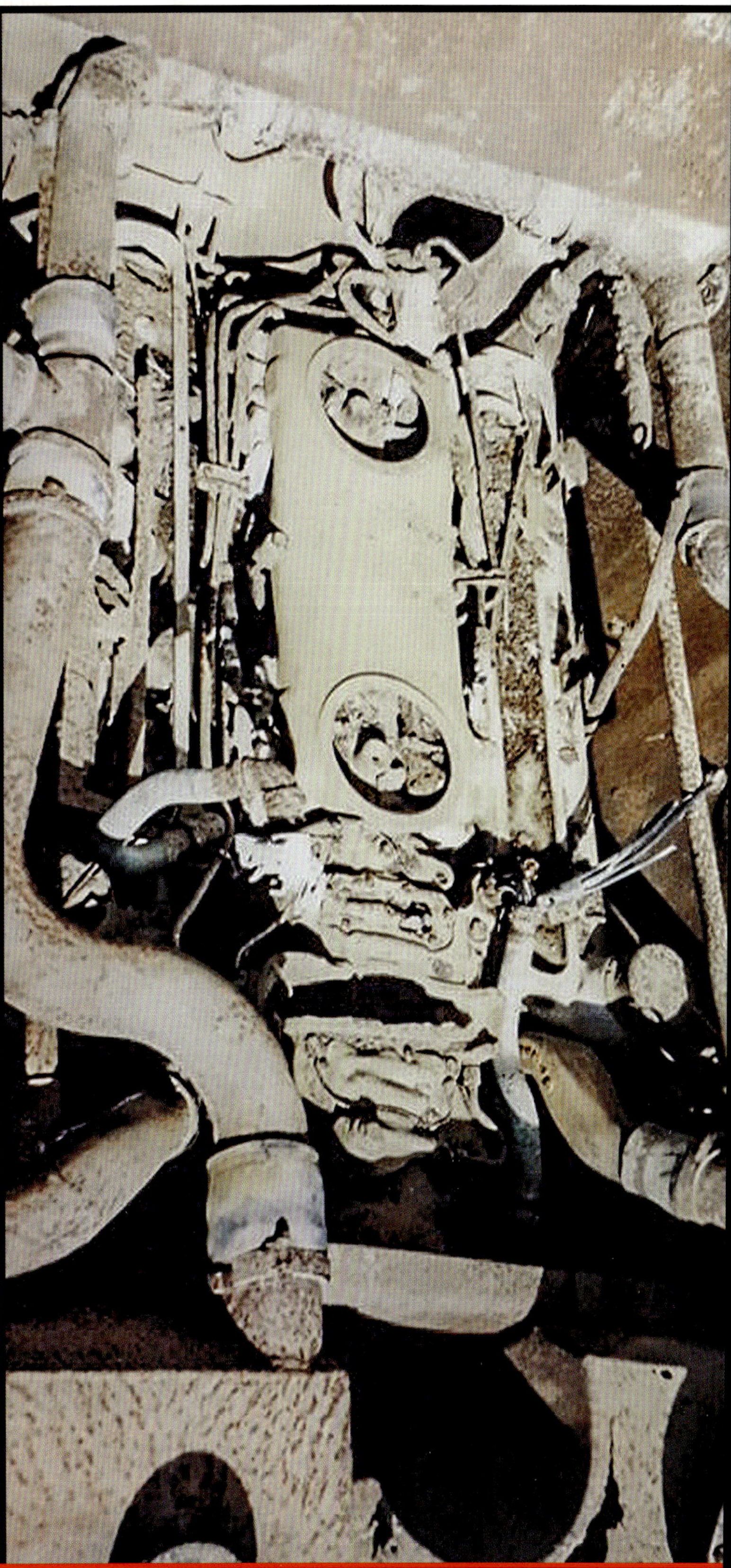

A look along the top of the LHS of an engine after the removal of the cylinder heads.

The underside of a LHS cylinder head. There is considerable corrosion to be seen.

Details of the rocker arms and rollers

A look down on the rocker arms and the valve gear.

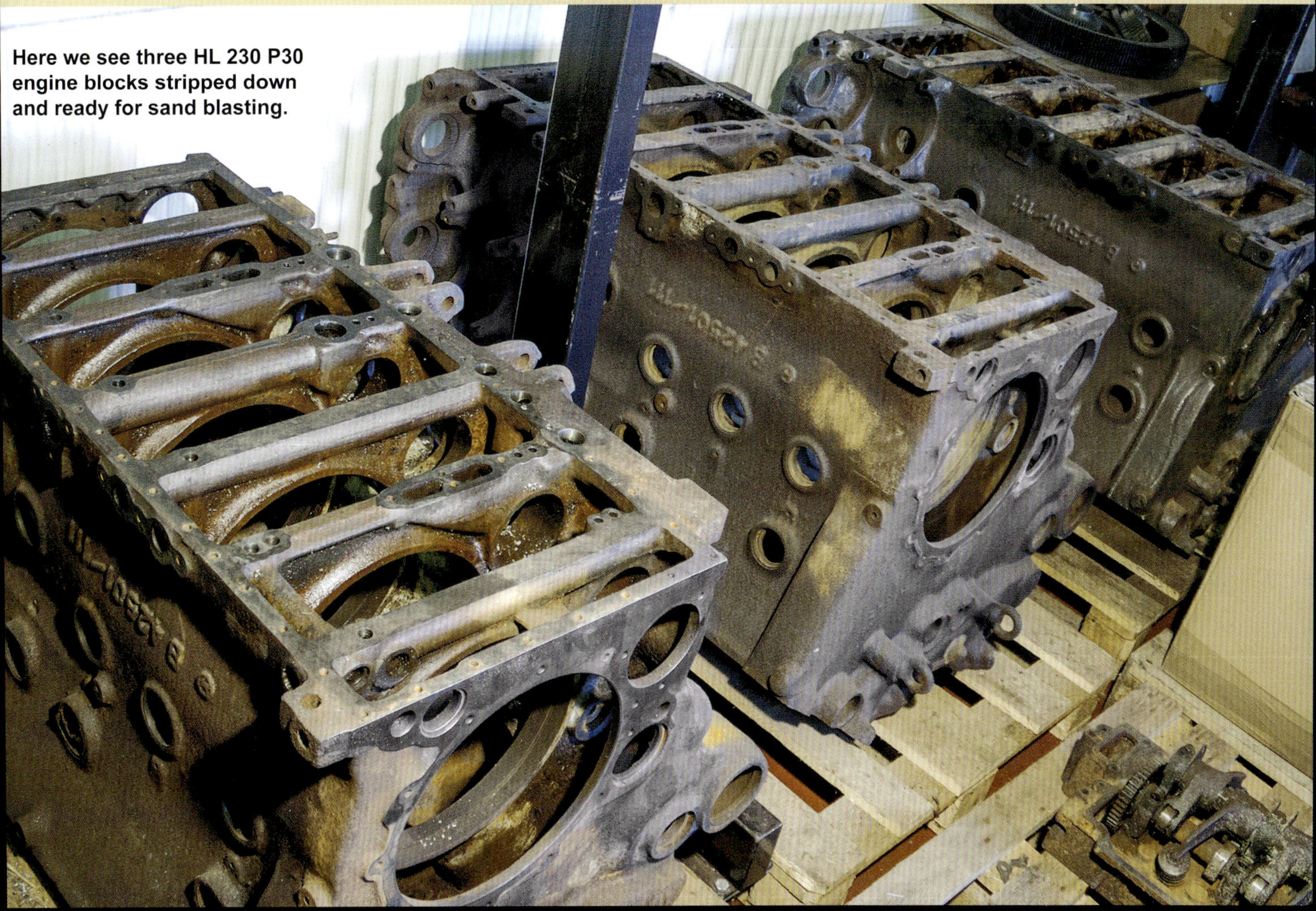

Here we see three HL 230 P30 engine blocks stripped down and ready for sand blasting.

The interior of each of the engine blocks are in remarkably good condition with no damage and only minor surface corrosion.

Pre-Restoration - Engines

A look down into a pair of Solex JFF carburettors.

By having the majority of the carburettor linkages still in place means the restoration process will be a lot simpler.

The oil cooler showing considerable corrosion damage.

The damaged oil cooler showing the oil pipe matrix.

The oil filter and a variety of the original piping still remains.

A look at the LHS cylinder bank after removal of the cylinder head.

The two original upper sponson fuel tanks.

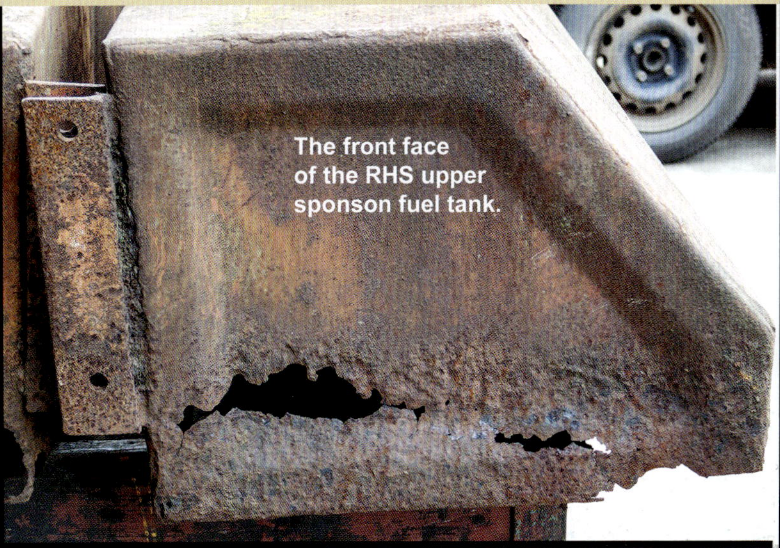

The front face of the RHS upper sponson fuel tank.

The front face of the LHS upper sponson fuel tank.

A close-up view of the corrosion that had damaged both fuel tanks.

Pre-Restoration - Fuel Tanks

A view of the fuel tanks looking at the rear sides.

The rear side of the RHS fuel tank.

The damage on the side of the RHS fuel tank was caused by a projectile entering the rear plate and then exiting the upper RHS hull.

The fuel tank pipe unions that connect to the lower hull fuel tanks.

The pipe union on the RHS fuel tank that connects to the fuel fille

The front section of the Zahnradfabrik Friedrichshafen AK 7-200 gearbox.

The rear section of the Zahnradfabrik Friedrichshafen AK 7-200 gearbox.

Pre-Restoration - Hull Crew Hatches

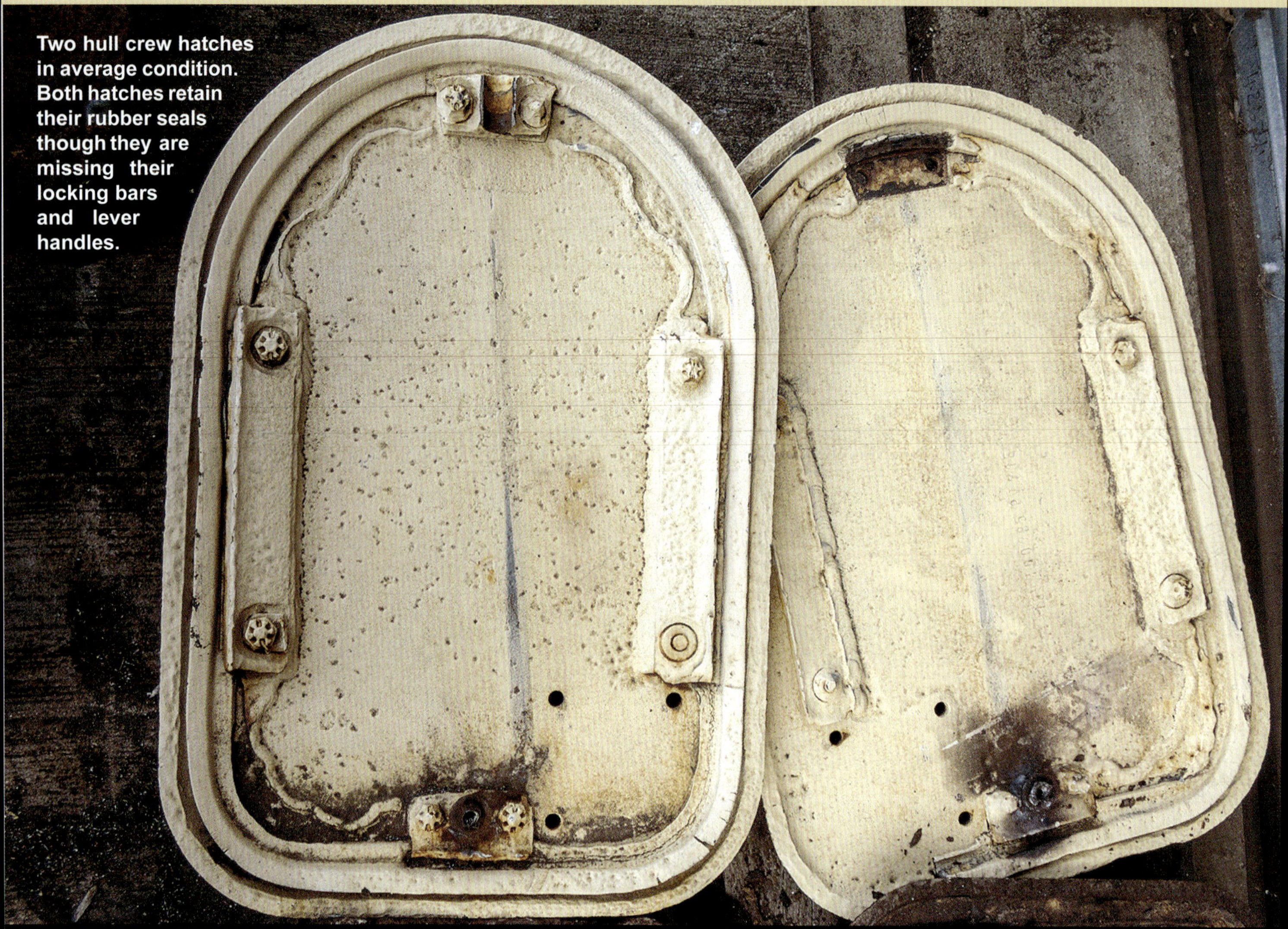

Two hull crew hatches in average condition. Both hatches retain their rubber seals though they are missing their locking bars and lever handles.

These two hull crew hatches are in very poor condition. Both hatches are missing their rubber seals although the hatch on the left-hand side still retains the short lever handle, and locking bar.

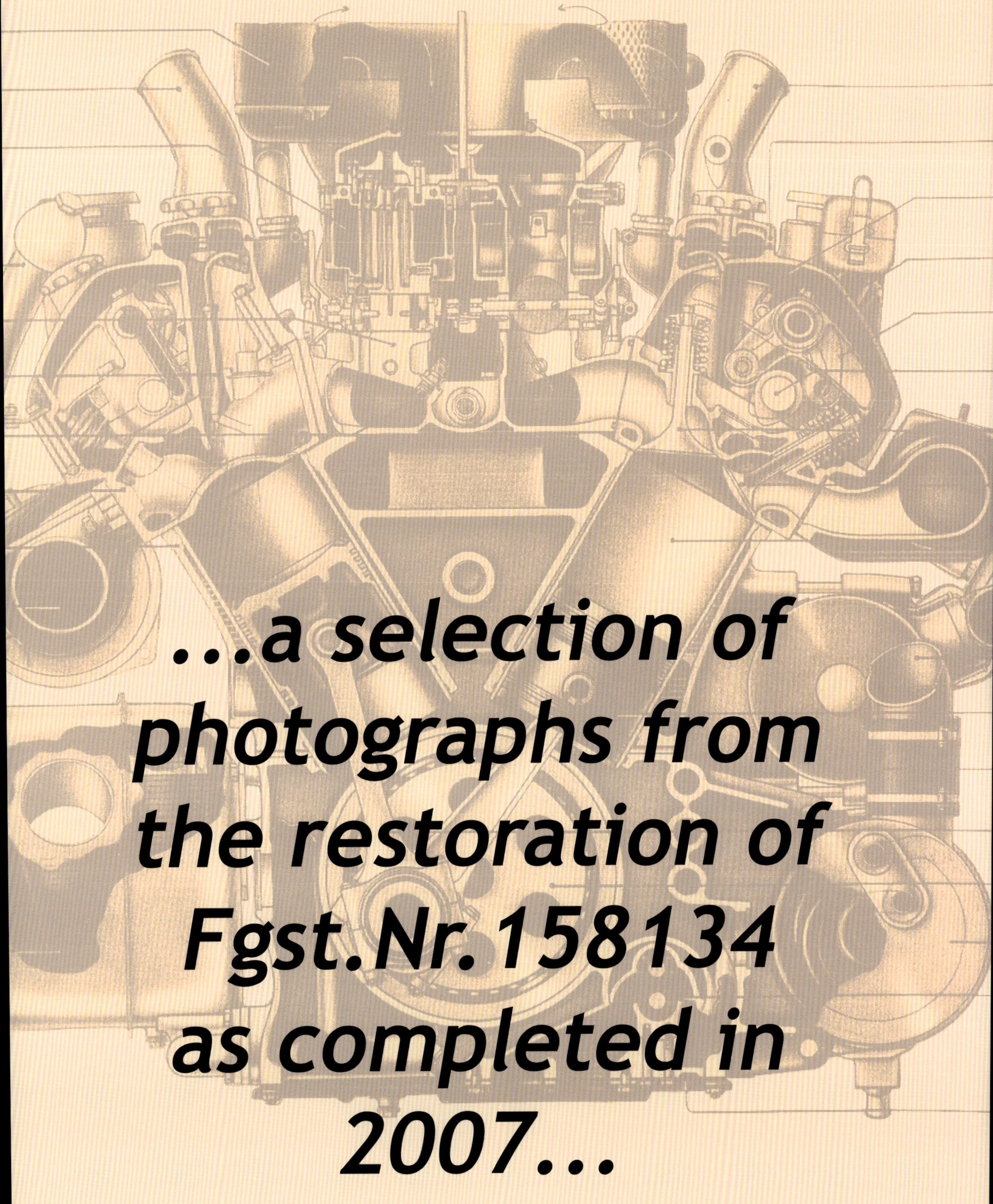

...a selection of photographs from the restoration of Fgst.Nr.158134 as completed in 2007...

Bild 24. Motor, Querschnitt

1: Starting in August 1943 new road wheels were introduced that incorporated 24 rim bolts to help solve the problem of road wheel failures that arose during **Operation Citadel** [13].

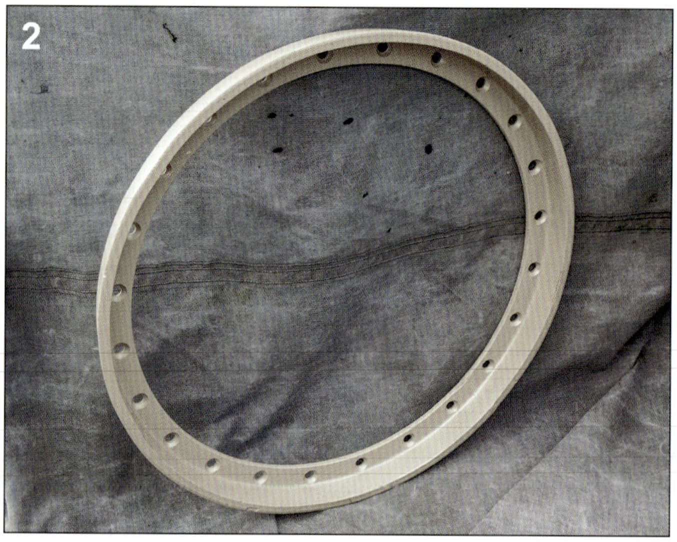

2: Each road wheel comprised of three main components: a large dished wheel, a solid rubber tyre and a tyre retaining ring. The assembled road wheel had a diameter of 850mm [14].

3: Utilising a separate road wheel tyre allowed for a relatively simple replacement of a tyre when they became worn. Steel wire was vulcanised into the rubber during manufacture of the tyre to provide additional strength.

4: The road wheels and retaining bolt rings on **Fgst.Nr.158134** have been restored from original wartime items. All rubber tyres are newly manufactured stock. Here we see a new tyre test fitted to a restored road wheel.

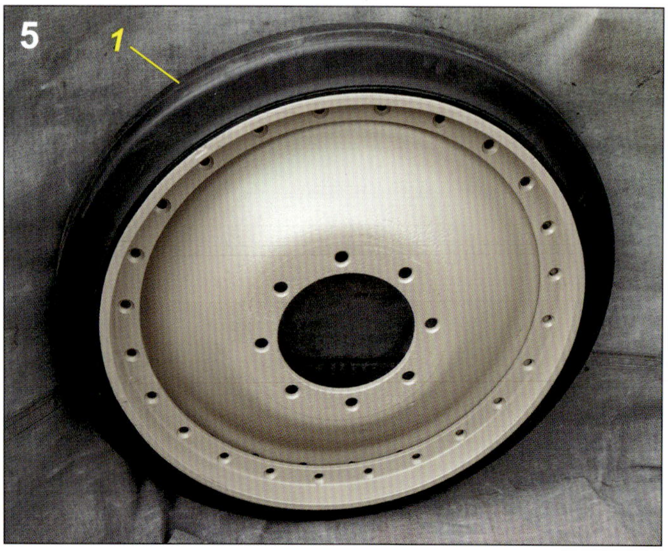

5: A look at the rubber tyre reveals the modern manufacturing process has also replicated the raised seam as seen on brand new wartime items ***1***.

6: A selection of Panther road wheels that are all candidates for restoration. The rubber tyres though all exhibit various degrees of wear and so will likely be discarded.

7: The original manufacturer of rubber tyres for the Panther was **Deka Pneumant AG**. This company was founded in 1906 and was the first recorded manufacturer to ever use synthetic rubber. In 1937 production was moved to a new facility in **Fürstenwalde** in **Brandenburg**. The Wheatcroft Collection has ensured that the original manufacturers logo has been replicated on the new tyres.

8: The markings here, **860/100 D** refer to the dimensions of the rubber tyre. **860** is the overall diameter of the tyre while **100** is the width of the tyre. One interesting point relating to these tyres is their weight. They are significantly heavier than one might expect although this is likely due to the steel banding vulcanised inside the rubber.

9: This final set of markings on the new tyres we have to assume are just original **Deka** manufacturers numbers. As a further point of history **Deka** continued producing tyres starting from 1946 in the **GDR** under a government monopoly. In 2005 the company was acquired by **Dunlop** and continues to sell tyres now under the **Goodyear-Dunlop** brand name.

10: Here we see examples of both early and late rubber tyre road wheels. The wheel at ***1*** is of the initial 16 bolt rim type that through experience in combat were discovered to be prone to early failure.

11: The Panther running gear on each hull side comprised of four inner and outer pairs of interleaved road wheels. In this photo we see one wheel of an outer pair that still has affixed the hub spacer tube, at ***1***.

12: A damaged 24 bolt road wheel that is not a good candidate for restoration. We can see here that the rubber tyre was not vulcanised to the road wheel rim.

13: Stories of tank wheels being removed from abandoned tanks in Western Europe to be used by the local populace are very common. Here we see an example of a 16-bolt road wheel where an axle hub has been welded into the road wheel centre.

14: A close-up view of the damaged road wheel as seen in photo **12**. Of interest is the exposed steel banding that was vulcanised into the rubber tyre at manufacture time.

15: This photo shows a road wheel that also been re-purposed for use by having a 6-bolt hub welded into the wheel centre, ***1***. Note also the original lock tabs used to prevent the wheel rim bolts from vibrating loose ***2***.

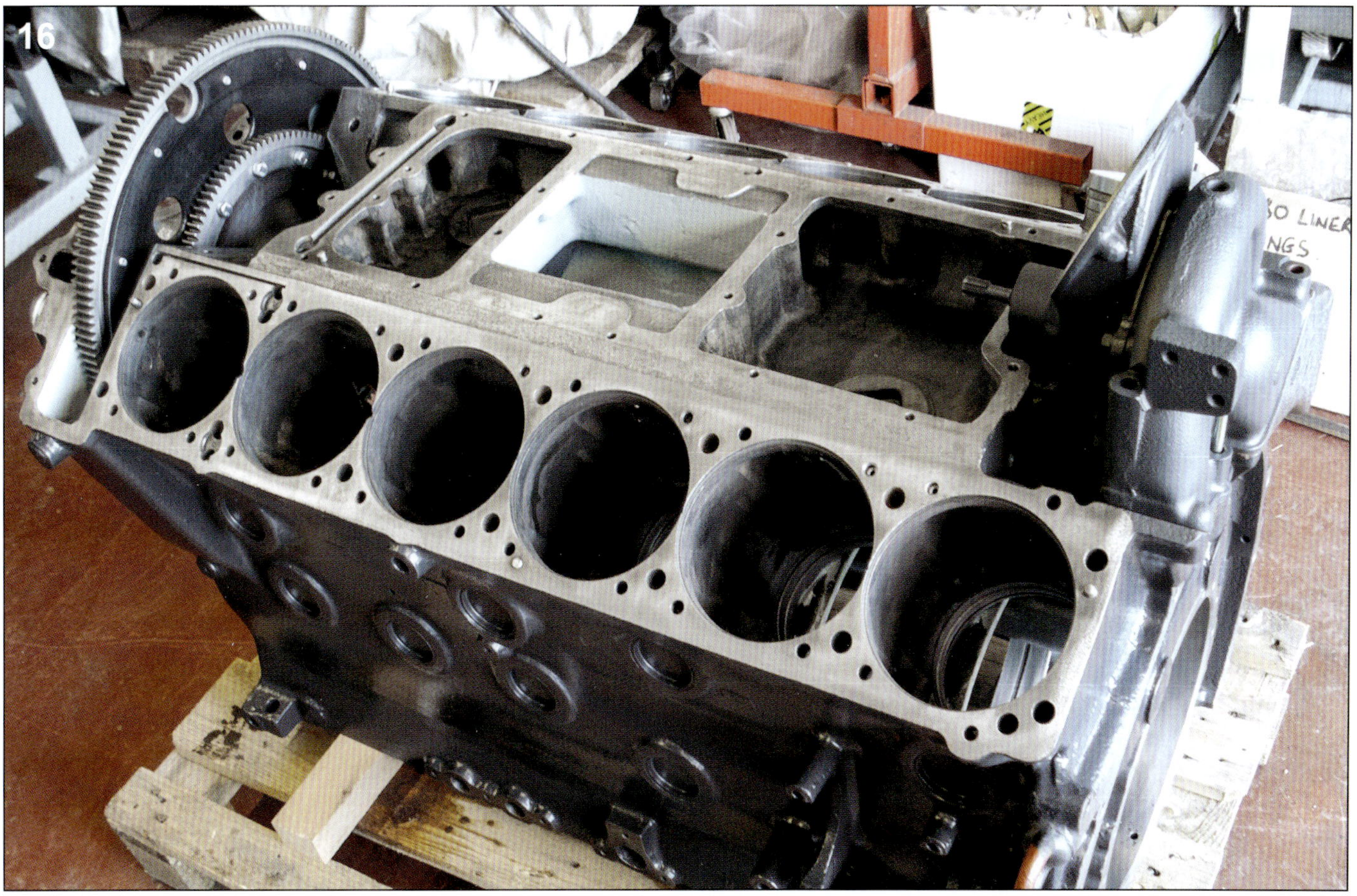

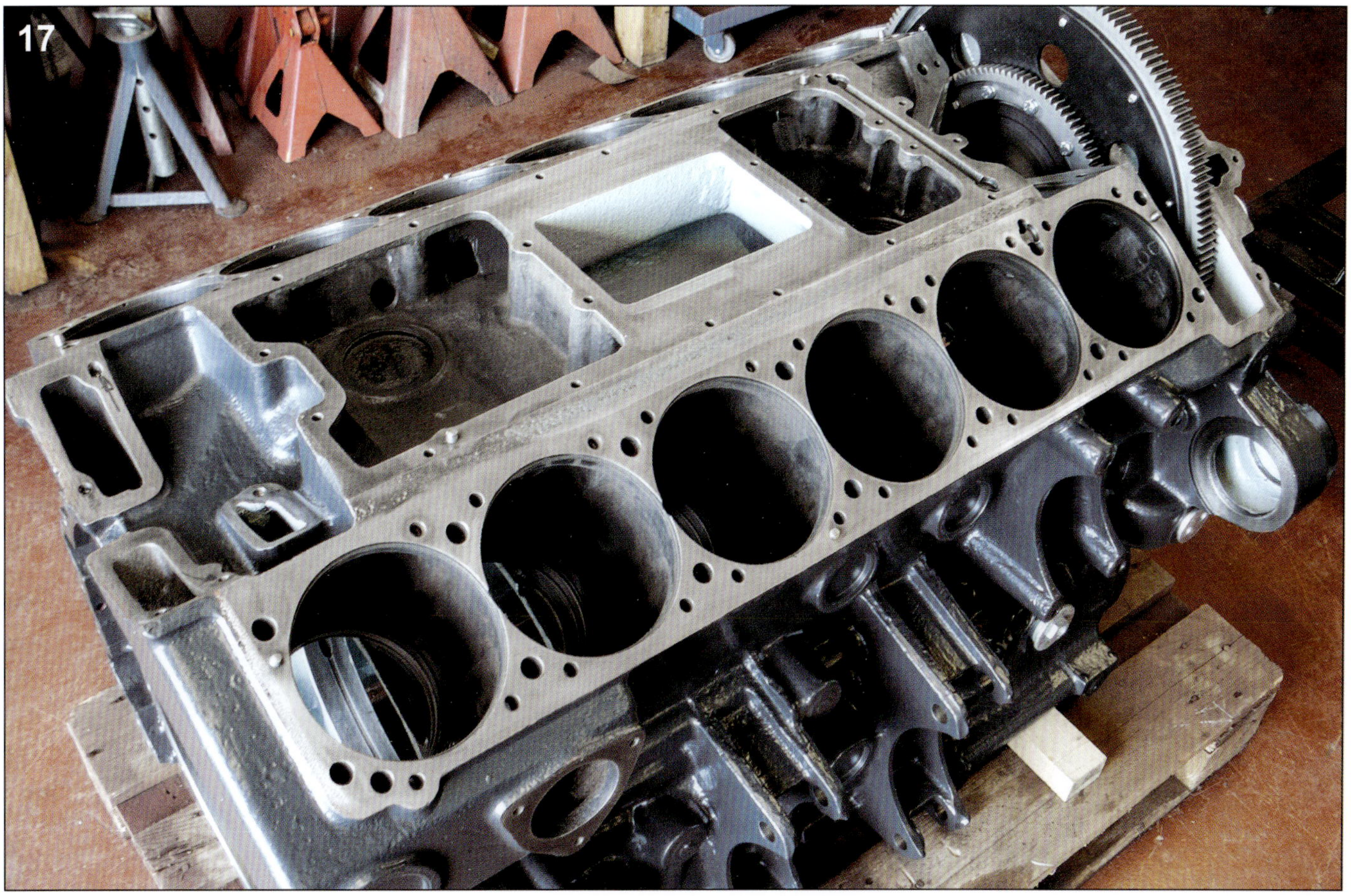

16-17: In May 1943 the **Maybach HL210 P30** engine was phased out to be replaced by the **Maybach HL230 P30**. This new engine can be simply identified by having only two multistage air filters instead of three. The **HL230** had an increased bore with the cylinder diameter now being 130mm and the total engine capacity being expanded to 23 litres. The Wheatcroft Collection has a number of **HL230** engines and as there are restoration plans for at least two Panther tanks the decision was made to concurrently restore a number of these engines at the same time. In these two photographs we see two blocks that are restored and ready for rebuilding.

18

18-19: The increase in cylinder diameter decreased the spacing between the cylinder liners. To retain the rigidity of the structural strength of the **HL230** engine block the entire assembly was now to be made from cast iron instead of a lightweight alloy. The new engine block increased the overall weight of the engine by 350kg. The **HL230** was rated at 700hp at 3000rpm. This was only a 50hp increase over the **HL210**. This minor increase in hp gave no extra speed but gave greater torque for accelerating, hill climbing etc.

19

20

21

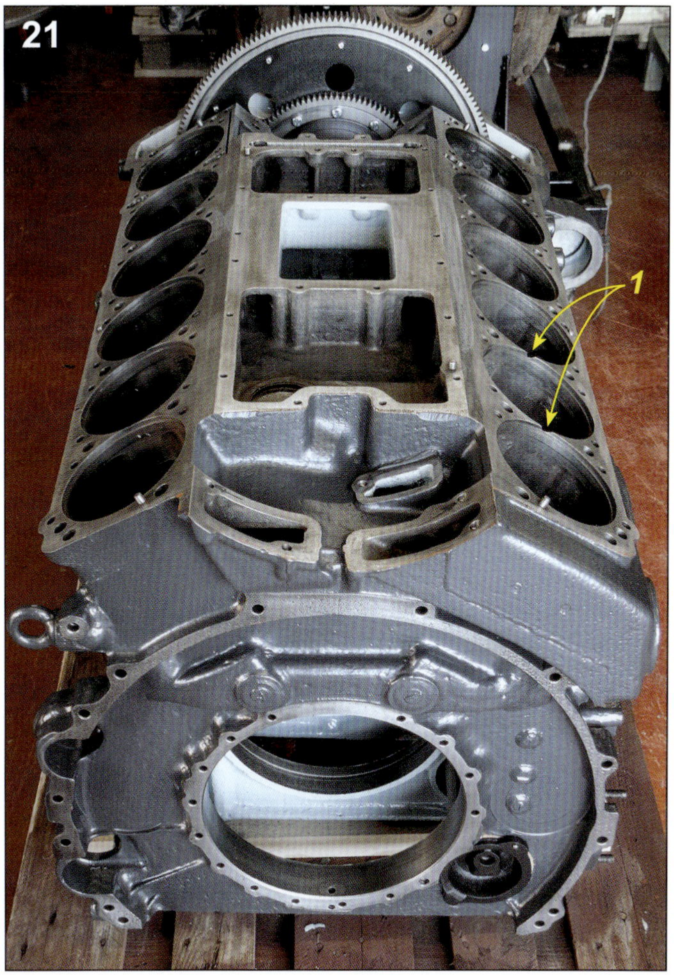

20-21: Here we see a side by side view of the two **HL230** engines that are to be restored looking from front to rear. Note that the engine seen in photo **20** is that which was ultimately decided upon to be fitted to **Fgst.Nr.158134**. What is interesting in these photos are the minor but significant casting differences. If you look closely there are a lot of differences to be seen. Also note the damage seen on both blocks between the cylinders, for example see ***1***, photo **21**. The addition of the copper compression rings, see illustration 22, meant that this damage to a certain degree could be ignored.

22

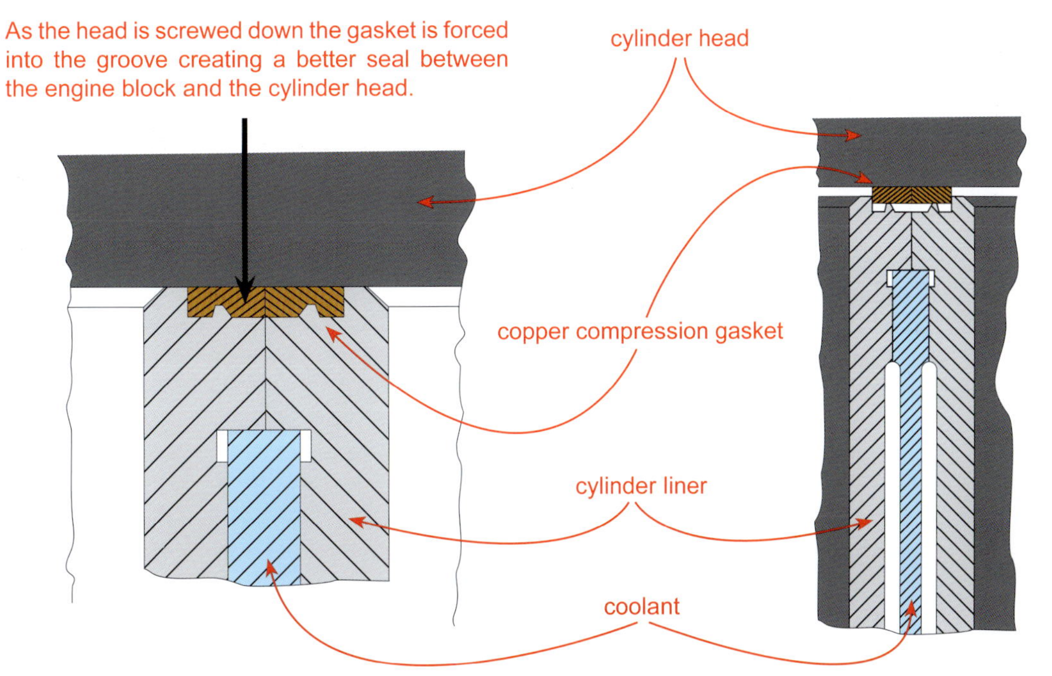

22: By September 1943 operational deficiencies of the HL230 led to a number of design changes. A significant number of blown head gaskets led to copper gaskets being fitted into grooves in the cylinder block to better seal the cylinder head.

23-24: A look down at the top of the engine blocks of both engines, showing the rear side of the flywheels. The engine in photo **23** will be the tank engine eventually used. Of interest again are the physical differences in the engine blocks. Note that at ***1*** the core plug is screwed into place using a square head key tool while the core plug at ***2*** has been press fitted into place.

25: A test fitting of a water pump, **Wasserpumpe**, on an engine block. The impellor drive shaft for this pump can be seen at ***1***.

26: Here we see a tool made by the restoration engineers to aid in pulling the new wet cylinder liners into place. A kinder process than driving them into place using a block of wood and a hammer as would have originally been done.

27: A view of the opposite side of the water pump as seen in photo **25**. The bolt at ***1*** is just in place to ensure the pump is lined up correctly on the engine block.

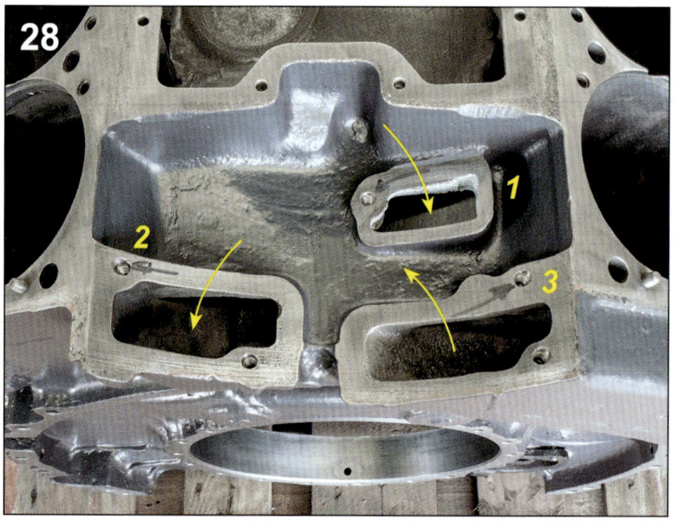

28: With the water pump removed we can see the water flow ports in the engine block. At ***1*** and ***2*** water flows from the pump and into the block. At ***3*** water flows into the pump from the oil cooler on the RHS of the block.

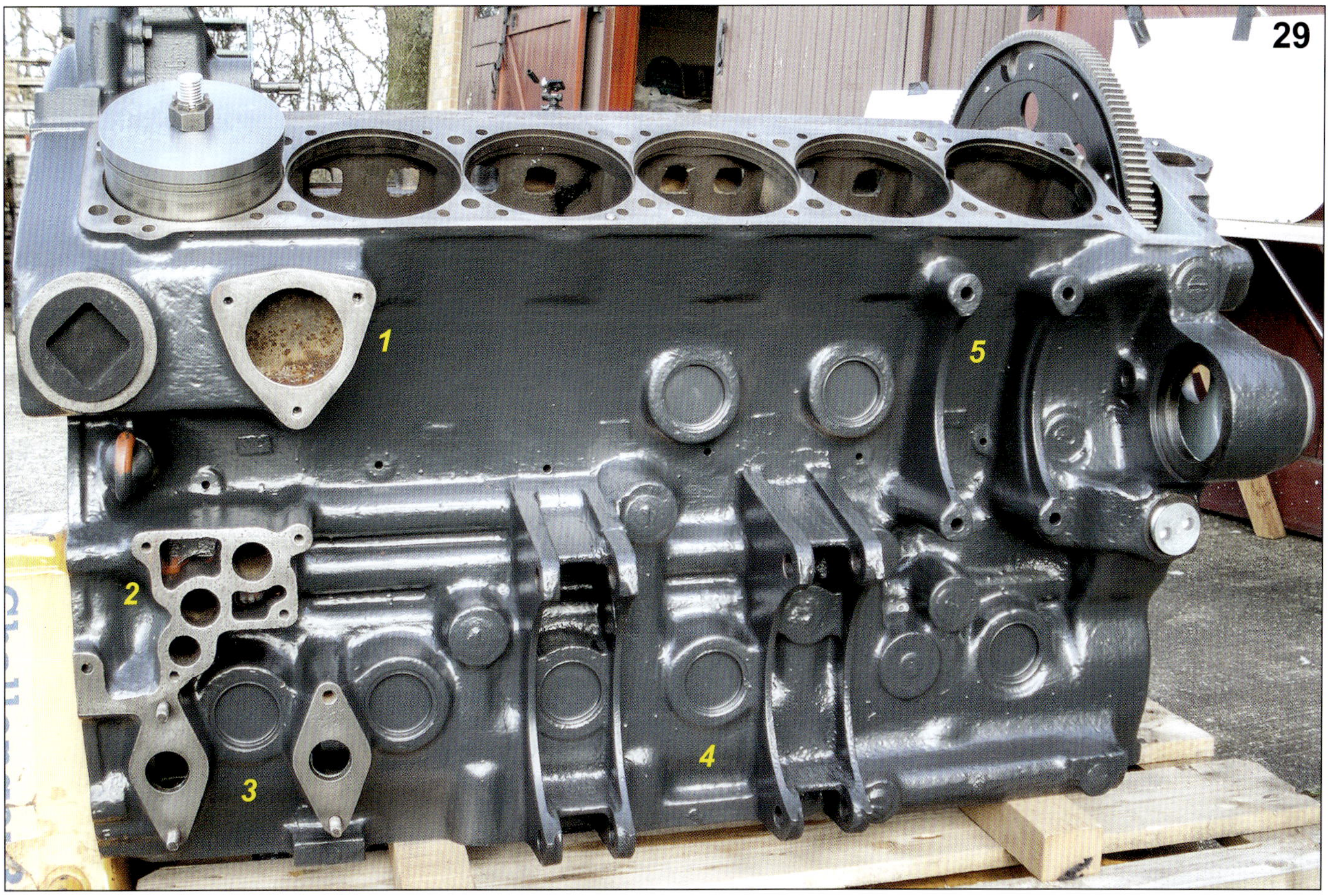

29: An overall view of the RHS of the engine that will be installed in the tank. Some location points of equipment to be fitted; ***1***: water pipe connected to oil cooler, ***2***: oil filter housing, ***3***: fuel filters, ***4***: oil cooler, ***5***: electrical generator.

30: The bottom of the engine block highlighting the races for the main bearings of the crankshaft. The crankshaft had seven main bearings but a series of failures led to an eighth bearing being added to the engine design starting in January 1944.

31: A close-up view of the RHS of the engine block showing a set of five sealed core plugs and a series of manufacturers part numbers: **021 B 42501-111 24**. Note that this is not the serial number of this engine.

32-33: Views of two reconditioned piston heads. The **HL230** piston carried four compression rings and two oil cleaner rings. The gudgeon pin was retained in place by using inner circlips, see ***1***, photo **33**.

34-35: Here we have two sets of photographs showing the piston heads side by side for comparison purposes. There is a gudgeon pin in place at ***1***, photo **34**. We can also see drilled lubrication holes for the gudgeon pin and cylinder wall at ***2*** and ***3***, photo **34**.

36: Stamped in the head of this piston are manufacturers marks, **12** and **3654**. Looking closely you can see the number **3** has been re-stamped over the number **2**.

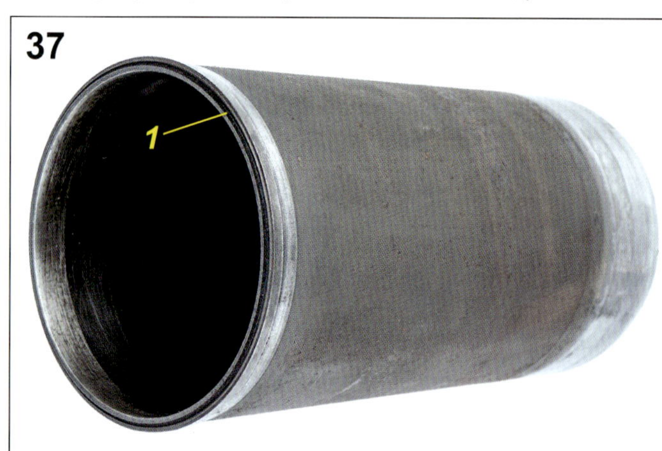

37: All twelve cylinder liners, **Zylinderlaufbüchse**, of a **HL230** were interchangeable. The groove at ***1*** seated the copper ring used for cylinder head sealing, see page **27**, illustration 22.

38

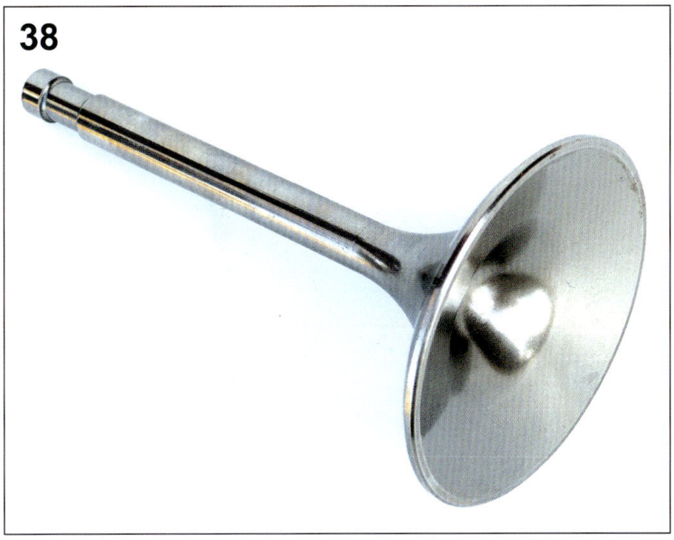

38: An example of a brand-new inlet valve. Spielberger states that in order to aid cooling the exhaust valves were hollow and filled with sodium [14]. The reason for this was as the exhaust valves run hotter the sodium acted as a heat sink thus reducing heat build-up and potential seizing of the valve.

39

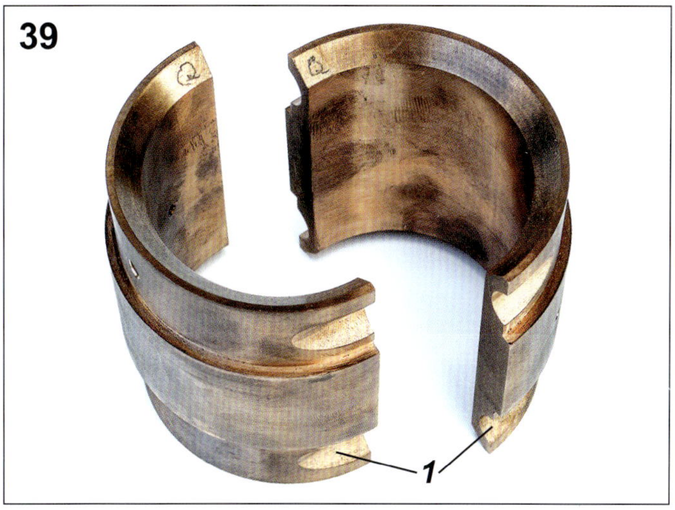

39: The big end piston arm bearings are made from new modern materials. From a restoration engineer: *'We used a material called Colsibro. It is used in high performance engines, i.e. Formula One engines, and is similar to the original material used. We found that some of the original bearings had a very fine/light white metal coating/flashing over the top of the bearing surface. This was probably an upgrade to help bearing performance. We replicated this on the new bearings. It was very expensive.'* [15].

40

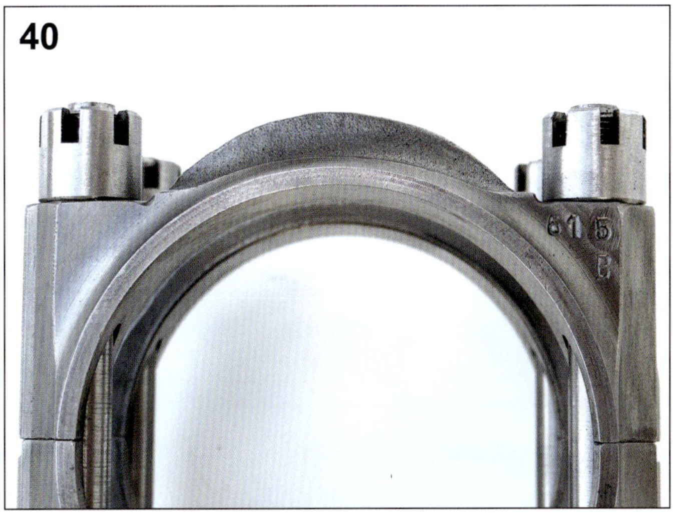

40: A close-up view of one side of a clamp for a big end bearing on a piston arm. We can see rounded castellated nuts that screw onto bolts that would be split pinned or lock-wired into place.

41

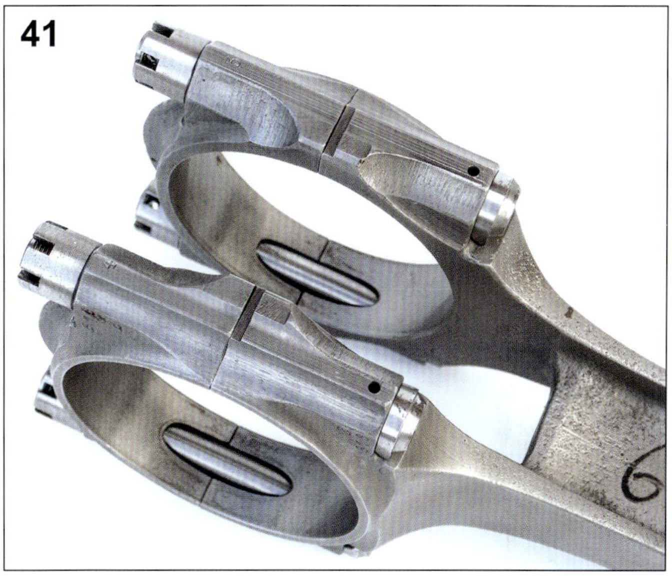

41: A general view of a piston big end minus any bearings. Note that the big end bearings are grooved thus preventing them from rotating in place, see ***1***, photo **39**.

42

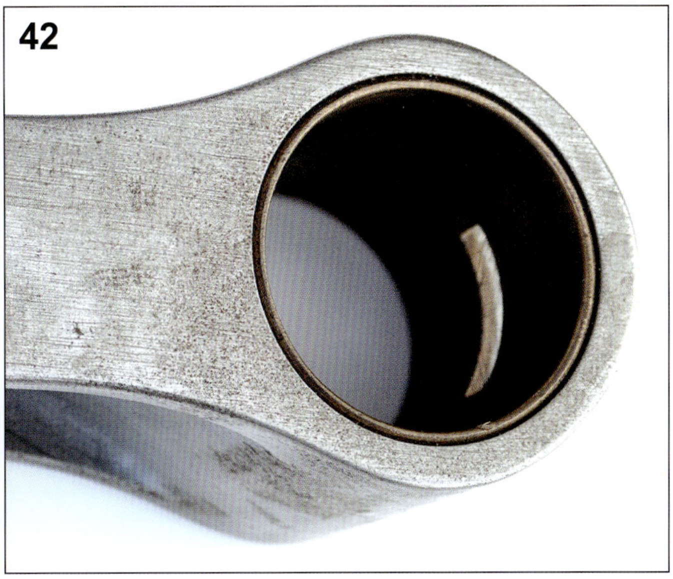

42: A close-up view of the little end of a piston arm. The bushing seen here is press fitted into place. The slot in the bush allows for oil lubrication of the bearing.

43

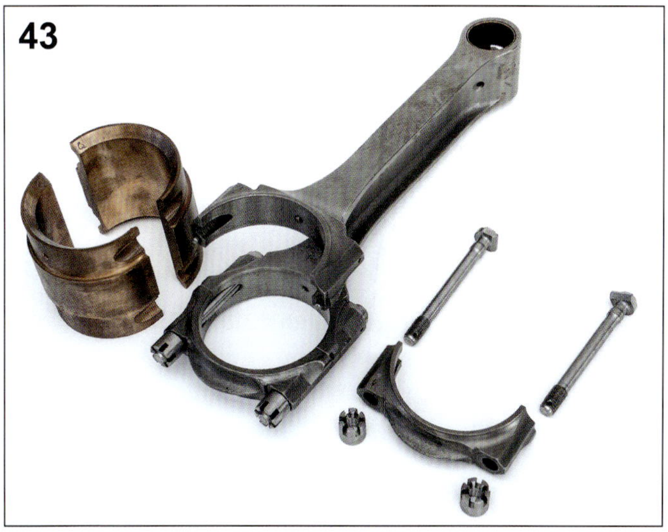

43: An overall view illustrating the primary component parts of a piston arm of a **Maybach HL 230 P30** engine.

44

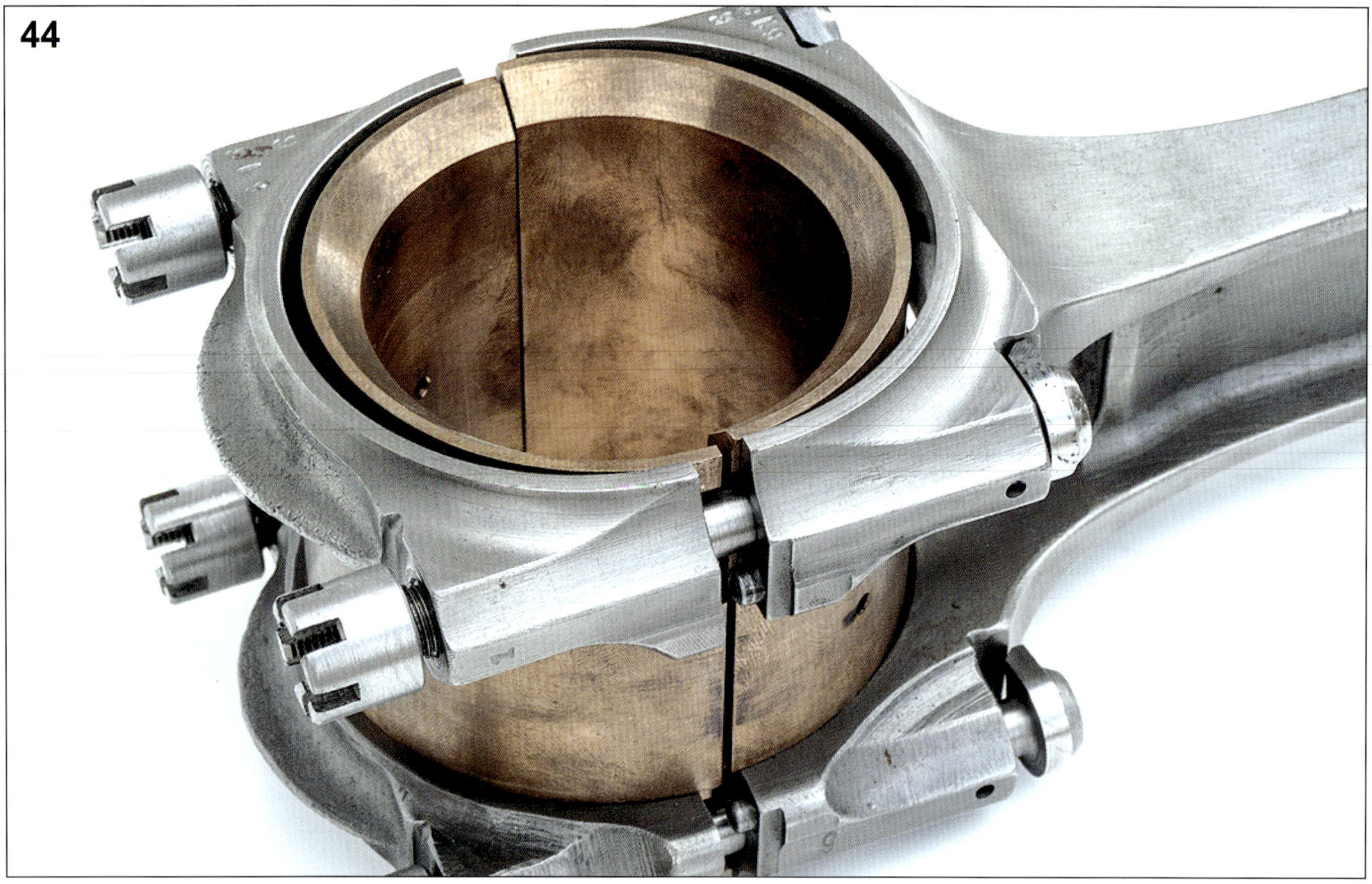

44: In this photo we can see a close-up view of a big end arm showing how all the component parts are assembled. Note how the bearings are aligned to fit either the piston arm or the piston clamp.

45

45: The complete piston assembly is presented here. All piston rings, gudgeon pin, bearings, clamps etc. are essentially ready to be fitted into a restored engine block.

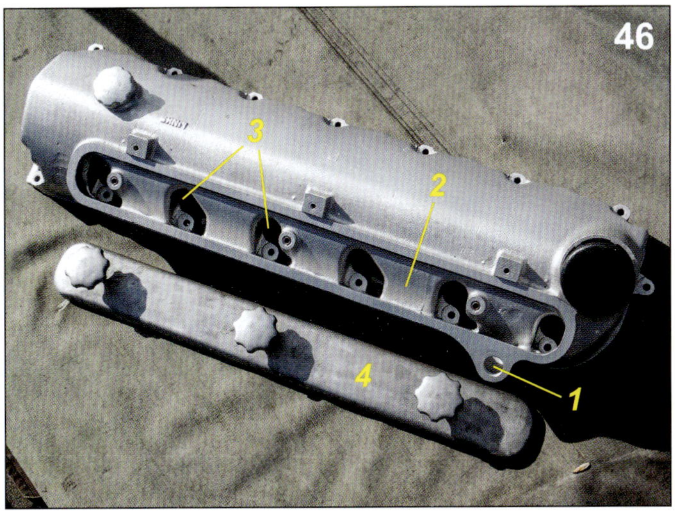

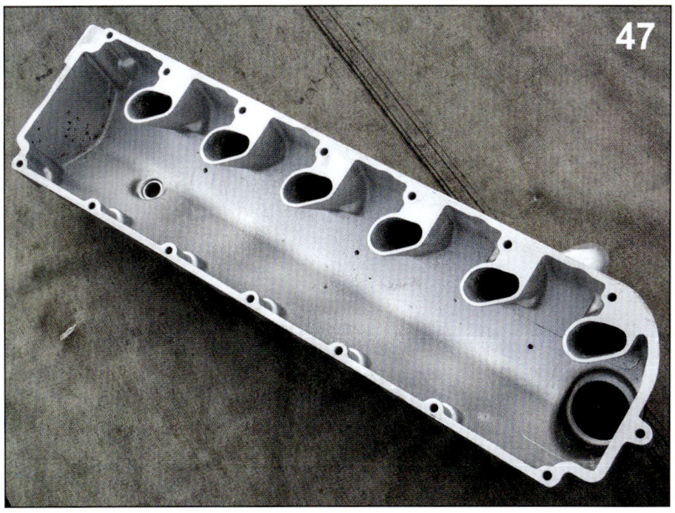

46: The LHS rocker cover. The two magnetos supplied power to the spark plugs, one for each cylinder bank. Six spark plug high tension cables were fed into the port at ***1***. The high-tension cables ran along the channel, at ***2***, with one of each cable being fed into the ports at ***3*** etc. The high-tension leads were protected by the radio-interference suppressor cover at ***4***.

47: Underside of the LHS rocker cover. A high-tension lead fed out of each port to a spark plug. The high-tension leads were copper cored and were enclosed in metal protective weave. Each cylinder had one spark plug that was centred between the inlet-exhaust values, see ***4***, page **45**, photo **102**, and was gap adjusted to **15 thou**.

48: Side view of a rocker arm. We again can see a press fitted bushing and can note that the camshaft roller wheel pin has been peened in place to prevent any pin movement.

49: The camshaft roller wheel is shimmed in place to prevent any longitudinal movement on the retaining pin. The flange at ***1*** is designed to restrict the total movement of rotation of the rocker arm, see page **45**, photo **100**.

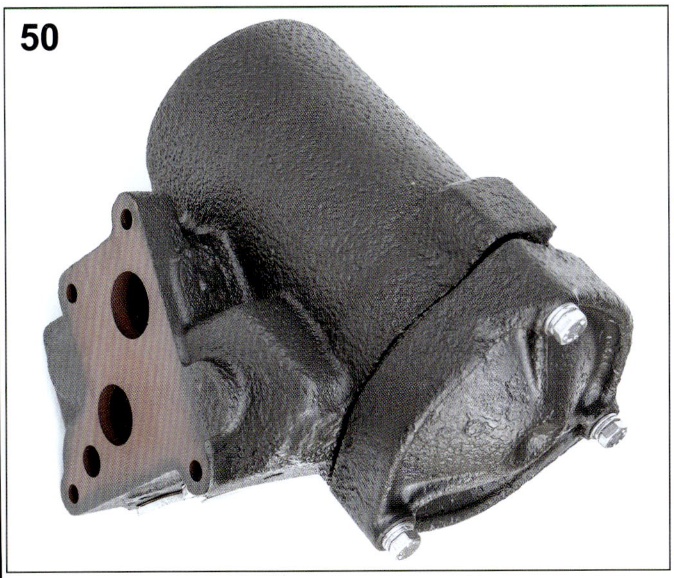

50: The oil filter housing was bolted to the RHS of the engine. This unit was located at **2**, page **29**, photo **29**, and we can see the complete housing in place on page **43**, photo **91**.

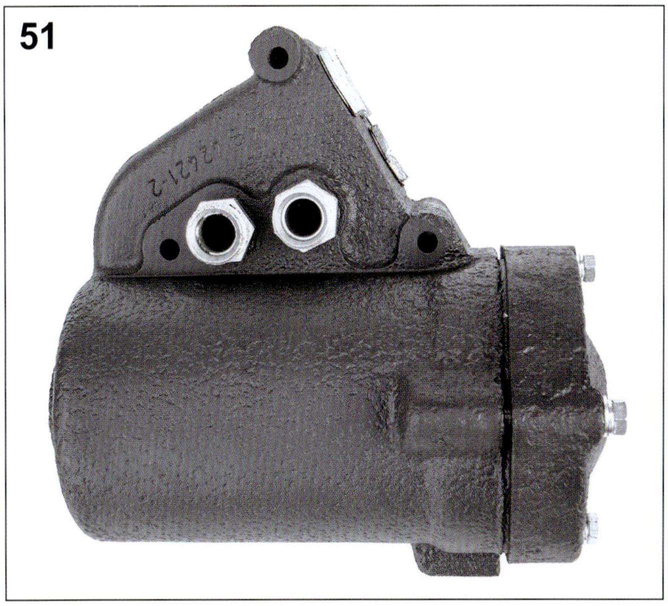

51: To change the oil filter itself is a simple matter of unscrewing the three end cap bolts and replacing the internal filter.

52

52: The electrical system of the Panther was serviced by a **12V Bosch** generator. This unit, together with a voltage regulator, was used to charge the two main **12V** lead acid batteries. The electrical connections to the generator are located at ***1*** and the port, at **2**, supplied cool air from the fighting compartment via a metal hose, see page **110**, photo **346**.

53

53: A close-up view of the generator gear that meshed with the timing gear at the rear of the engine. Spielberger states that this generator had a rated output of **700W** [14] and this is confirmed by the information as recorded on the data plate, at ***1***.

54

54: At the top front of the engine is a fuel cut-off valve. This is designed to only allow fuel into the carburettors once oil pressure has reached a specific level. This prevents the carburettors from being flooded before the engine has started.

55

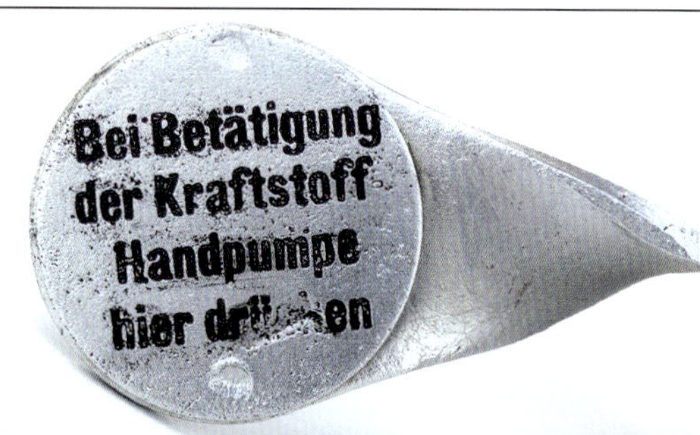

55: On the operating handle of the fuel lift pump is the text: **Bei Betätigung der Kraftstoff Handpumpe Hier Drucken** which translates to: *Press the fuel hand pump when operating*.

56

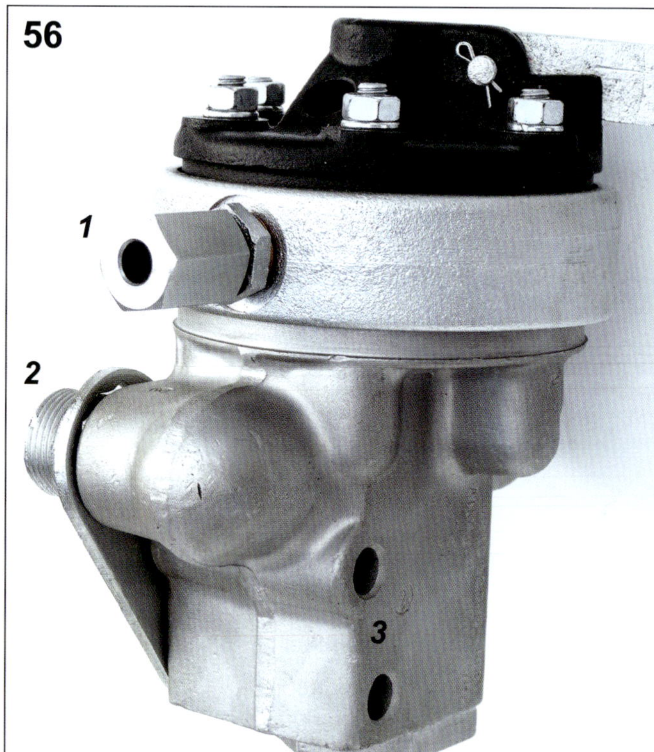

56: The oil feed line into the fuel cut-off valve is seen at ***1***, with one of the fuel line connections being seen at **2**. Bolts are fitted into the holes, at ***3***, for securing the fuel valve to the engine, see page **43**, photo **95**.

57

58

57-60: The water pump is responsible for circulating coolant throughout the engine and radiators. This water pump is driven, at ***1***, photo **59**, from the engine governor which is of a centrifugal type that is itself driven from the timing gearing. Coolant flows into the pump via the port at ***2***, photo **60**, from the oil cooler and out into the engine block via ports ***3*** and ***4***, photo **60** and ***5***, photo **58**.

59

60

61: The engine had two identical **Bosch** magnetos used for the generation of electrical current supplied, via twelve high-tension leads, to the spark plugs. These magnetos were located at the top rear of the engine, see page **41**, photos **83** and **84**.

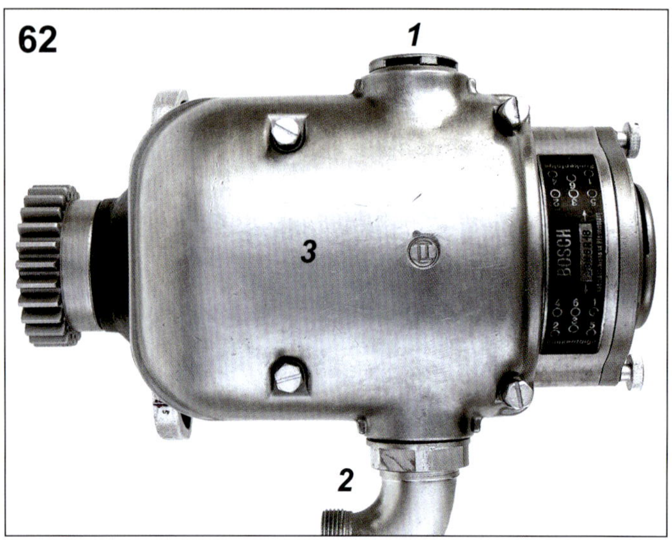

62: Each magneto was responsible for the supply of current to a single bank of spark plugs. A curved tube carried the shielded high-tension cables out of the magneto at either position ***1*** or ***2***. In this image this magneto is configured to supply power to the spark plugs on the LHS cylinder bank of the engine.

63: A close-up of a **Bosch** data plate on a magneto that refers to how the high-tension cables would be connected up inside the body of the magneto, ***3***, photo **62**, depending on which side of the engine the magneto was to supply power to.

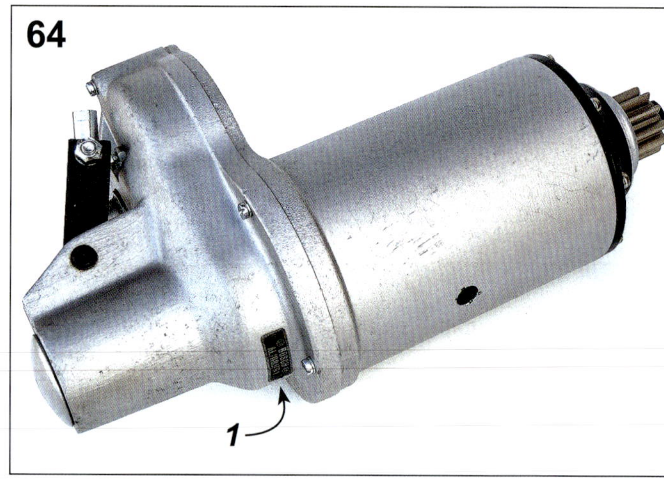

64: The engine could be started with either a crank starter or an electrical starter. Here we see the crank starter, manufactured by **Bosch**, and designated as type **AL/RBI/RI** as seen on the plate at ***1***. This device was operated by a hand crank which engaged the pinion to the engine flywheel. This crank passed through a port in the rear plate, see page **50**, photo **130**.

65: Spielberger states the reduction ratio of the spur gearing in the housing at **2**, photo **64**, was **140:10000** [14]. The pinion would engage the flywheel and then a series of plates would gradually mesh for smooth transfer of kinetic energy.

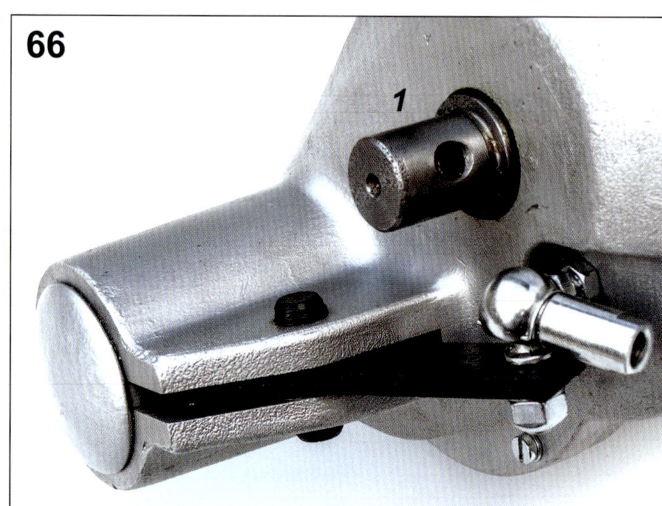

66: The hand crank used to turn the crank starter was connected at ***1***. We see the hand crank shaft in place at ***1***, page **40**, photo **79**. Once the rpm of the flywheel overtook the pinion the plates would slip and a return spring would pull the pinion out of mesh.

67: Examples of both newly manufactured and existing wartime starter pinions. Both pinions on the crank starter and electrical starter were interchangeable items and were of a softer metal than the flywheel.

68: When looking at the wartime pinion in the bottom of the photo we can see how worn the pinion teeth are. This is designed so that the pinion will wear out first and not the flywheel. It is easier to change a starter pinion than an engine flywheel.

69: Here we see a new pinion at the front of the electrical starter motor. This starter is still undergoing reconstruction. The split pin holding the pinion on the central shaft is not yet bent into place.

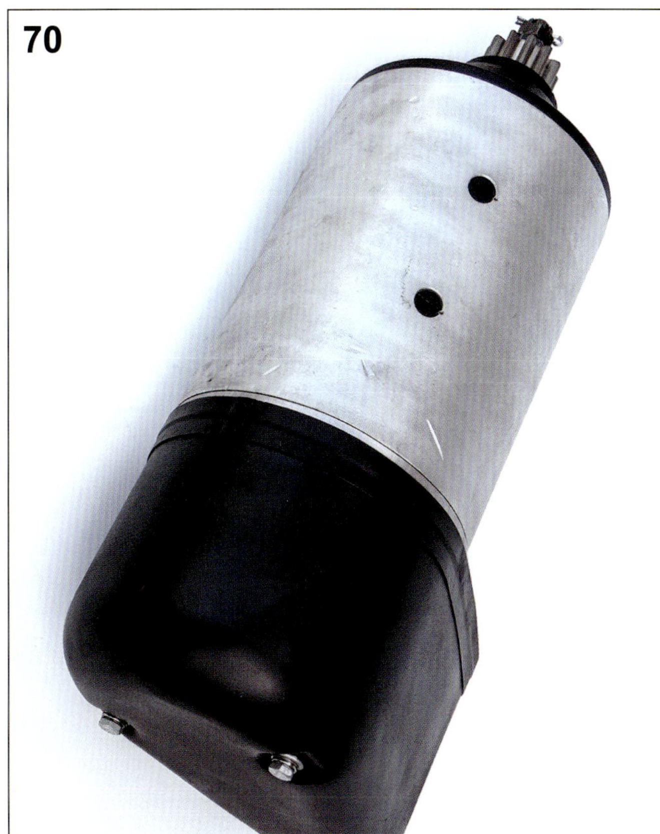

70: A full length view of the **Bosch** manufactured electrical starter motor, designated as type **AI/ZMI**. Both the crank and electrical starters were mounted on the LHS of the engine.

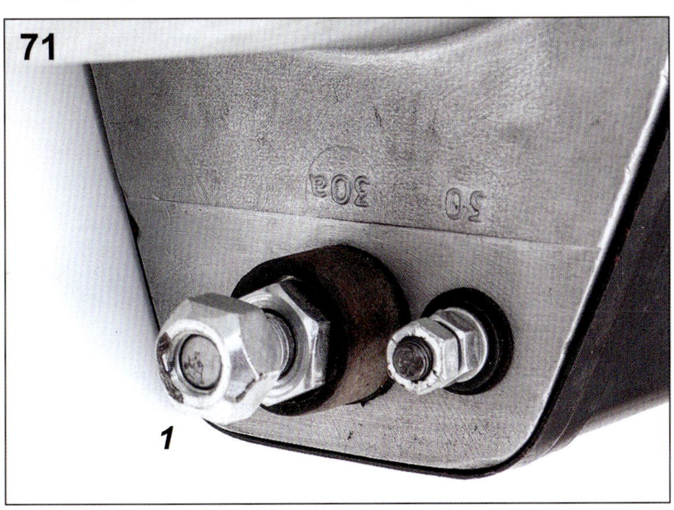

71: The electrical system of the Panther was **12V** and ran from two **12V** lead acid batteries. The electrical starter used **24V** and was connected to the engine using a heavy-duty cable at *1*.

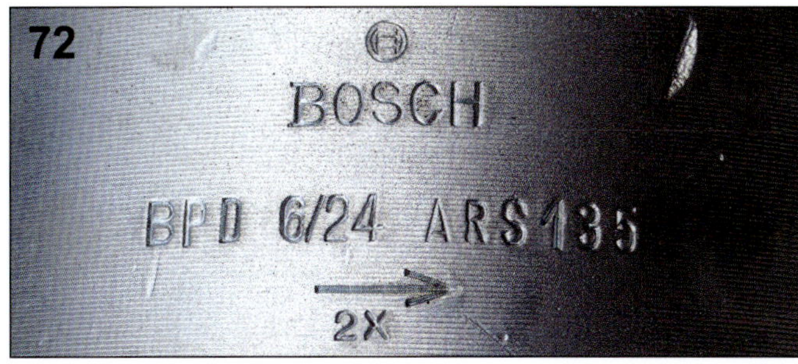

72: Stamped on the body of the electrical starter is the **Bosch** name and logo together with the manufacturers part number, **BPD 6/24 ARS135**.

73: The Panther used two fan drives, each driven by a cardan shaft, at ***1***. There was one fan drive per compartment at each side of the engine. The configuration of a fan drive located in respect to the radiators can be seen on page **132**, photo **387**.

74: Here we see the top of the fan drive unit. The actual fan is sandwiched between the cap, at ***1***, and the lower plate, **2**, photo **73**. Eight bolts are used to secure all elements together.

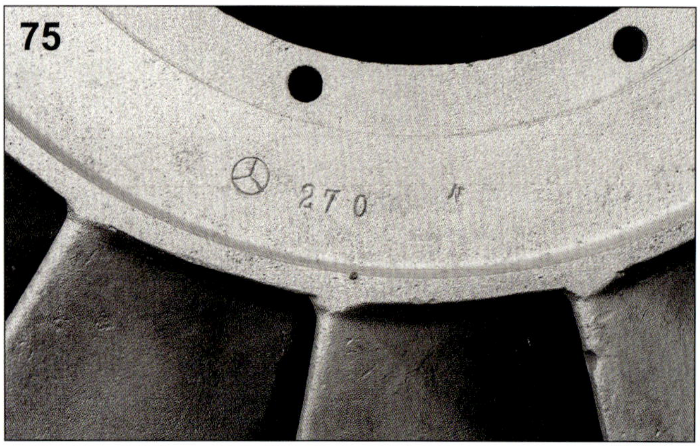

75: A close-up view of the fan showing a manufacturers logo, possibly **Mercedes**?, and some manufacturers marks, **270** and **N**. This fan unit was manufactured from a light alloy.

76: With the top cap removed we can now see how the fan sits upon the base plate, **2**, photo **73**.

77: Finally we see the cap in place on top of the fan. All that is required now is to bolt all component parts together.

78: The skeleton frame of the radio rack. This frame sits inside an outer solid panel box. The brackets at ***1*** above are mounting points for the bolt holes seen at ***1*** on page **74**, photo **244**.

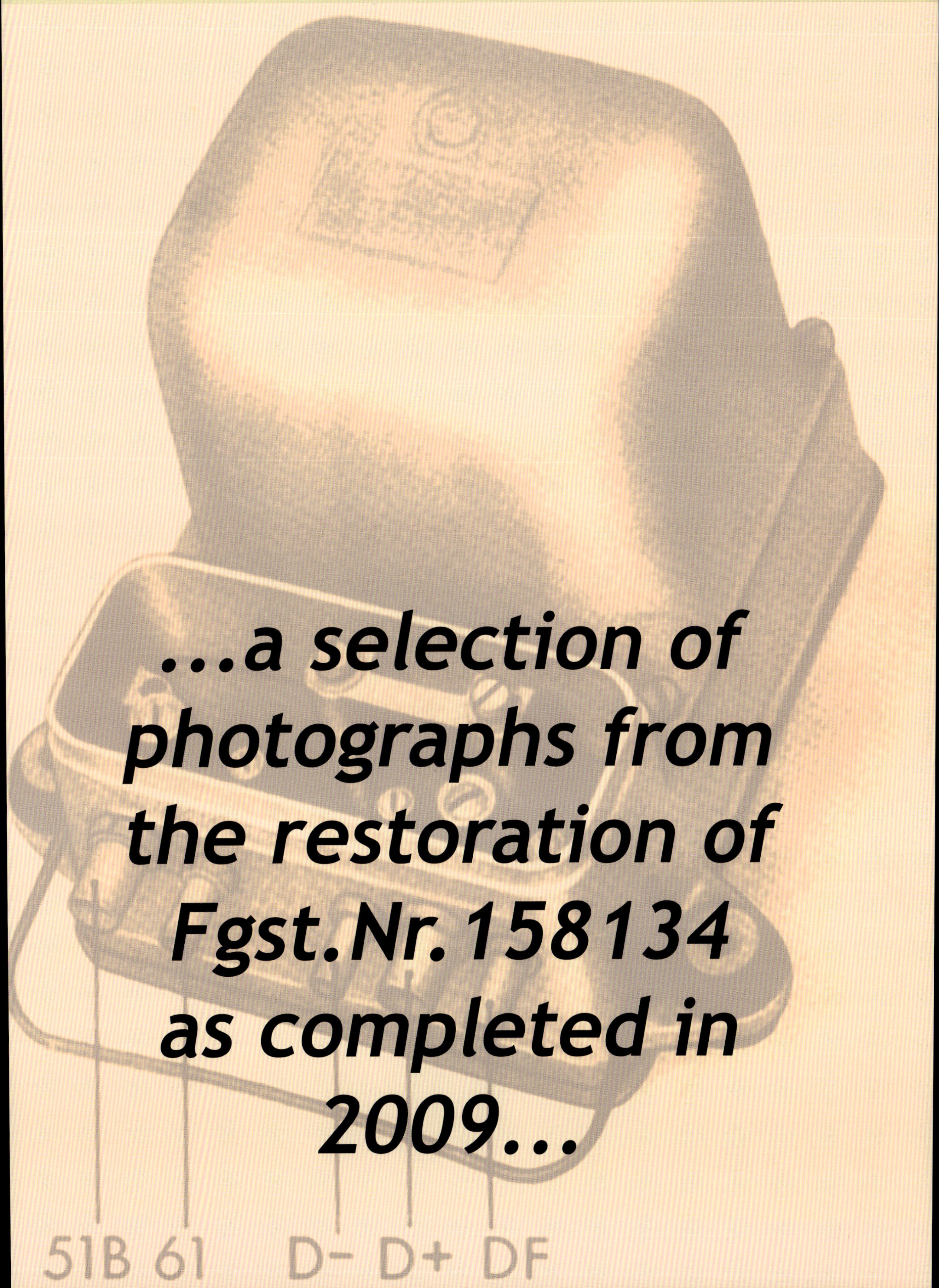

...a selection of photographs from the restoration of Fgst.Nr. 158134 as completed in 2009...

79-80: By 2009 the bulk of all restoration work on the engine had been completed. I do not think any of The Research Squad will forget our first sighting of this engine. The quality of work achieved was just stunning in the attention to detail of the finished result. To remember that this engine was over sixty years old and now appeared in this state was just incredible. The Wheatcroft Collection team of restoration engineers have to be congratulated on the excellence of work completed here.

81-84: In these four images we walk around the engine as it sits in a test bed frame. Photos **81** and **82** show the front of the engine while photos **83** and **84** show the rear. The **Maybach HL230 P30** once in the engine compartment was secured to the hull by a set of rubber mounts to dampen vibration. Power was transmitted via a cardan shaft to a power take-off under the turret and then via another cardan shaft to the rear of the gearbox. All timing gearing was mounted to the rear of the engine.

85: Here we see both the **Bosch** magnetos mounted at the top rear of the engine. Note the blanking plugs with air vent holes, at *1*, closing off each side of the magneto not being used. These magnetos could be rotated on their central axis to ensure correct timing against the engine.

86: Still to be fitted here is the curved tube, at *1*, that carried the shielded high-tension spark plug cables from the magneto into the rocker cover. When the bolts at *2* are loosened we can see how the body of the magneto can then be rotated to set up the correct ignition timing.

87: The upper rear top of the engine. The gearing in the housing, at *1*, is used to drive the flanges seen at *2* and *3*. These flanges are connected to the cardan shafts that propel the fan drives in the radiator compartments.

88: The housing onto which are bolted the magnetos used for the ignition system. At *1*, page **102**, photo **331**, we can see into this housing and observe how the gearing of the magnetos is timed to the engine.

89: The gearing, seen at *1*, at the rear of the engine is where all drive is sourced for the camshafts, the magnetos and the fan drives. See technical illustration, page **201**.

90: The rear engine mount. The pipe, at *1*, feeds water to the oil cooler. The butterfly valve, at *2*, aids with cold starting. When closed the oil will reach the operating temperature much faster.

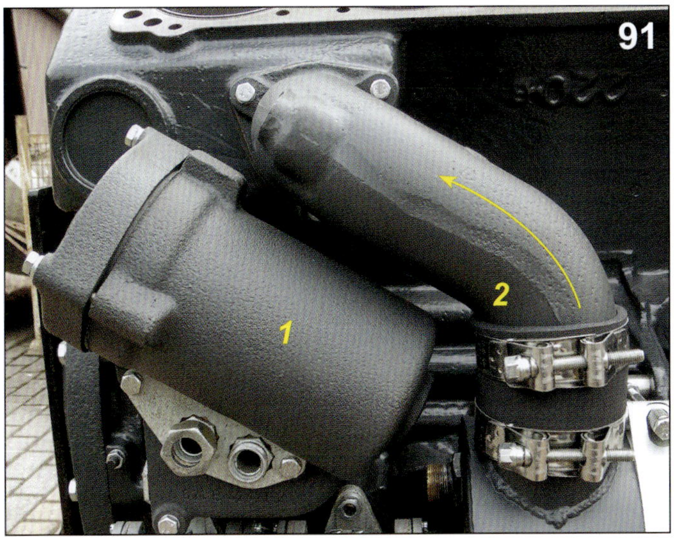

91: The oil filter housing is seen at ***1***. The pipe that carries water from the oil cooler into the water pump is seen at ***2*** with the arrow denoting the direction of water flow.

92: The engine oil cooler. This acts as a heat exchanger where hot oil is cooled by water cycled from the coolant system. See the damaged oil cooler on page **16**.

93: The engine oil tank. A dipstick tube was bolted to the flange at ***1***. The dipstick was accessible for use when the engine hatch on the hull deck was opened.

94: Here we can see both the crank starter, ***1***, and the electrical starter unit, ***2***, as fitted to the LHS of the engine. Both units are secured by large U-shaped clamps.

95: Here we see the fuel cut-off valve as was bolted to the front top of the engine. The fuel line connections to this valve, sealed with tape to prevent the ingress of dirt and water, are at ***1***.

96: The **Bosch 12V** generator was secured to the RHS of the engine using two large clamps. The junction box for the electrical connector unions can be seen at ***1***.

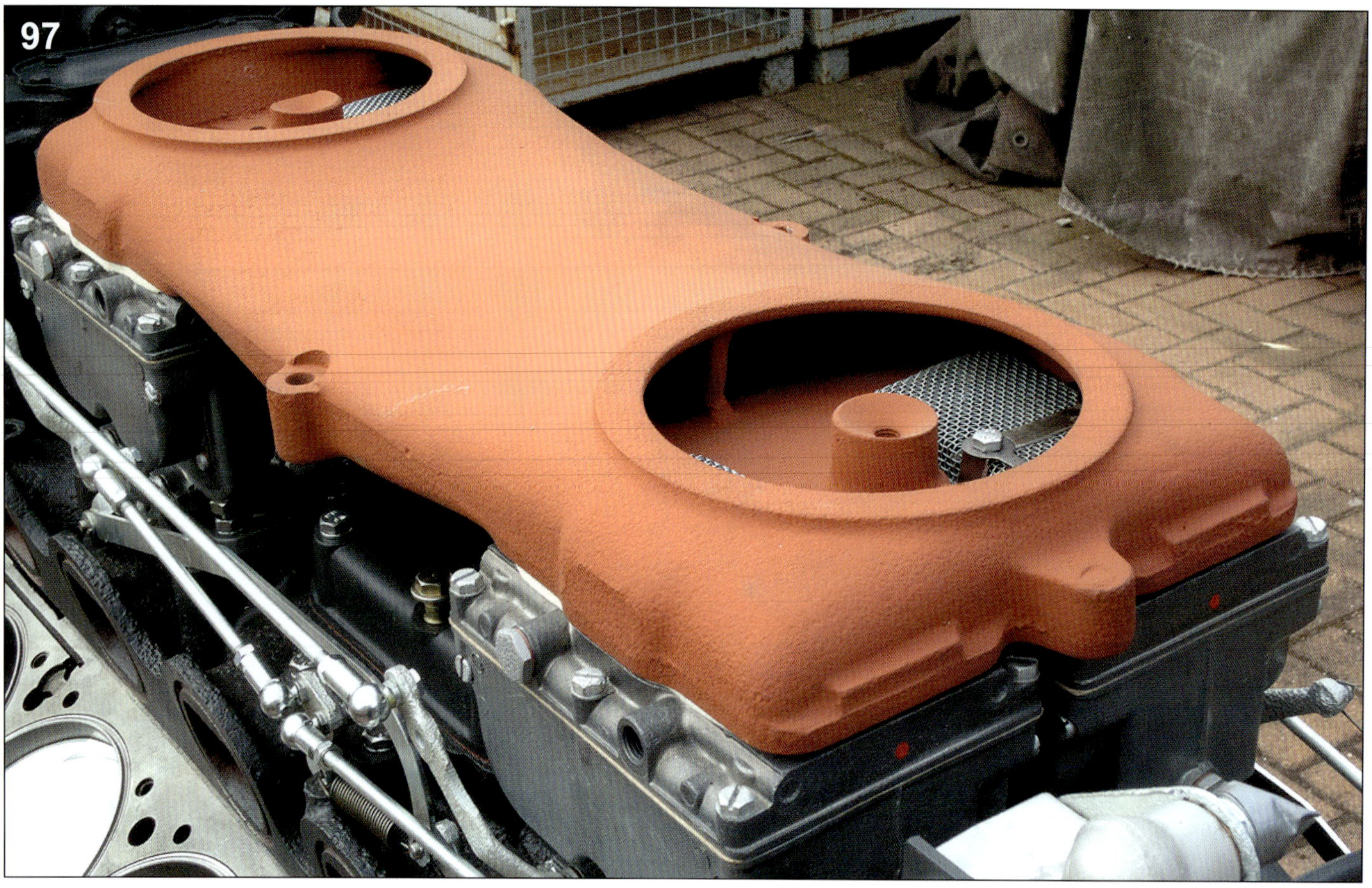

97: The introduction of the **Maybach HL 230 P30** brought several improvements to the engine design. A major external change was the introduction of two combination air intake filters that were installed in box housings as opposed to the three-drum type oil bath air filters as previously used. This necessitated a physical change in the air intake manifold to accommodate this as we see here.

98: Here we see the two **Solex** fuel filters as were bolted to the bottom front of the LHS of the engine. All fuel input and output ports here are sealed with tape to prevent the ingress of dirt and water.

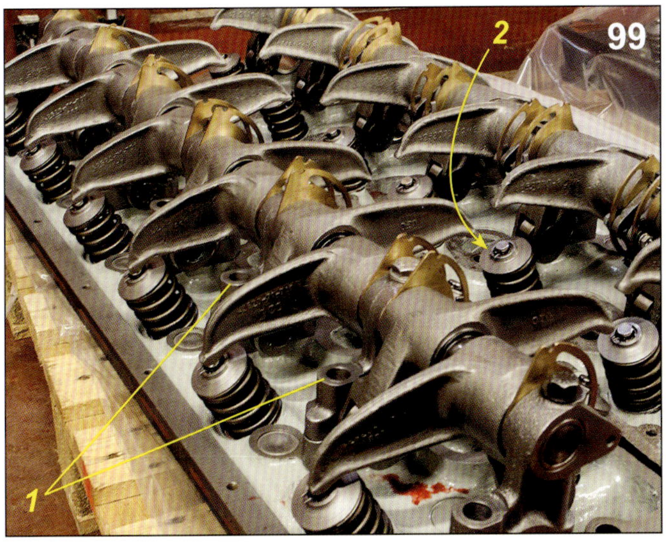

99-100: In these two photographs a test fitting of the rocker gear on a cylinder head is being carried out. The rocker arm shaft is not bolted in place at present, see ***1***, photo **99**. All the inlet and outlet valves, valve return springs and retainers are in place. Each valve is secured by a spring clip, see ***2***, photo **99**.

101: Here we see a section of a restored overhead camshaft. Some minor surface pitting can still be seen on the cams, at ***1***, but this will have no effect on the performance of the engine.

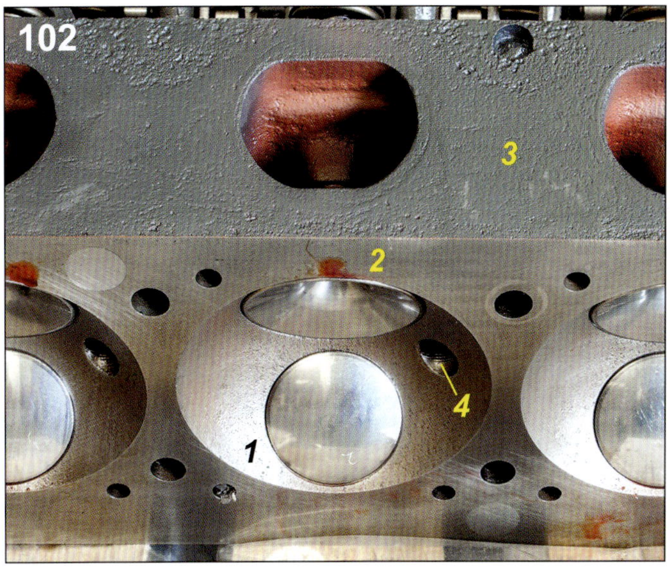

102: A view of the underside of a cylinder head. The exhaust valves have a convex surface, ***1***, whilst the inlet valves have a concave surface, ***2***. Part of the inlet manifold is seen at ***3***.

103: A close-up view of a cylinder head mounted to the restored engine. We can see how the rocker arm rollers interact with the cams on the camshaft, see ***1***. The exhaust manifold is at ***2***.

104: A general view of the overall configuration of the valve gear as seen against the carburettors, carburettor controls and the air intake manifold.

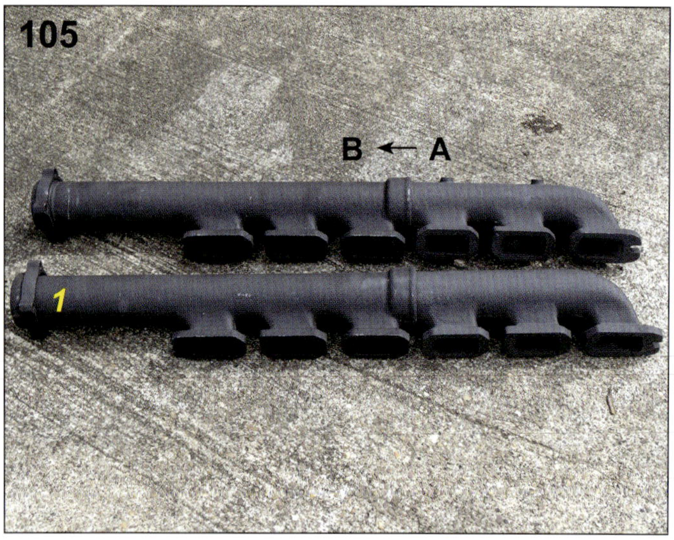

105: The exhaust manifolds that are bolted one to each side of the engine. These manifolds are comprised of two parts, with part **A** slotting into part **B**. They are not bolted together.

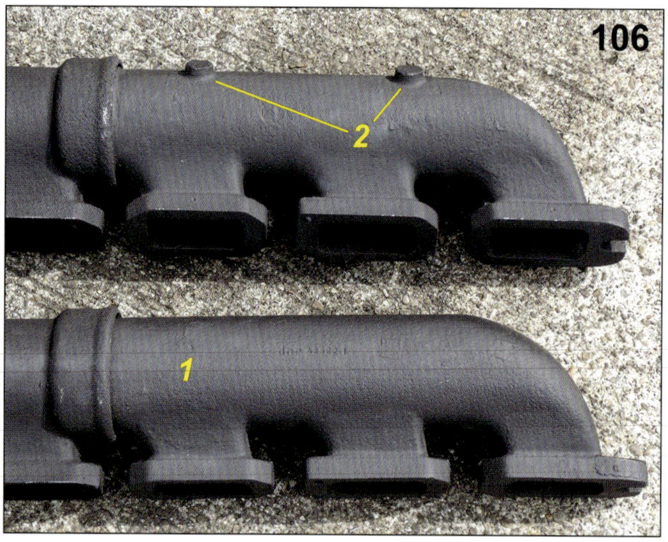

106: The manifold at ***1*** would be fitted to the RHS of the engine. The cast projections at ***2*** aid in keeping the sheet metal heat shield from coming in direct contact with the exhaust manifold.

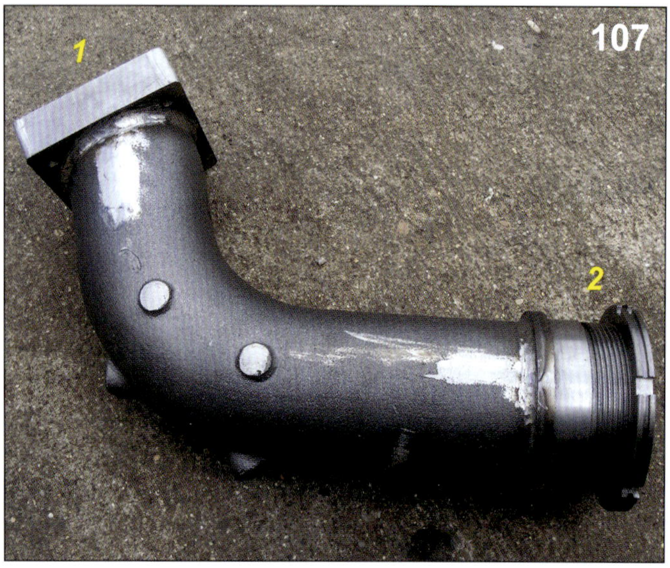

107: This section of exhaust is fitted into the external armoured exhaust cover, see page **51**, photo **133**. To complete the exhaust system there is a short section of pipe fitted between the flange at ***1*** above and to the exhaust manifold flange, see ***1***, photo **105**.

108: A close-up of the threaded section of exhaust pipe seen at ***2***, photo **107**. This threaded section protrudes out of the external armoured exhaust cover, see ***1***, page **51**, photo **138**. The lock ring at ***1*** secures the pipe in place, see ***2***, page **51**, photo **138**.

109-110: A montage of all the restored pistons as to be replaced into the restored engine block. The care and attention to detail of all aspects of work carried out on the overall restoration project of **Fgst.Nr. 158134** is evident when regarding items like these.

111

112

111-114: Two **Solex** fuel filters were fitted to a **Maybach HL 230 P30**. This filter was designed for aircraft engines and then modified for use on vehicles engines. We can see two different types of mesh filter that were used in photos **112** and **113**. The filters sat in a housing that could be fitted to either side of the fuel filter, see ***1***, photo **114** or ***1***, photo **111**, depending on the orientation of how the filter was to be bolted to an engine.

113

114

2009 - Compressor

115: An improved version of the bore evacuator was fitted to the Panther **Ausf. A**. This **Rohrausblasevorrichtung** was a small compressor that was designed to clear the gunpowder gases from the breech of the gun tube after the firing of the main gun.

116: The small air tank of the bore evacuator is seen at ***1***. On recoil after firing of the main gun a valve was actuated that forced a volume of compressed air into the gun tube. This air forced the spent gunpowder fumes out of the forward end of the main gun.

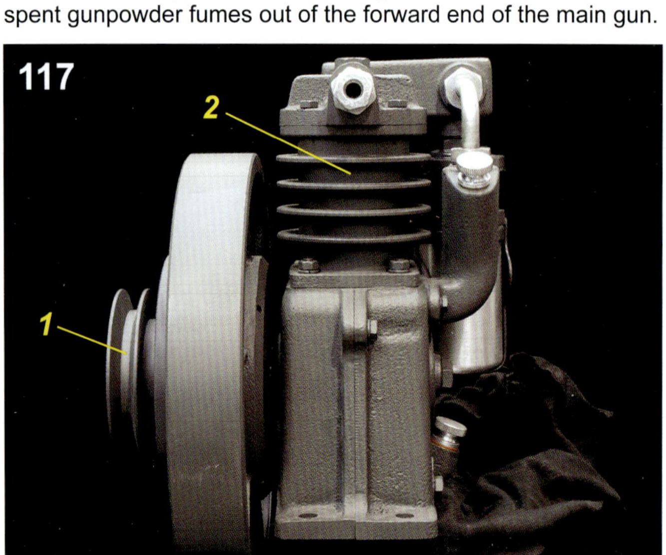

117: The bore evacuator was driven via a pulley belt that was connected to the hydraulic motor on the floor of the turret basket, see ***1***, page **89**, photo **309**. The pulley wheel is seen at ***1***.

118: The Wheatcroft Collection are a team of people who are never one to do anything by halves. Why just restore one item when you can restore several at once? Here we have a collection of six fully restored bore evacuators.

119: Here we see both the flywheel and pulley wheel of the bore evacuator before fitting to the main compressor body. This unit was bolted to the LHS of the turret floor underneath the Gunners station, see page **88**, photo **305**.

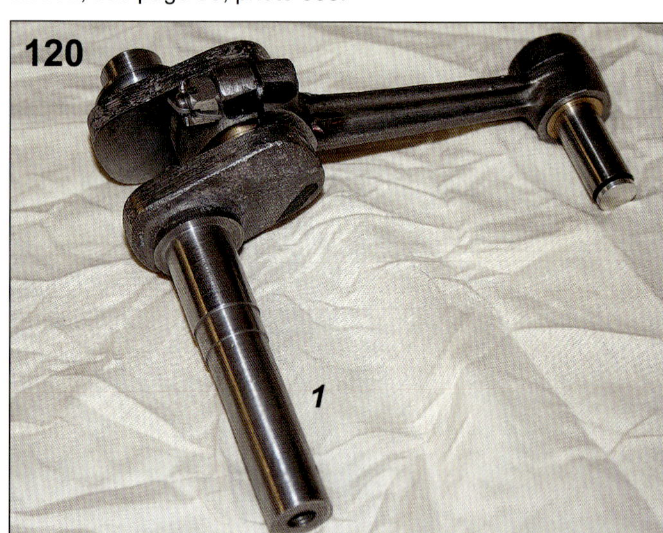

120: The crankshaft of the bore evacuator. The pulley wheel is connected directly to the shaft at ***1***. The piston arm is connected to a piston head that is installed in the chamber at **2**, photo **117**.

By 2009 the bulk of all the work on the exterior of **Fgst.Nr. 158134** had been completed. There were still a few outstanding items to be sourced or manufactured and also by this time all hull zimmerit had been applied. The focus of the restoration had now switched to the turret and as we have covered the hull in more detail in [12] we only present a small selection of images in this section.

121: A general view of the configuration of items on the rear plate of the tank. A heat shield, at ***1***, still has to be fitted on the same corresponding position on the RHS storage pannier.

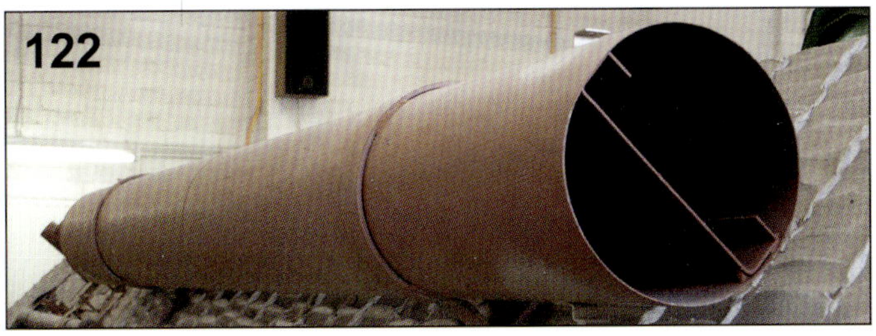

122: The gun barrel cleaning rods were stored in the tube as mounted to the upper LHS sponson side. Four cleaning rods were stored here along with a spare antenna when required.

123: A view of the LHS tracks. Examples of the cotter pins that hold the track pin retaining ring on a track pin can be seen at ***1***.

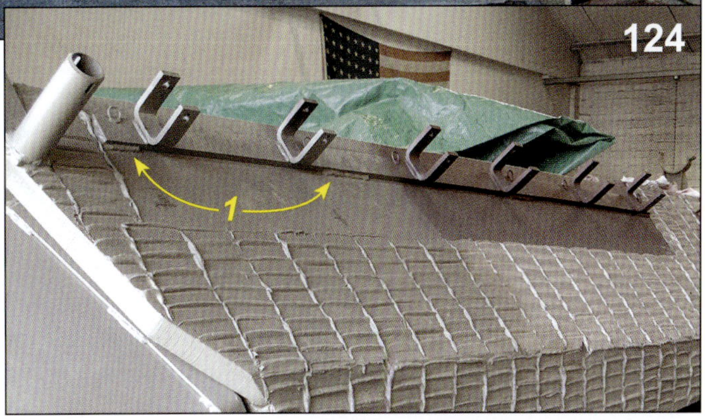

124-125: Note the spare track hanger on the RHS of the tank as ***welded*** to the hull side, at ***1***, photo **124**. When the Panther was first acquired by **The Wheatcroft Collection** the track hangers had been welded to the upper hull sides. The decision was made to correct this and have the track hangers bolted to the upper hull deck as was originally carried out by **Demag**, see the rework on page **121**, photo **365** and **366**. At **2**, photo **125**, we can see two of the radiator compartment hull deck plates.

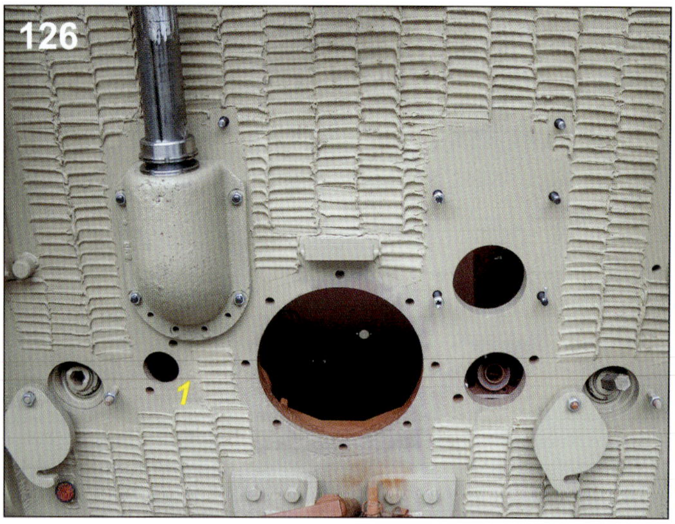

126: A view of the ports in the rear armoured plate. At ***1*** we can see the cold-water heating port, **Kühlwasser Heizgerät**. To aid cold weather engine starting a blowtorch would be inserted into the port and would be used to heat up the engine coolant, see technical illustration, page **199**.

127: Here we see the armoured plate that covers the port for the track adjuster, **Kettenspanner**, on the LHS of the tank. In order to increase tension on the LHS tracks the adjuster would be turned in an anti-clockwise direction.

128: Here we have an adjuster tool in the track adjuster port on the RHS of the tank. To adjust the tension on the RHS tracks the adjuster tool would be turned in a clockwise direction.

129: A general view of the RHS of the rear plate showing the RHS exhaust pipe port and the port for the crank starter at ***5***, **Schwungkraftanlasser**.

130: In order to manually turn the engine over a hand crank would be inserted into the guide tube at ***1***. This would mesh with the cardan shaft that runs from the rear of the crank starter, at ***1***, page **40**, photo **79**, that fits into the rear of this guide tube.

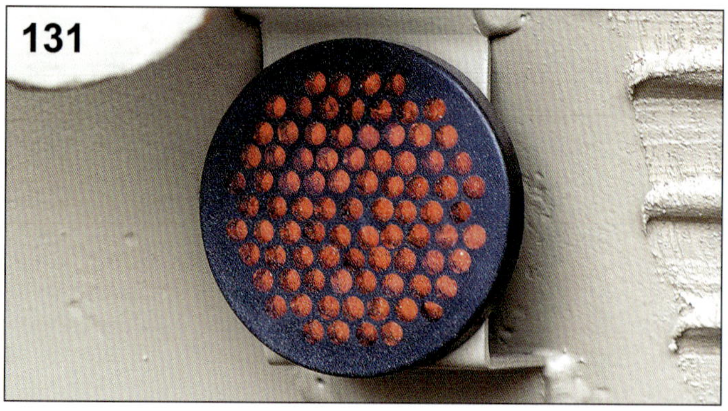

131: The vehicle reflector as located at the bottom corner of the LHS rear plate. Note that this reflector is a brand new ***original*** item. This is not a restored or newly manufactured part.

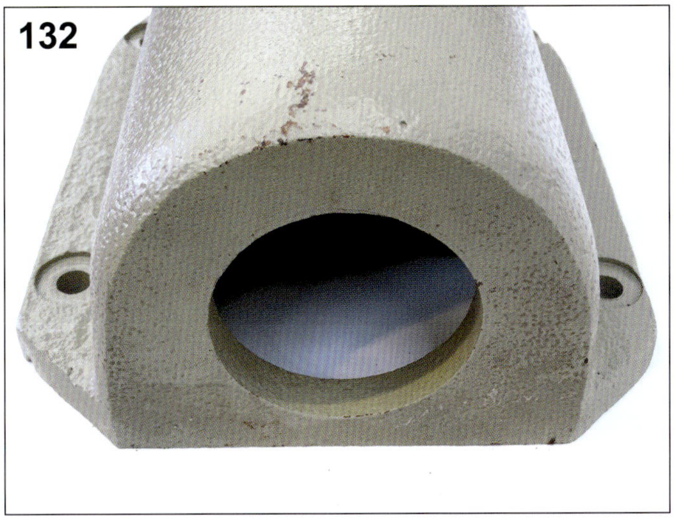

132: The twin Panther engine exhaust pipes that exited through the rear hull plate were protected by two large armoured covers. Here we are looking down at the top of the armoured cover that was to be fitted to the LHS of the tank.

135-136: The external exhaust pipe, **Auspuffrohr**, that was screwed onto the pipe inside the armoured exhaust cover is seen at ***1***, photo **136**. In the end of this exhaust pipe, at ***2***, photo **136**, is a small rod that acts as a stiffener for the pipe.

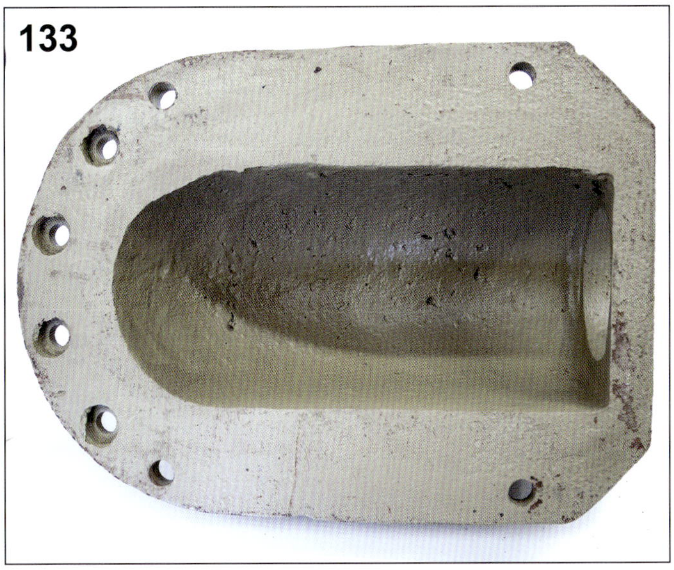

133: Looking into the same armoured exhaust cover as seen in photo **132**. The exhaust pipe section, page **46**, photo **107**, fits inside this cover, see page **46**, photo **108** and photo **138**.

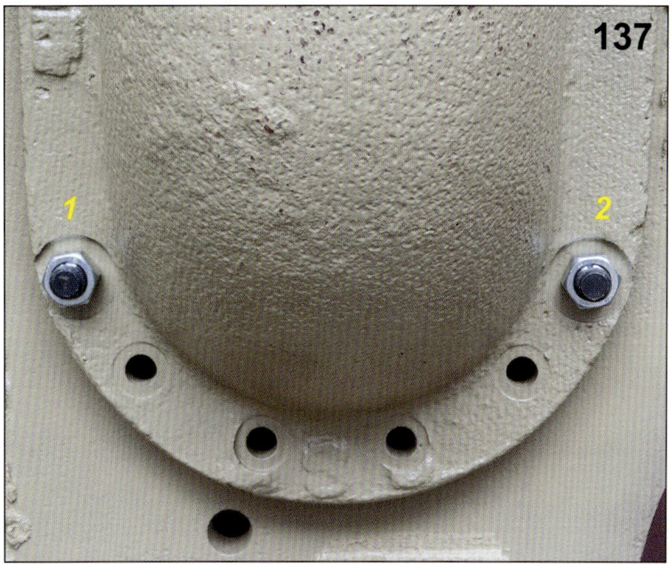

137: Here we see the armoured exhaust cover now bolted to the tank over the LHS exhaust port in the rear hull plate. Note that only the bolt holes, at ***1*** and ***2***, are used for securing the cover.

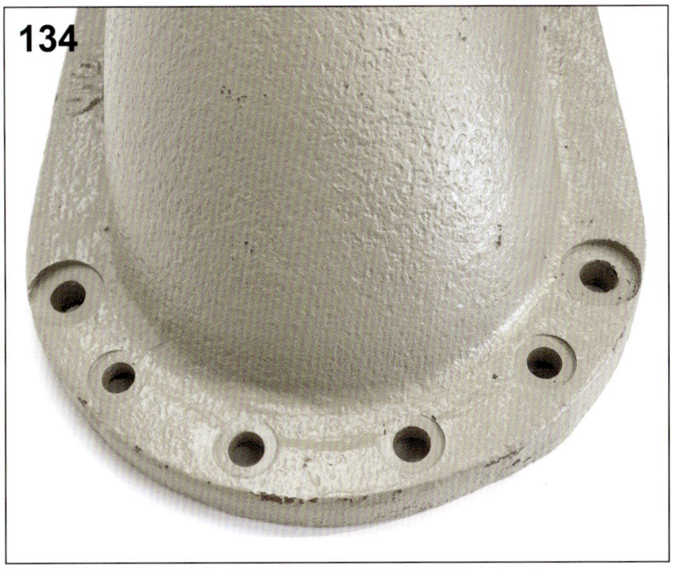

134: The bottom outside edge of the same armoured exhaust cover. Note all the drilled holes. Only four actual bolts secured this cover to the rear plate, see ***1-4***, page **50**, photo **129**.

138: The external exhaust pipe is screwed onto the pipe inside the armoured exhaust cover using the large circular pipe union at ***3***. This is tightened down by using a large c-spanner.

2009 - Gearbox Access Plate

139: As has been stated that two Panthers will be rebuilt we see in photos **139** and **140** the process of restoring two of the hull roof gearbox access plates. The gearbox access plates here are of the type that could be fitted to either the **Ausf. D** or **A**.

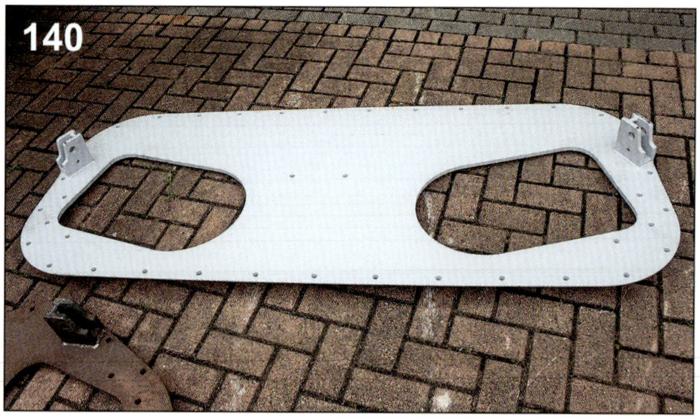

140: Here we see one of the gearbox access hull roof plates that has already been sandblasted and primed. This plate is still to be painted in red primer.

141: Now we have the plate red primed and in place. The plate is bolted down using countersunk bolts. These can be seen quite clearly in photo **142**.

142: The hatch retaining mechanism for the Radio Operator. This was use to prevent the crew hatch swinging free when open.

143: Each crew hull hatch was mounted onto a spring-loaded piston. This was spring balanced in such a way that a crewman could raise and lower the hatch quite easily. Three bolts secured a hatch to the plate on top of the piston.

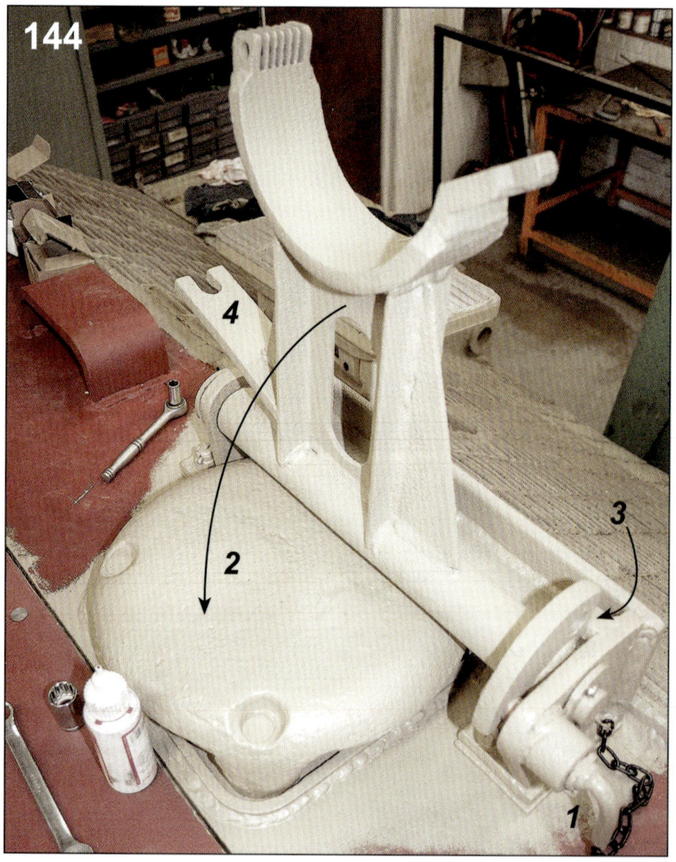

144: The upper hull main gun travel lock. For stowage in combat the pin at ***1*** would be withdrawn, the travel lock would then be folded back flat on the hull, ***2***, and the pin reinserted back into the hole locking the unit down, at ***3***.

145
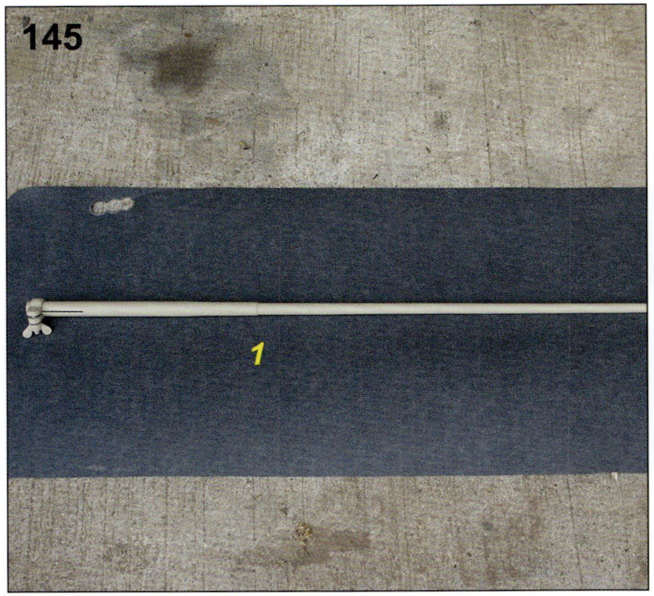

146
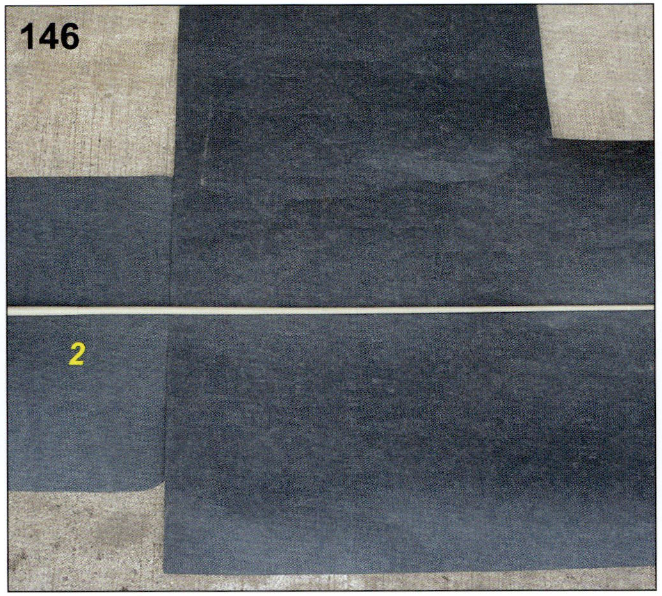

147

145-147: Here we see a montage of images showing the full length of the aerial but this is mainly to show the taper of the overall rod. The diameter of the lowest section of the aerial shaft measures **27mm** which tapers to **18mm** at the top with the overall length being **2m**. This aerial was not a one-piece item but was comprised of three separate sections. You can see where these three sections join at ***1***, photo **145**, and **2**, photo **146**.

148

149
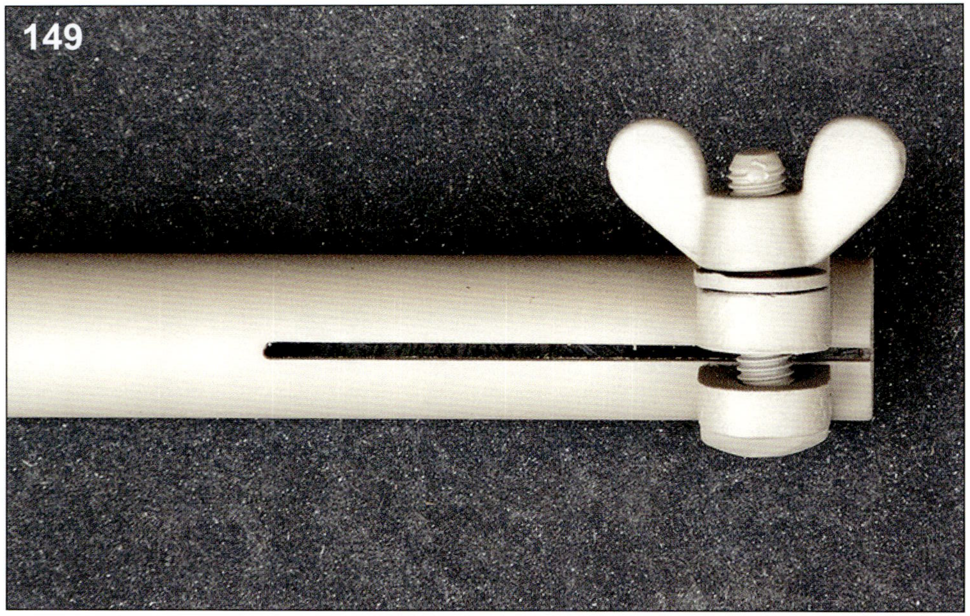

148-149: In photo **149** we can see the simple wing nut clamp that was used to secure the aerial to the hull base mount, **Antennfu.B.2**, see ***1***, page **122**, photo **367**. Early versions of the aerial were manufactured from a composite of fibre and copper strip while later versions were made from steel. The aerial seen here is of the late variety.

150: Looking down at the rear end of the lower hull fuel tank as fitted to the LHS of the tank. This tank was not interchangeable with the lower hull fuel tank on the RHS due to the cut out in the box shape designed to fit around the rear LHS shock absorber.

151: The forward end of the lower hull fuel tank as fitted to the LHS of the tank. Note the rubber strapping, at ***1***, that was used to prevent vibration, wear and ultimate splitting of the fuel tank due to operation stresses.

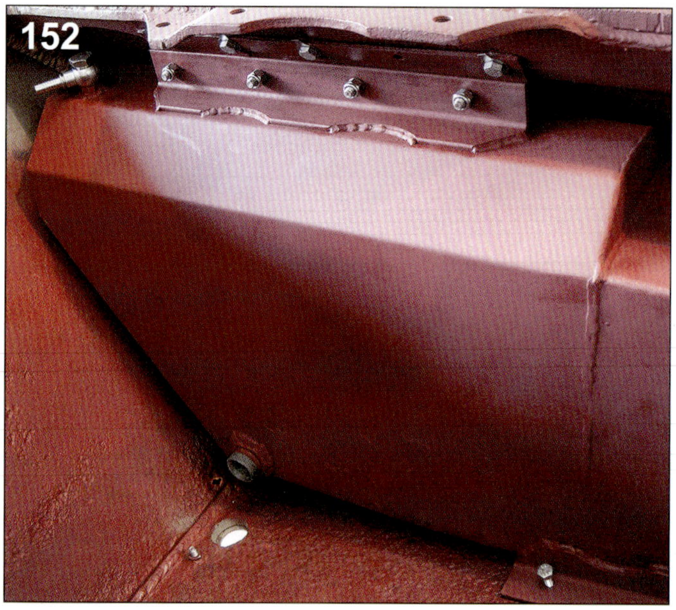

152: The rear end of the upper LHS fuel tank as located in the LHS hull sponson. All five fuel tanks, in either the upper or lower hull, were suspended from brackets with none making any direct contact with the hull floor or sides.

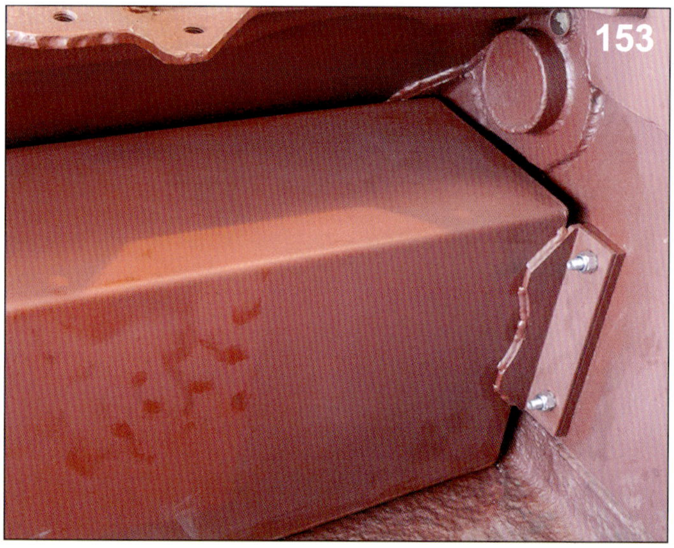

153: In this photo we see the front end of the upper LHS fuel tank as located in the LHS hull sponson.

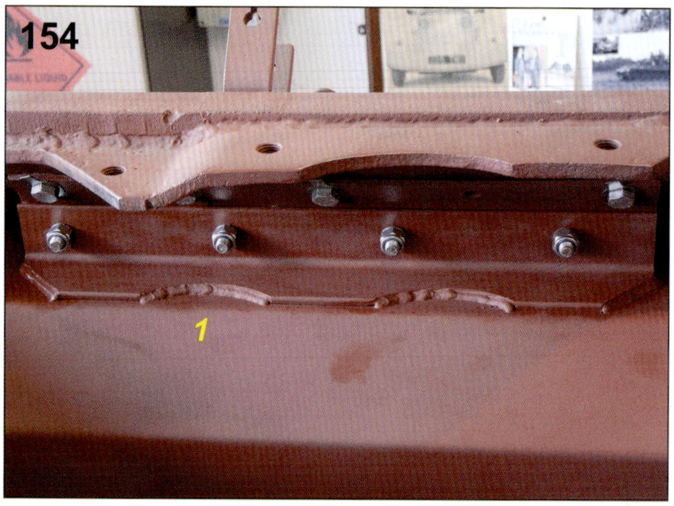

154: A close-up view of the mounting bracket as seen in photo **152**. The scalloped sections, at ***1***, were designed to create a longer section of edge contact between objects thus allowing for a longer run of welding to be employed.

155: The welded pipe conduit, at ***1,*** runs into the RHS forward radiator compartment and is connected to a pipe that carries oil and runs back to the oil cooler on the LHS of the engine.

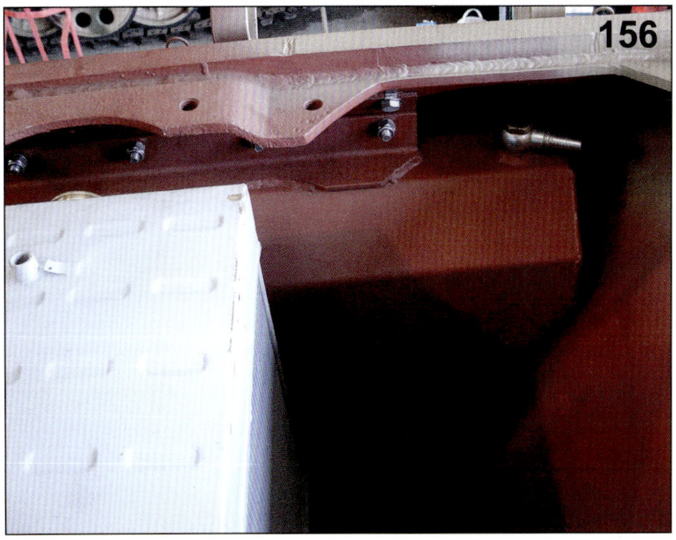

156: Here we see the rear end of the upper RHS fuel tank as located in the RHS hull sponson. The radiator was at this time being test fitted to ensure all clearances were correct.

157: A selection of modern fuel pipe connector unions are shown here. Modern materials should prevent issues with fuel leaks, an issue that was common on early Panther **Ausf. D** variants and that was only corrected as part of later vehicle series rebuilds.

158: This union is part of the overflow piping that runs from the rear top of the upper RHS sponson and back to the fuel system header tank. The pipe can be seen at ***1***, page **131**, photo **385**.

159: Here we can see piping connected to the rear RHS radiator, ***1***. This piping carries hot water from the engine block into the top of the rear RHS radiator, see ***1***, page **57**, illustration 166.

160: Of interest seen in this photo is the inner flange section of the exhaust pipe at ***1***, see also page **46**, photo **107**, that is fitted into the armoured exhaust housing.

161: There were four radiators used for water cooling that were fitted into a Panther. Three of these radiators were identical with the fourth being of a smaller width.

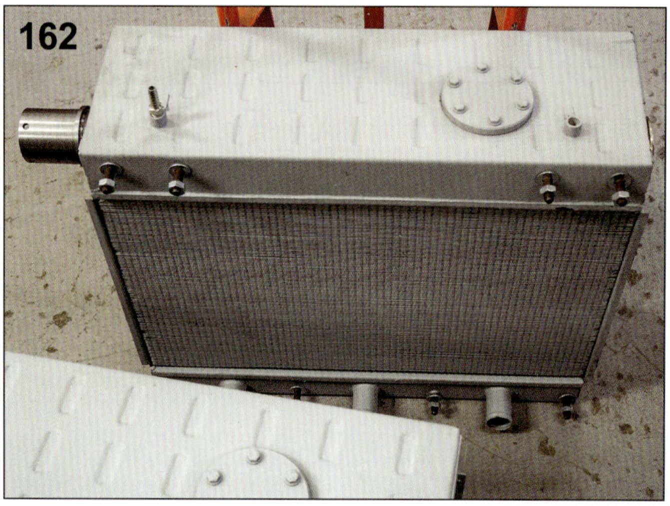

162: The three large radiators were all interchangeable items. They each had along one bottom edge three tubes, seen clearly at ***1***, photo **161**. These tubes would be for either the input or output of water depending on how the radiators ended up being positioned. The side of the radiator with the bottom edge tubes always faced inwards towards the fan units.

163: One side of each large radiator would be fitted with a brass blanking plug while the other was fitted with a steel tube that would be connected to a coolant hose. On the top of each large radiator were two threaded ports. Once it had been determined into which configuration a radiator would be fitted one of these top ports would be blanked off while the other would be fitted with a pipe union. This union would form part of the overflow piping, see ***1***, page **132**, photo **387**.

164: The side of a radiator with a large brass blanking plug. In this configuration this radiator could be either the forwardmost LHS or the rearmost RHS radiator. The bolts seen at ***1*** are connected to the upper fan drive cradle, see **2**, page **132**, photo **387**.

165: The large steel tube seen at ***1*** would protrude through a side wall of the engine compartment. This would be connected to a coolant hose for circulation of either hot or cooled water. Note the overflow pipe union connector seen at ***2***.

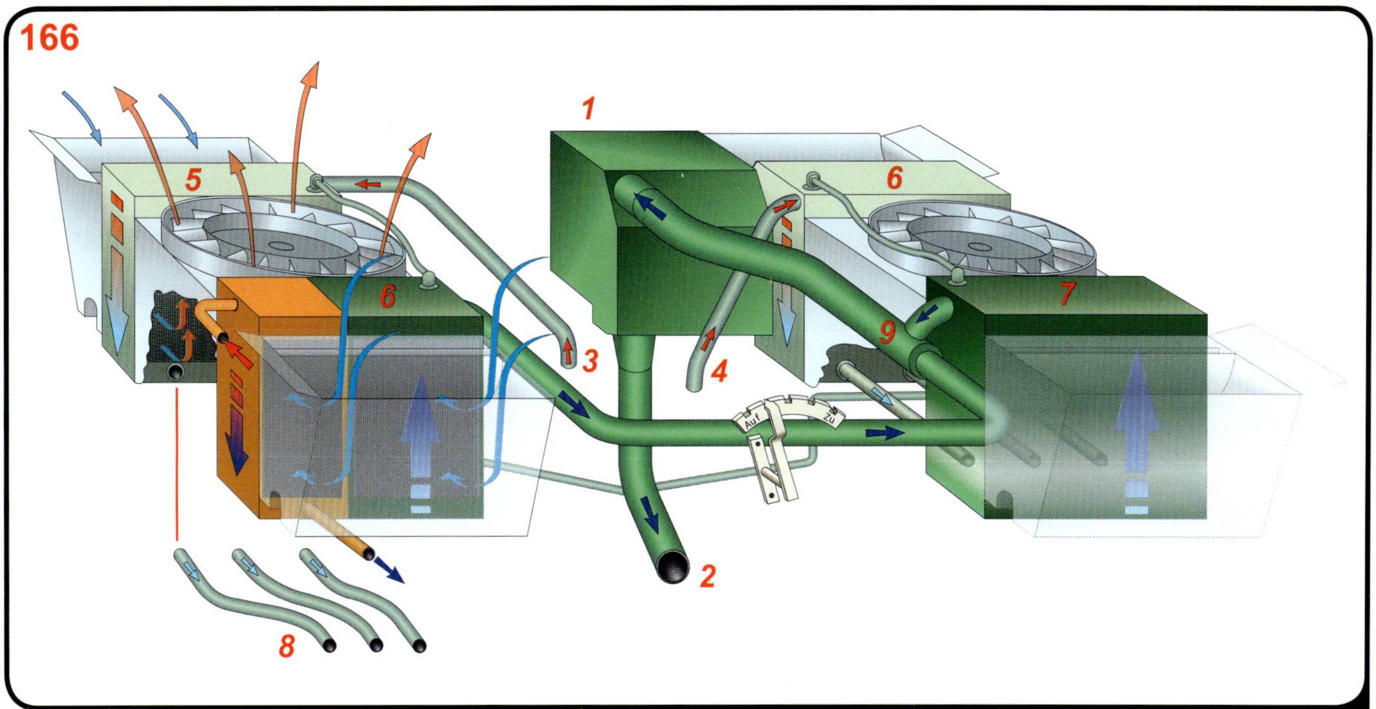

166: Here we see the coolant flow system of the Panther. Water flows from the header tank, *1*, into the oil cooler at *2*. From the oil cooler water is moved into the water pump and then through the engine block. Water exits the engine block at two points, *3* and *4*, and flows into the two rear radiators, *5* and *6*. Water flows down through these radiators and into the forward radiators, *6* and *7* via three connecting pipes, *8*. Water then flows up through the forward radiators and then back into the header tank, *9*.

167: Here we see both the oil cooler radiator, at ***1***, and the small water coolant radiator, at ***2***. This small water coolant radiator could only be installed in one configuration. There were three tubes at a bottom edge that were used for input of cooled water. This radiator also only had one overflow port on the upper surface, at ***3***. The oil cooler radiator could also only be installed in one configuration. This radiator had a single input port for hot oil, at ***4***, and a single output port for cooler oil, at ***5***.

168: In the photographs on this page we lucky to be able to watch the restoration engineers as they worked on test fitting all the elements of the coolant system in the radiator compartments. You can see how the fan drive is enclosed in a sheet metal box, designed to ensure any air drawn into this box will only be blown out up through the fan.

169: To prevent movement of the fan drive in the fan box the base of the fan sits in the dished section, at ***1***, while the top of the fan is bolted to the fan cage, at **2**, and the lower flange rim of the fan drive, at ***3***, page **38**, photo **73**. For the coolant overflow piping the radiator port at ***3*** will be blanked off with the ports at ***4*** and ***5*** being connected.

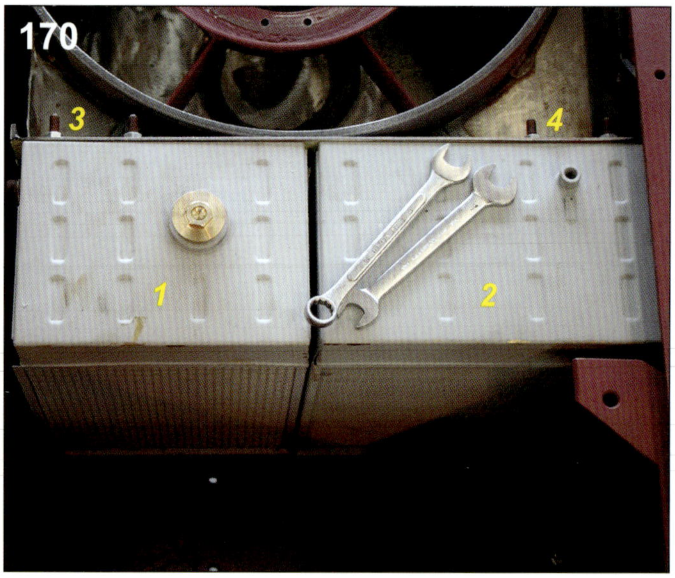

170: Here we can see how the oil cooler radiator, at ***1***, and the small coolant radiator, at **2**, are situated next to each other. All radiators in each compartment were bolted to the top of their respective fan drive box, at ***3*** and ***4***.

171: A look down into the fan drive box. This still has to be primed and painted. The port in the engine sidewall, at ***1***, is used by the cardan shaft that drives the fan directly from the engine.

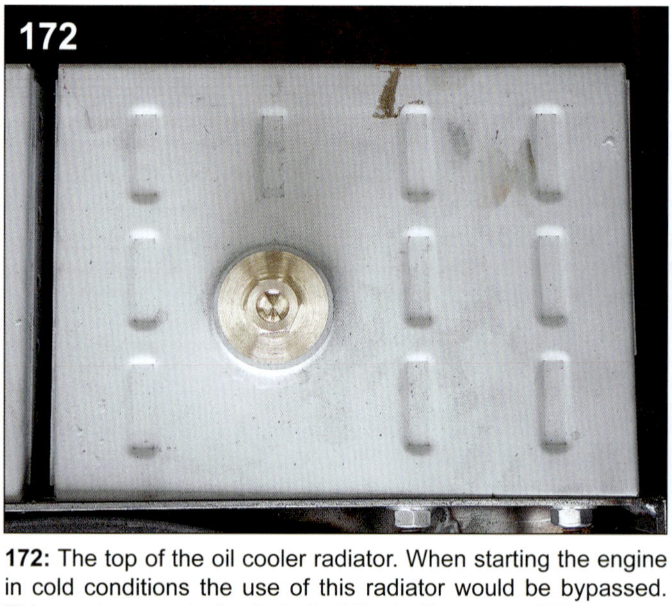

172: The top of the oil cooler radiator. When starting the engine in cold conditions the use of this radiator would be bypassed. This can be seen in the technical illustration, page **199**.

173

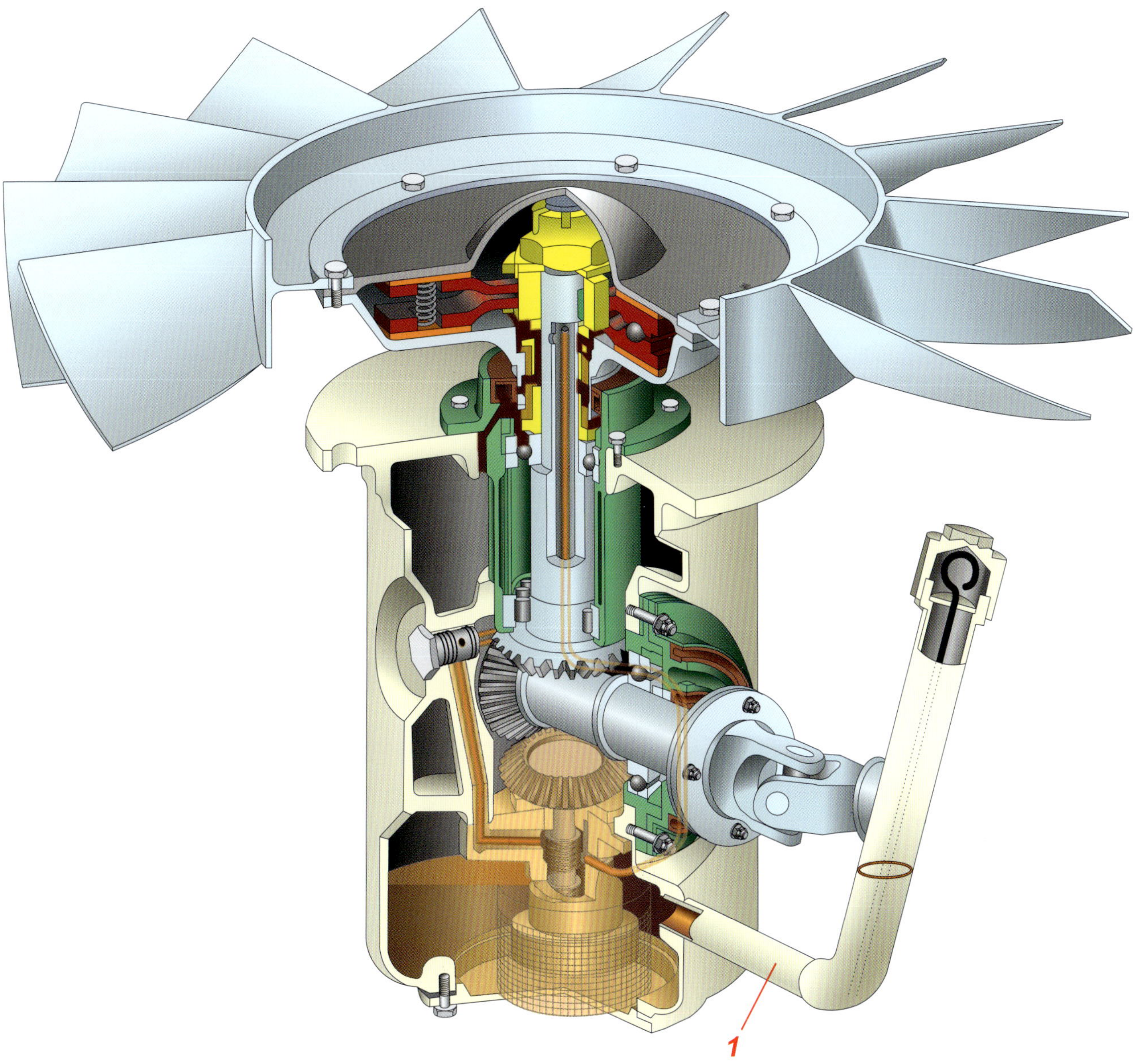

173: The Fan drive unit. This was powered directly from the engine using a cardan shaft. A technical illustration showing the general connection to the engine of a fan drive can be seen on page 201. Torque from the engine was transmitted to the fan drives through the use of a slip clutch. This slip clutch was designed to prevent sudden acceleration or deceleration of the engine being directly transmitted to the fan drives thus reducing the risk of damage [14]. Each fan drive unit had a dipstick used to measure the internal oil level. The horizontal section of a dipstick tube, *1*, was aligned with and passed through a small sealed port in the engine compartment side wall, see *1*, page 128, photo 380 and *1*, page 128, photo 381. To each pipe was fixed a vertical dipstick tube which was then bolted to the engine compartment sidewall. This vertical dipstick tube came up between the engine and the side wall to the top of the engine. When the engine deck hatch was raised you then had easy access to be able to dip the fan drive oil level. If the engine was to be removed both the vertical fan drive dipstick tubes had to be removed otherwise the engine would foul on them when lifted.

174-177: Here we have four views of the coolant system header tank. This tank is bolted to the upper edge rear plate bracket seen at ***1***, page **127**, photo **378**, using the brace at ***1***, photo **175**, and can be seen in situ on page **133**, photo **388**. The coolant system held a total of **150** litres of water but in very cold conditions this would be changed to a **50:50** mixture of water and **Glysantin**. **Glysantin** is a coolant that is designed to protect an engine from the effects of overheating, corrosion and frost. The filler port for the coolant is at ***1***, photo **174**. Cool water from the radiators flowed into the header tank at ***2***, photo **177**, and out into the oil cooler via a large port on the bottom of the tank. This is depicted clearly in the technical illustration, page **200**.

178: A general look down view into the fighting compartment showing all work as was completed by 2009. In this view we look towards the front of the tank. All the floor panels are in place. The ammunition panniers are all new items modelled from the corroded original items. It is worth noting that the new wooden retainers seen on top of each pannier were still in good condition on the original items.

179: Here we are looking towards the rear of the tank. Again all floor panels are now in place. The blue panels we see are designed to provide safe step areas for the restoration mechanics to stand upon to prevent damage to the surrounding equipment as well as providing a safe working area for themselves.

180-181: All photos on page **62** are a montage of images looking into the fighting compartment towards the rear of the tank. In photos **180** and **181** we can see the tank battery trays, at ***1*** and ***2***, and the battery isolation system at ***3***, photo **181**. The Panther employed two lead-acid batteries that incorporated two sets of lead plates enclosed in a heated casing. The two types of batteries that could be used were used referenced as either **12 B 150, (150Ah capacity, 12V)** or **12 B 120, (120Ah capacity, 12V)** [16].

182-183: Of main interest in these photos are the two original spent main gun round cases that are test fitted into the three-round under turret basket floor ammunition pannier. At ***1***, photo **183**, we see a frame that held a flat tray and a storage box, at ***2***, photo **183**. The tray held a variety of vehicle and main gun tools. The storage box was used to hold tools for track maintenance [17].

184-185: Also of interest is the floor of the fighting compartment. The tread plate, also known as diamond plate, has been faithfully reproduced and was designed to give a non-slip platform on which the turret crew could operate. At ***1***, photo **185** we can see the hydraulic oil reservoir for the turret traverse mechanism.

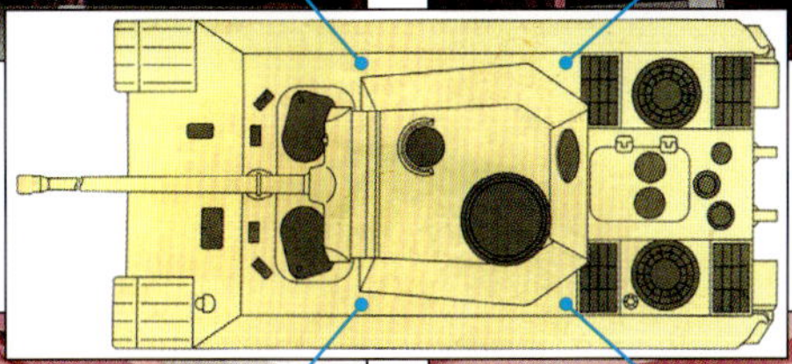

186: Continuing a tour around the fighting compartment looking at the sponsons and engine firewall. The diagram indicates the area of interest in the tank being viewed.

187: The RHS rear sponson ammunition pannier. The small box, seen at ***1***, stores the tools for the servicing and maintenance of the turret mounted **M.G.34**.

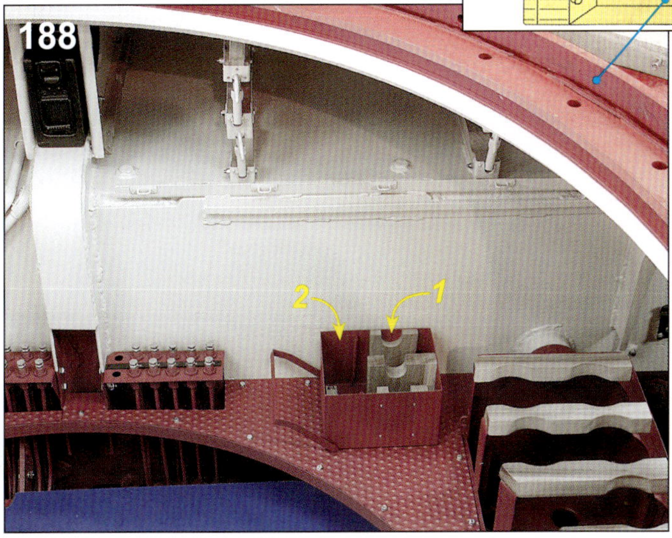

188: The front LHS sponson ammunition pannier. The box on the floor was used to store the breech shell case ejection finger assembly, at ***1***, and a spare periscope vision block for the loader, at ***2***, see also page **84**, photo **288**.

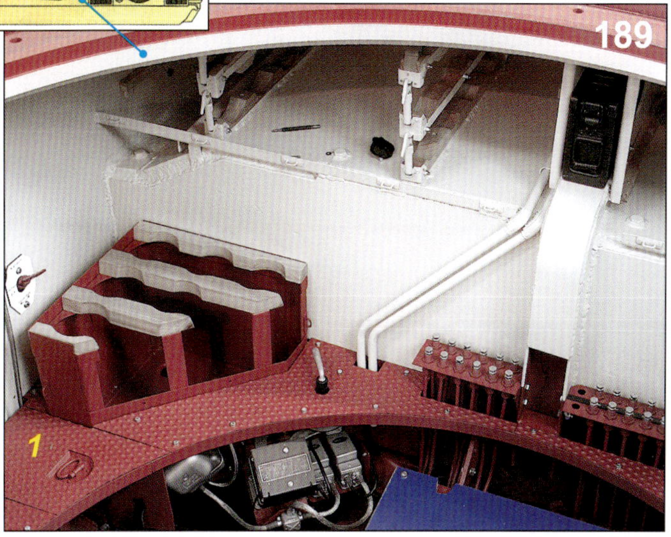

189: The floor panel, at ***1***, could be lifted and the panel in the LHS firewall could be removed, at ***1***, photo **191**, see also **2**, page **135**, photo **391**. This gave access to the fuel and oil filters at the bottom LHS of the engine.

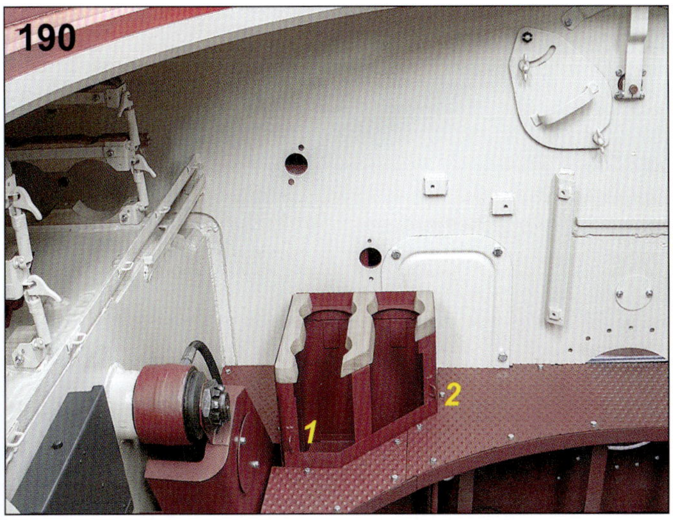

190: Note the small loops, at ***1*** and ***2***, photo **190** and ***3*** and ***4***, photo **191**, on the floor mounted ammunition panniers, seen more clearly at ***1*** and **2**, page **64**, photo **193**. Canvas sheets were secured here to cover the sponson ammunition panniers.

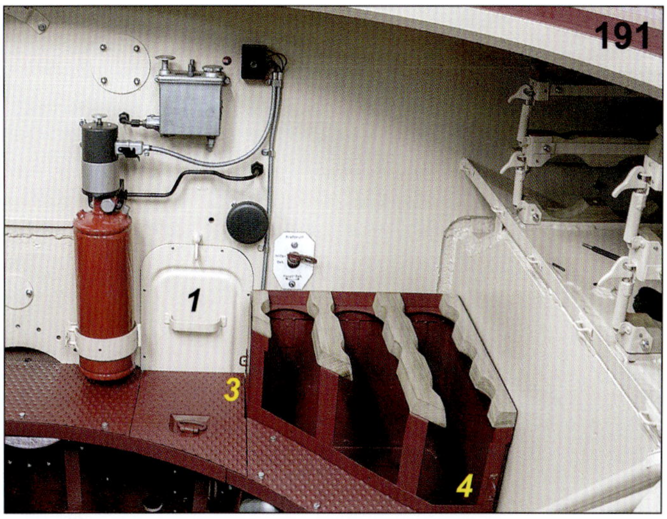

191: These canvas sheets also covered the sponson ammunition panniers and were used to protect the main gun rounds from dirt and damage etc. These were often discarded as they interfered with the ability to remove main gun rounds quickly in combat.

192: A general view showing how the turret floor at the rear RHS of the fighting compartment is built around the rear RHS shock absorber and ammunition pannier.

193: Looking down at the three-round ammunition pannier at the rear RHS of the fighting compartment. All main gun rounds stored vertically in the fighting compartment are oriented nose down.

194: Mounted to the lower hull side on the RHS of the tank is a box used to store the tool kit and spare parts for the turret mounted **M.G.34**. The tools are still to be placed in the box.

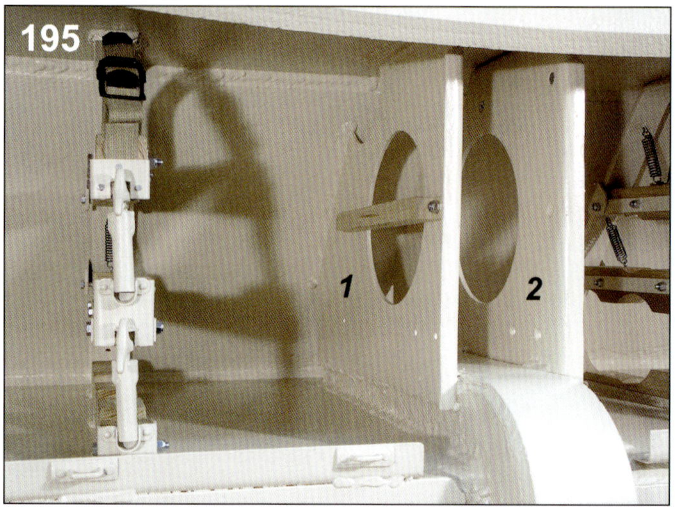

195: At the mid-point in the sponsons in the fighting compartment are two vertical support braces, at ***1*** and ***2***. The brackets defined the limits of the sponson ammunition panniers and provided a compartment for the stowage of an **M.G.34** ammunition box.

196: A close-up view of the catch used to close the **M.G.34** tool kit box. This is a simple push button that releases a small latch that clips to the inside of the box lid.

197: In the LHS sponson we can see an **M.G.34** ammunition box in place. The wooden strip, at ***1***, was used to prevent excessive longitudinal movement of a main gun round when stored in the mid-level layer of a sponson ammunition pannier.

198: This section of hull flooring can be removed to gain access to the small panel in the LHS engine compartment firewall. This panel gives access to the oil filter housing and the fuel pumps.

199: Here we see two original expended main gun rounds that are being test fitted in place in the three-round under turret floor ammunition pannier.

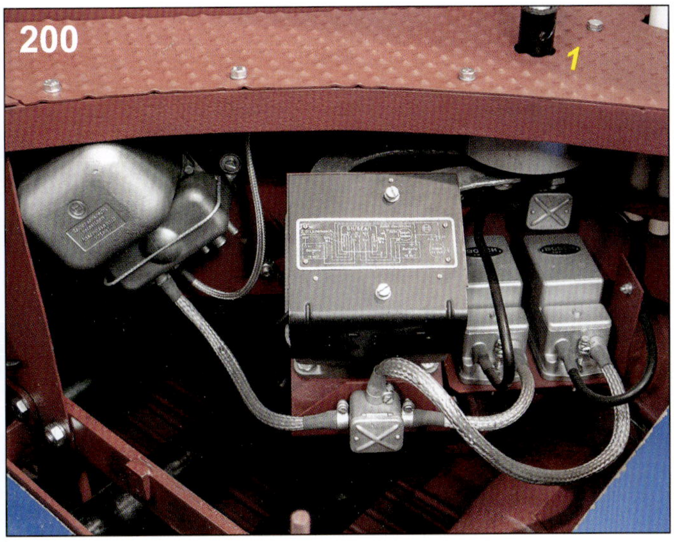

200: The battery isolation system is mounted under the turret floor to the rear LHS of the fighting compartment. This switch is operated by a square headed key, at ***1***, and is seen more clearly at ***1***, page **61**, photo **179**.

201: A close-up view of two of the Bosch suppressor/filters that form part of the battery charging circuit.

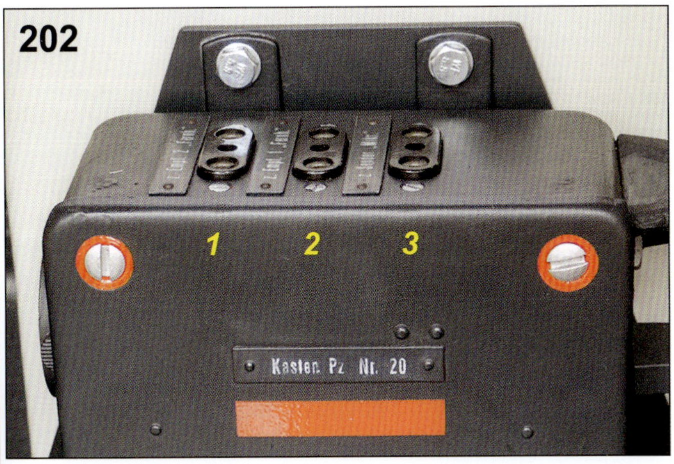

202: At the rear of the radio frame is the intercom connection box, **Kasten Pz. Nr. 20**, see ***1***, page **66**, photo **207**. This box is powered via the cable, seen at ***1***, page **74**, photo **242**. At ***1*** is the plug for the **UKw.E.e 2 (secondary receiver)**, page **74**, photo **240**. At **2** is the plug for the **UKw.E.e 1 (primary receiver)**, page **74**, photo **242**. At ***3*** is the plug for the **Fu 5 10 W.S.c Sender**, page **74**, photo **243**.

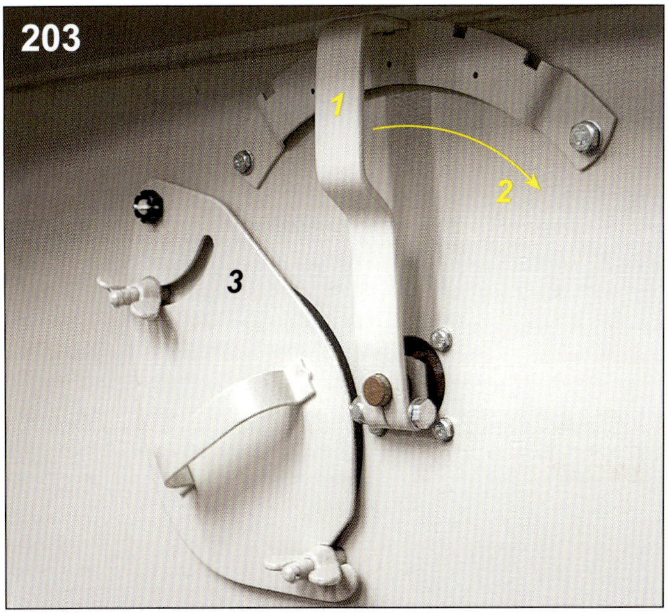

203: At the upper mid-section of the engine firewall we have the control lever for the opening and closing of the fan louvres, at ***1***, see also page **130**, photos **383** and **384**. Movement of the lever clockwise, at **2**, closed the fan louvres. Behind the access panel, at ***3***, is the control lever for engaging or disengaging the fan drives, see technical illustration, page **201**.

2009 - Fighting Compartment

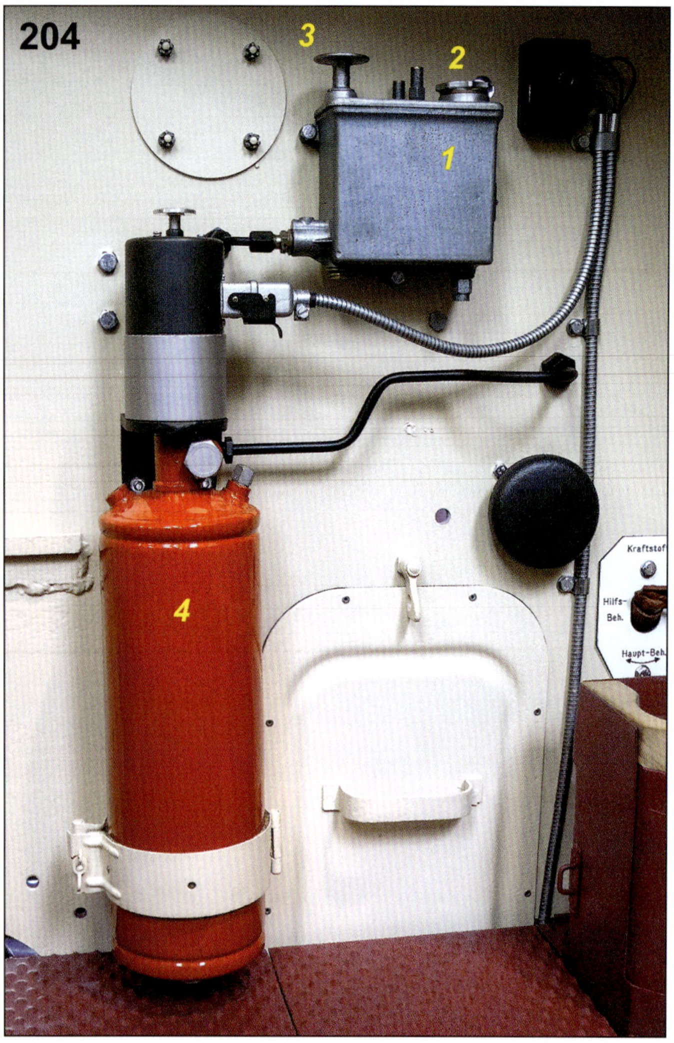

204: At *1* we have the cold start injection pump that is used to aid in starting the engine. **Gasolin** is poured into the port at *2*. The handle, at *3*, is then pumped which thus causes fuel to be injected into the inlet manifolds. This air/fuel mix in the manifolds then helps the engine to fire immediately upon first turn over.

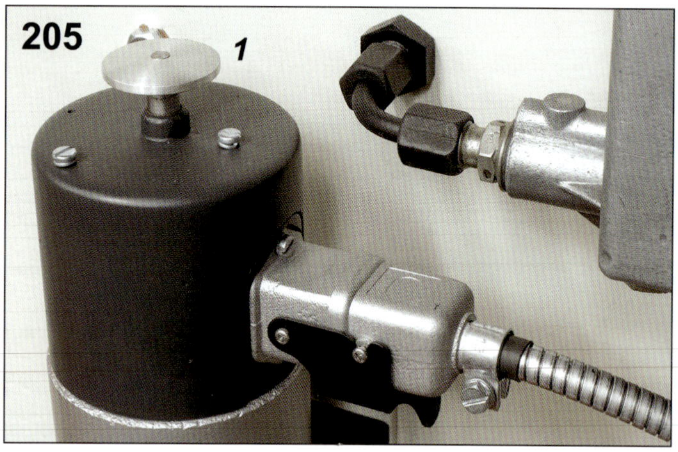

205: The upper section of the automatic fire extinguisher system for the engine compartment. The full unit is seen at *4*, photo **204**. If the temperature in the engine compartment exceeded **160°C** a mixture of **CB** (carbon-chlorine-bromine) was sprayed for seven seconds at specific hazardous areas on the engine. The system could also be operated manually using the push knob at *1*.

206: Here we can see the vent plug that provided cool air to the electrical generator in the engine compartment, at *1*. At *2* we can see the master switch for the fuel system.

207: A view from the centre of the fighting compartment looking forward to the front of the tank. The whole area appears spacious but once all the ammunition panniers are filled with shells and the turret is in place, it became extremely difficult for either the driver or the radio operator to egress from their stations and exit through the turret if their crew hatches were blocked or jammed in place.

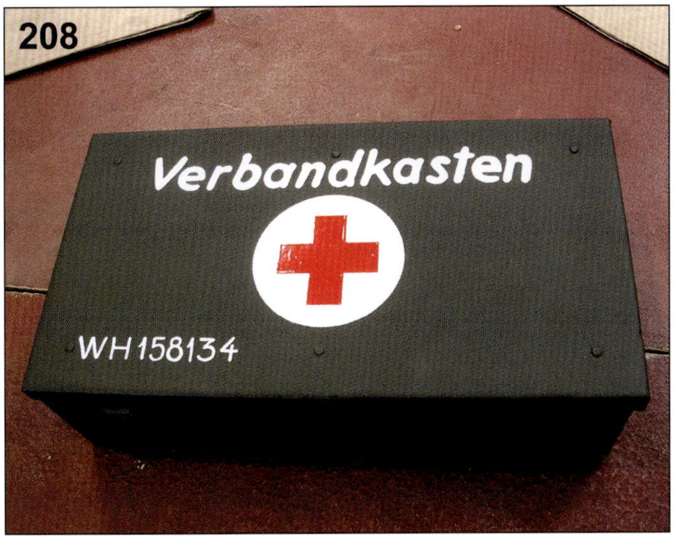

208: The tanks first aid kit, **Verbandkasten**, is located at the front of the fighting compartment, between the ammunition panniers situated directly behind the driver and radio operators station.

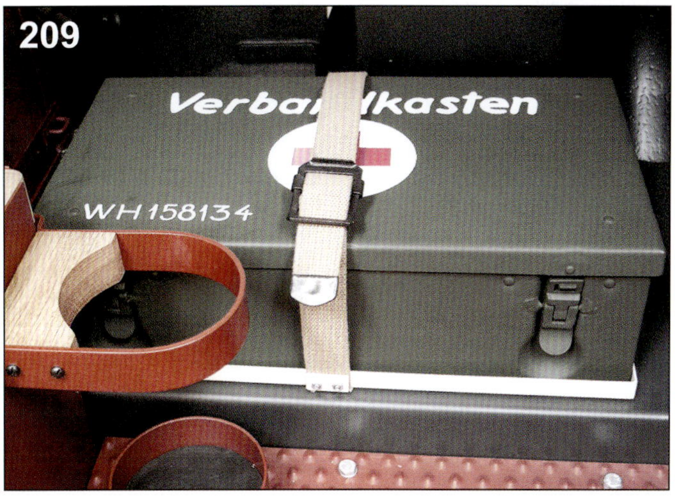

209: The box of the first aid kit is an original wartime item that has been fully restored. Note that the box is marked with the **Fahrgestellnummer** number of the tank. The canvas retaining strap and buckle are new items patterned on original parts.

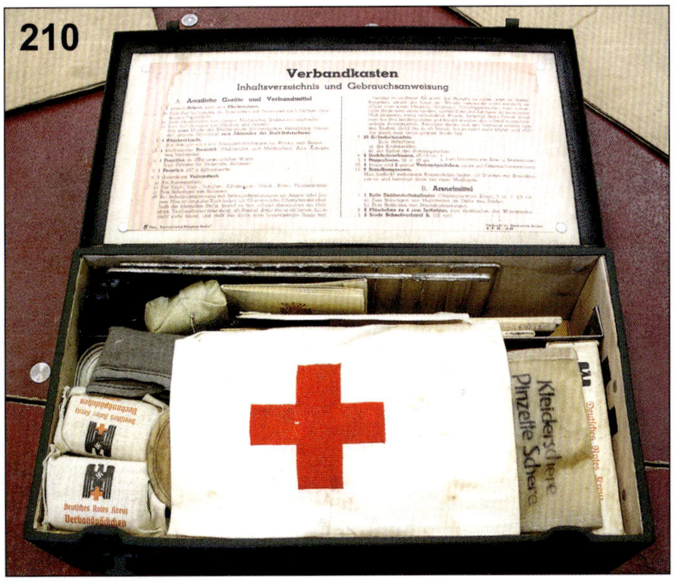

210: The label on the inside of the box lid is an original inventory list of what the first aid kit should comprise of. All items in the box are original and are still in their original packaging.

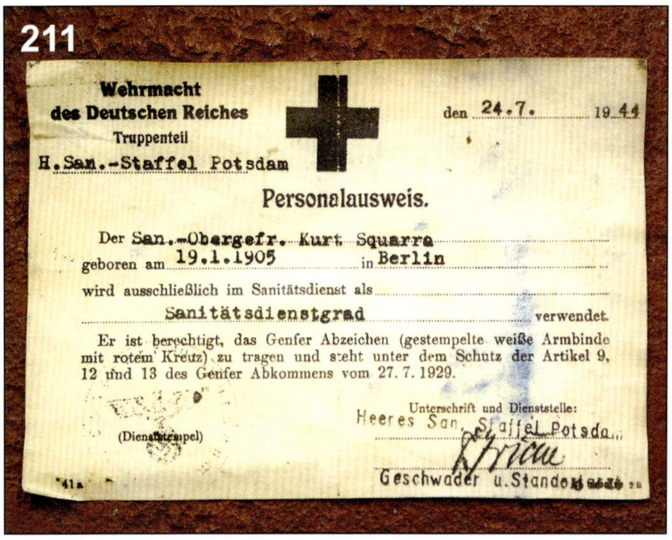

Wehrmacht des Deutschen Reiches
Truppenteil H.San.-Staffel Potsdam
den 24.7. 1944

Personalausweis.

Der San.-Obergefr. Kurt Squarre geboren am 19.1.1905 in Berlin wird ausschließlich im Sanitätsdienst als Sanitätsdienstgrad verwendet.

Er ist berechtigt, das Genfer Abzeichen (gestempelte weiße Armbinde mit rotem Kreuz) zu tragen und steht unter dem Schutz der Artikel 9, 12 und 13 des Genfer Abkommens vom 27. 7. 1929.

(Dienststempel)
Unterschrift und Dienststelle:
Heeres San. Staffel Potsdam
Geschwader u. Standort

211: Also in the box is an identify card for a **Kurt Squarre**, born in 1905 in Berlin, whose military rank was **San.-Obergefr.** (Lance Corporal) and was a member of the Medical Services. The lower section of text roughly translates as '*He is entitled to wear the Geneva badge (armband with a red cross) and is protected by Articles 9, 12 and 13 of the Geneva Convention*'.

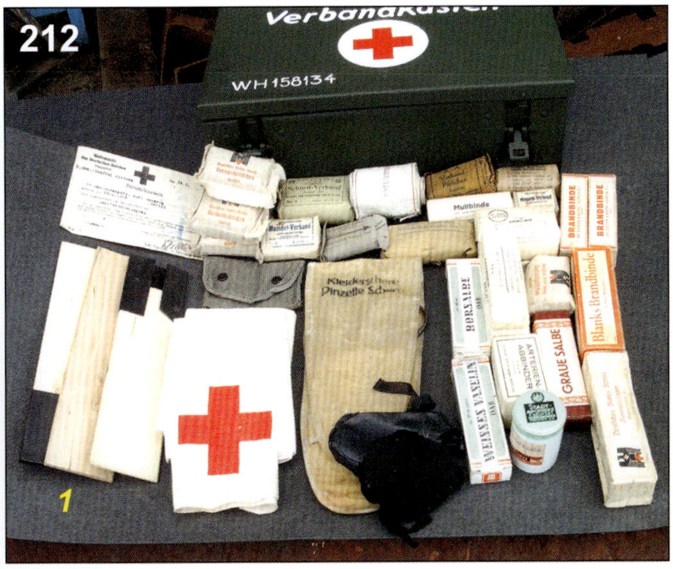

212: Here we see a selection of the majority of the items from inside the first aid box. Note the wooden splints, at *1*, that can be slotted together, for aid in setting broken bones etc.

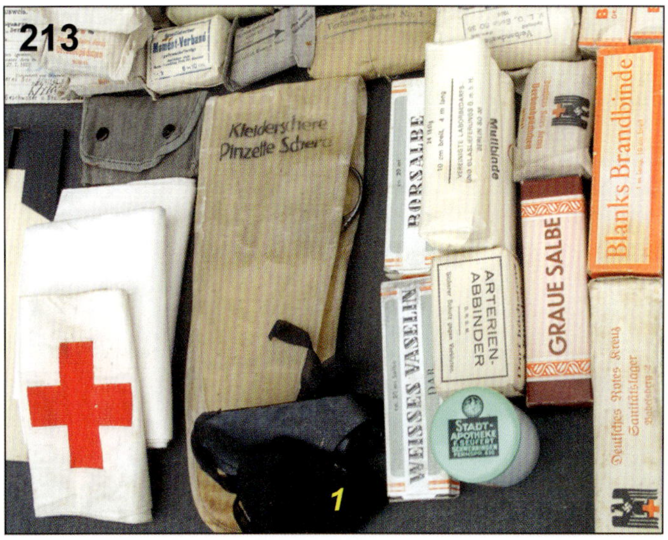

213: Of interest also in the contents of the box is an eye patch, at *1*. Not something you might expect but in combat situations head and eye injuries would be a lot more common.

214

214: In this photo we can observe an original demolition charge storage container. This container is heavily corroded but as all parts are intact it can be used as a pattern for the fabrication of new items.

215

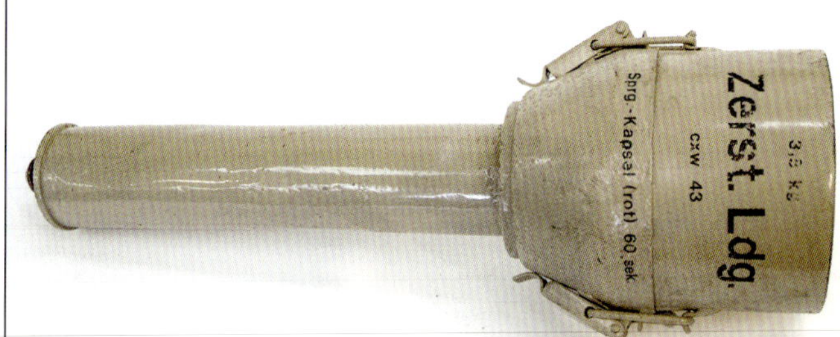

215: An original demolition charge, **Zerstörungs-Ladung**, (with all explosives having been removed) complete with dunkelgelb paint and original label markings.

216

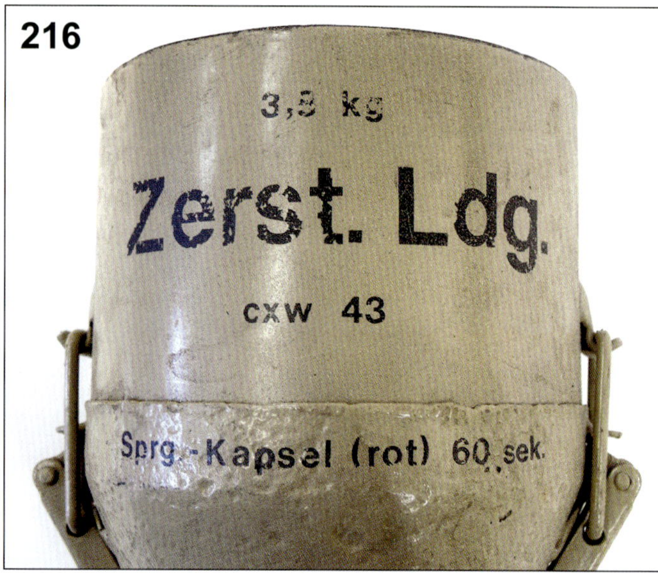

216: The labelling on the demolition charge can be interpreted as follows: a) the device contains 3.5kg of explosive; b) **Zerst. Ldg.** in full is **Zerstörungs-Ladung**, meaning demolition charge; c) **cwx 43** would appear to be a manufacturers code = **Ludwig Braun, Schmalkalden in Theuringen (1943)**; d) **Sprg-Kapsel (rot) 60 sek**. in full is **Spreng-Kapsel (rot) 60 sekunden**, and means detonator cap, detonator (red) 60 sec. (delay).

217

217: A close-up view of the end cap of the demolition charge container. The hole we see here is due to corrosion and is not an actual feature of the cap.

218

218: To activate the fuse the red knob would be pulled and then the charge would be placed. The crew would have a short while to evacuate the vicinity before the explosive detonated.

219: A close-up view of the top lid and a tension clasp of a newly manufactured demolition charge container.

221: In order to protect the demolition charge from moisture the cap of the charge container sits in a rim that has a rubber seal, at ***1***. Note the small brackets, at ***2***, that hold the demolition charge in place to stop it moving around in the storage container.

223: A side by side comparison of the original demolition charge container, page **68**, photo **214**, next to a newly manufactured container. We can clearly see the level of skill and workmanship that has been achieved.

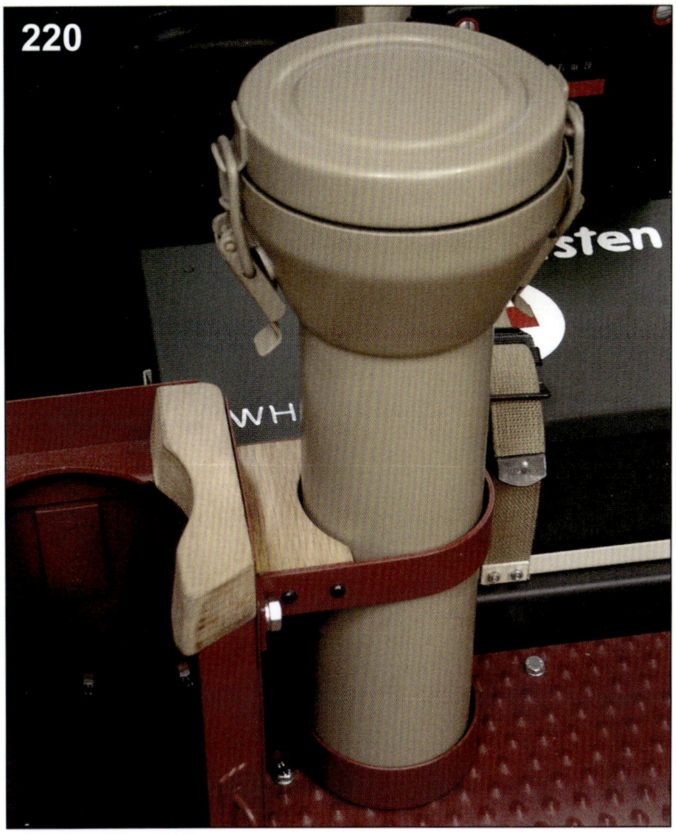

220: The demolition charge container is stored centrally in the tank, just behind the first aid kit. The upper retaining loop is fixed to the front LHS ammunition pannier that is bolted to the fighting compartment floor.

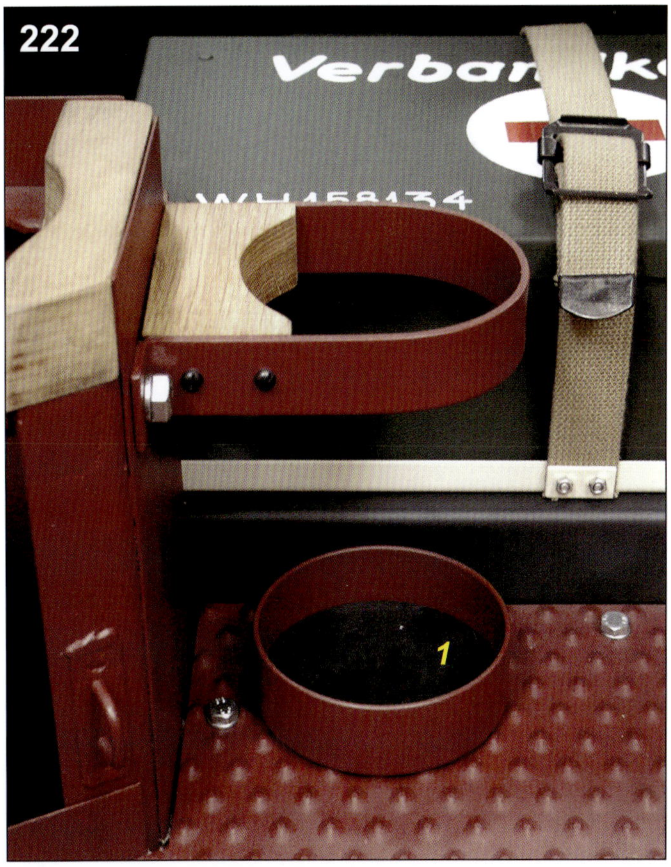

222: To prevent as much shock as possible to the demolition charge the container sits on a small rubber mat in the base of the locating bracket, ***1***. The actual charge container is not strapped in place to allow crew members to access it as fast as possible in the event of an emergency.

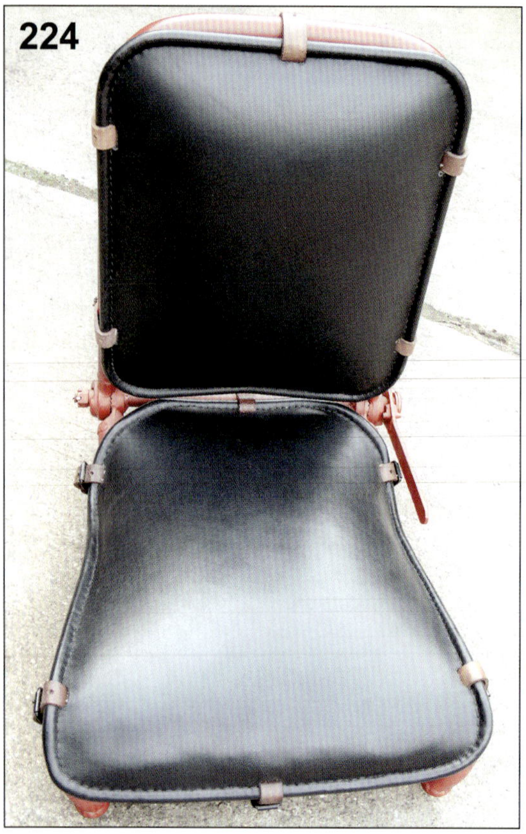

224: The driver and radio operators crew seats were identical items. These seats could not be raised above their floor position. For the driver this meant he could not operate the tank with his head out of the hull crew hatch.

225: A general view of both the underside of the seat and rear of the backrest of a crew seat. A total of eleven straps and buckles hold the cushions in place.

226: Both seat and back rest cushions are new manufactured items. These have been replicated from leather in the same manner as the original items would have been.

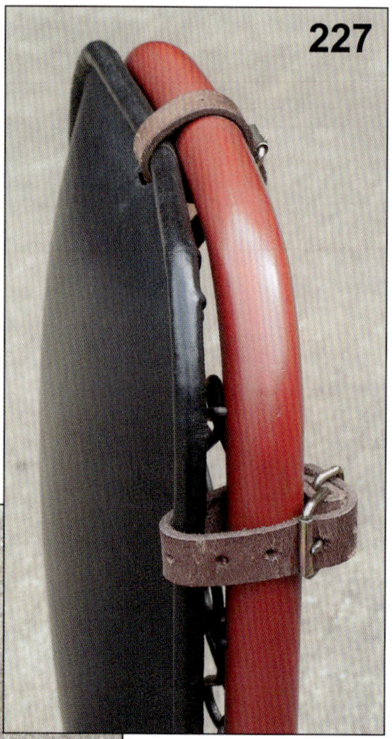

227: Here we have a close-up view of two of the cushion straps and buckles.

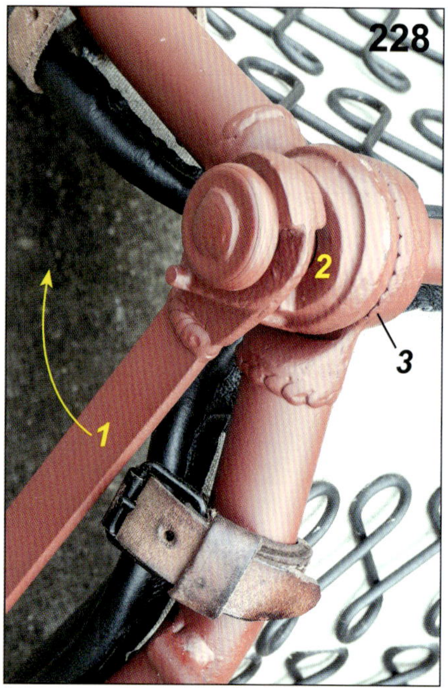

228: The seat back could be adjusted by lifting the lever, at ***1***. This lever acts on an interference cam, ***2***, which when freed allowed the teeth meshed at ***3*** to be freed up and the seat back moved.

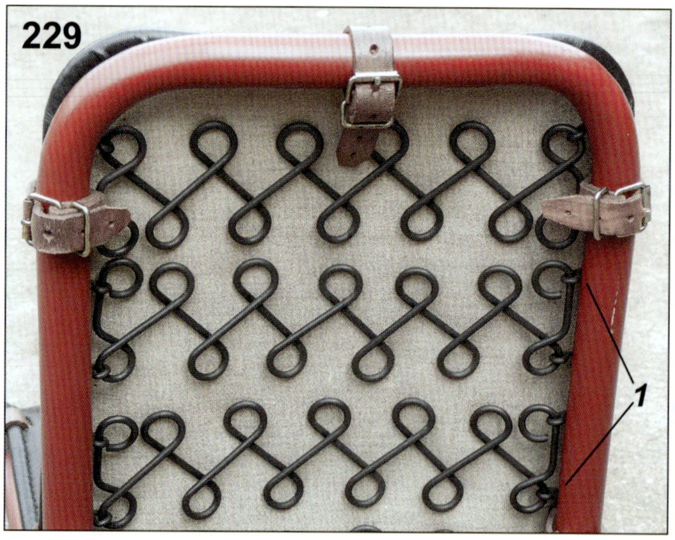

229: The seat springs are a one-piece item that are fixed to the sides of the seat frame, at ***1*** etc. These are made from spring steel and provided a good deal of support.

230

230-231: Here again we just show two images of the Drivers Station as this area was extensively covered in **The Panther Project Vol.1** [12]. New work is limited here to the drivers instrumentation and electrical wiring, that is still not all in place, and the directional gyrocompass, **Kurskreisel**.

231

232: The Driver had two periscopes, **Winkelspiegel**. One vision block faced directly forward while the other block, on the drivers left hand side, was angled at **45°** to the left from the 12 o'clock direction.

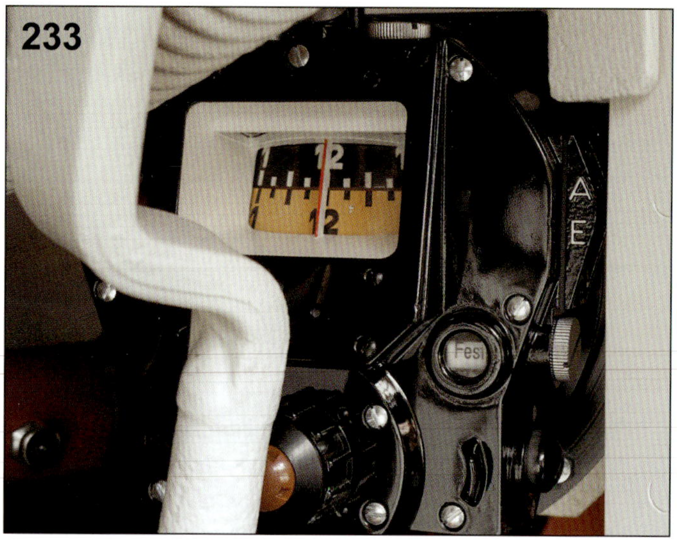

233: Here we can see the directional gyrocompass mounted in place, **Kurskreisel**. This unit could be locked to a preset bearing that would be kept on station by the use of an internal electrically powered gyroscope.

234: Still to be fitted to the instrument panel next to the engine starter button, at ***1***, is the oil pressure gauge, at ***2***, the coolant temperature gauge, at ***3***, and the engine compartment on fire warning light, at ***4***.

235: A direct translation of the label directly above the engine starting button reads: "**Do Not Start**, as long as the engine or starter is moving. As soon as the engine starts, **Release the Push Button**."

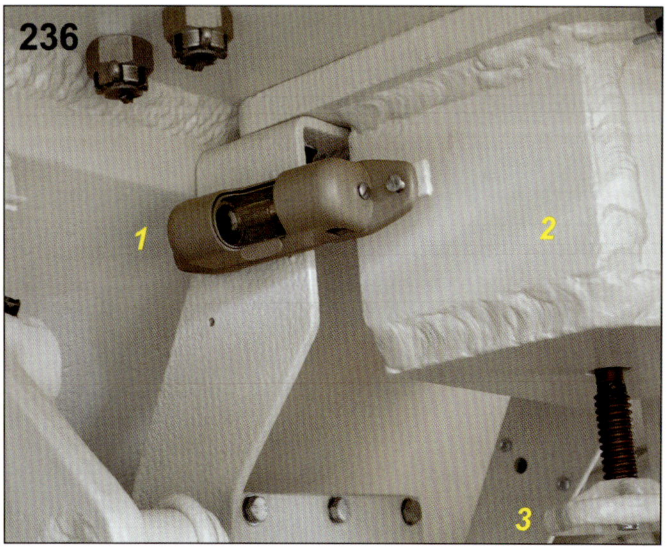

236: Here we have one of the adjustable lights, at ***1***, fixed to the body of the forward hull ventilator, at ***2***. The valve inside the hull ventilator could be sealed by screwing in the spigot, at ***3***.

237: To the RHS of the Driver is a frame with the tachometer, at ***1***, and the odometer, at ***2***. What is interesting here is the fact that the numbering on the dials has been hand painted!

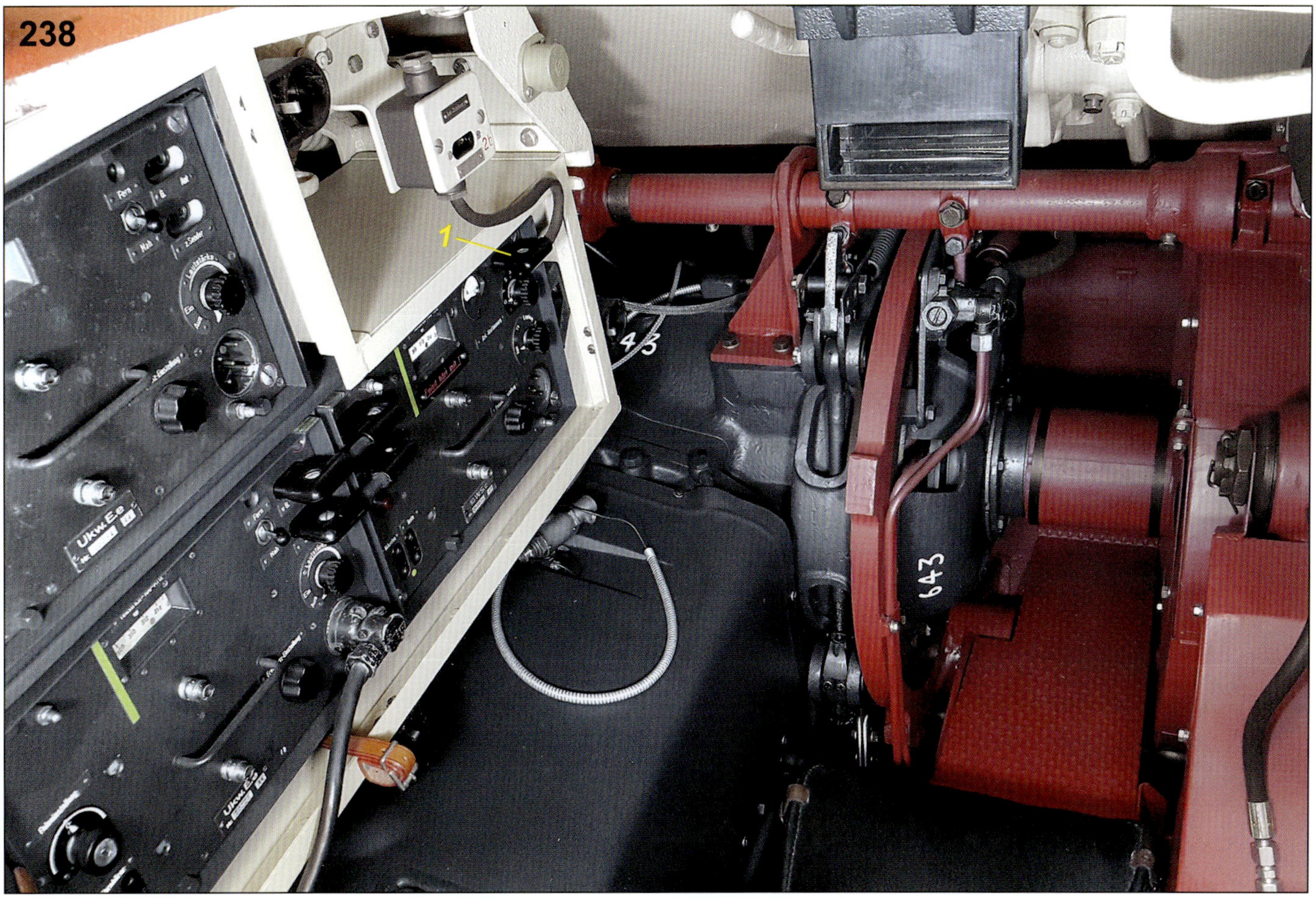

238-239: Here we have a general view of the essentially completed Radio Operators station. We have all radio equipment in place and in the rack, at ***1***, photo **239**, are the covers for each of the radio sets. Of worth noting here is the fact that all the radio sets are in full working order. For more information on the operation of this radio equipment the reader is directed to [18] and [19].

240: Here we look at each radio set as mounted within the radio frame. The unit shown here is the **FuG 2 Ukw.E.e 2 (secondary receiver)**. This unit was a receiver that operated within the range of **27.1-33.3MHz**.

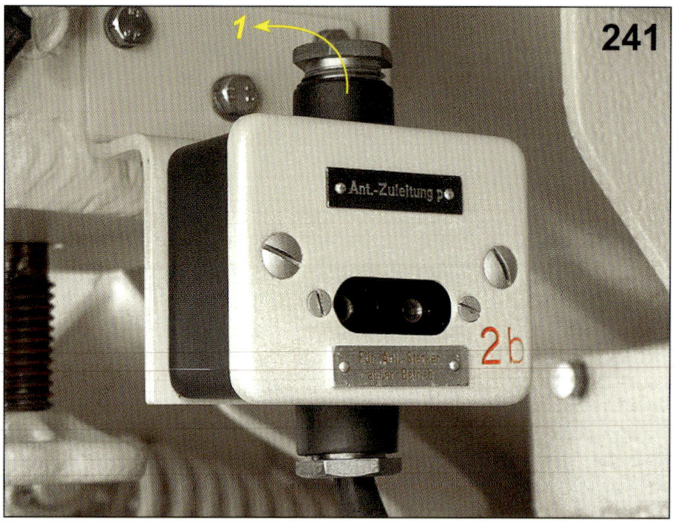

241: Bolted to the forward hull ventilator is the aerial connection box. The cable to the aerial feeds out of this box, at ***1***, and is routed back to the external aerial mount on the hull deck, at ***4***, page **122**, photo **368**. This box is connected to the **Fu 5 10 W.S.c Sender** at ***1***, page **73**, photo **238**.

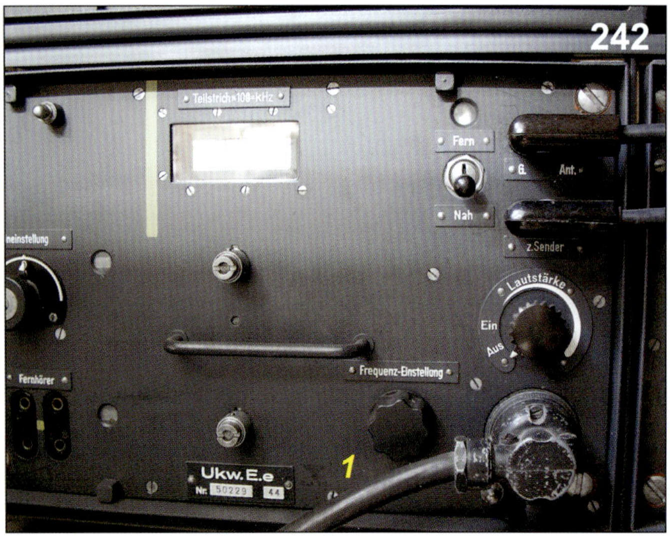

242: The **FuG 2 Ukw.E.e 1 (primary receiver)**. This unit was an ultra-short wavelength receiver set that operated within the frequency range of **27.2-47.8MHz**.

243: In this photo we have the **Fu 5 10 W.S.c Sender (10 Watt transmitter)**. This unit operated within the frequency range of **40.6-47MHz (10 Watt c band VHF)**. Typical radio transmission and reception ranges were **~6km** for voice and **~9km** for Morse.

244: A view of the outer box frame that covers the skeleton frame that holds the radio equipment, see page **38**, photo **78**. We can see this box painted and in place on page **73**, photo **239**.

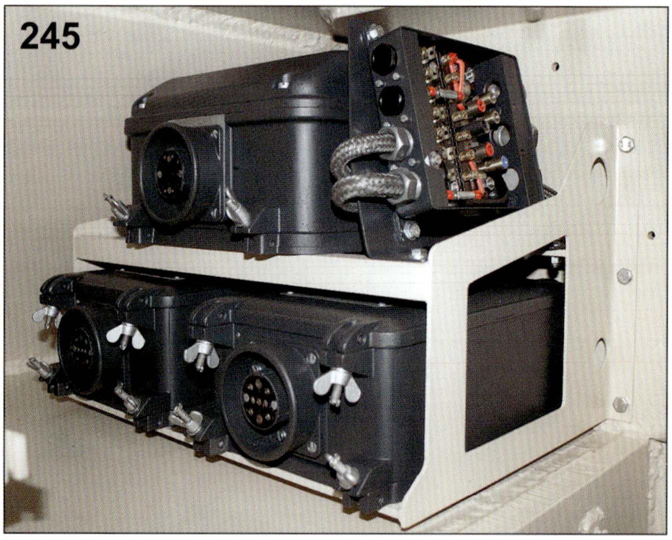

245: In the forward RHS sponson we have the three electrical transformers that allowed the three radio sets to be powered from the **12V** battery system of the tank.

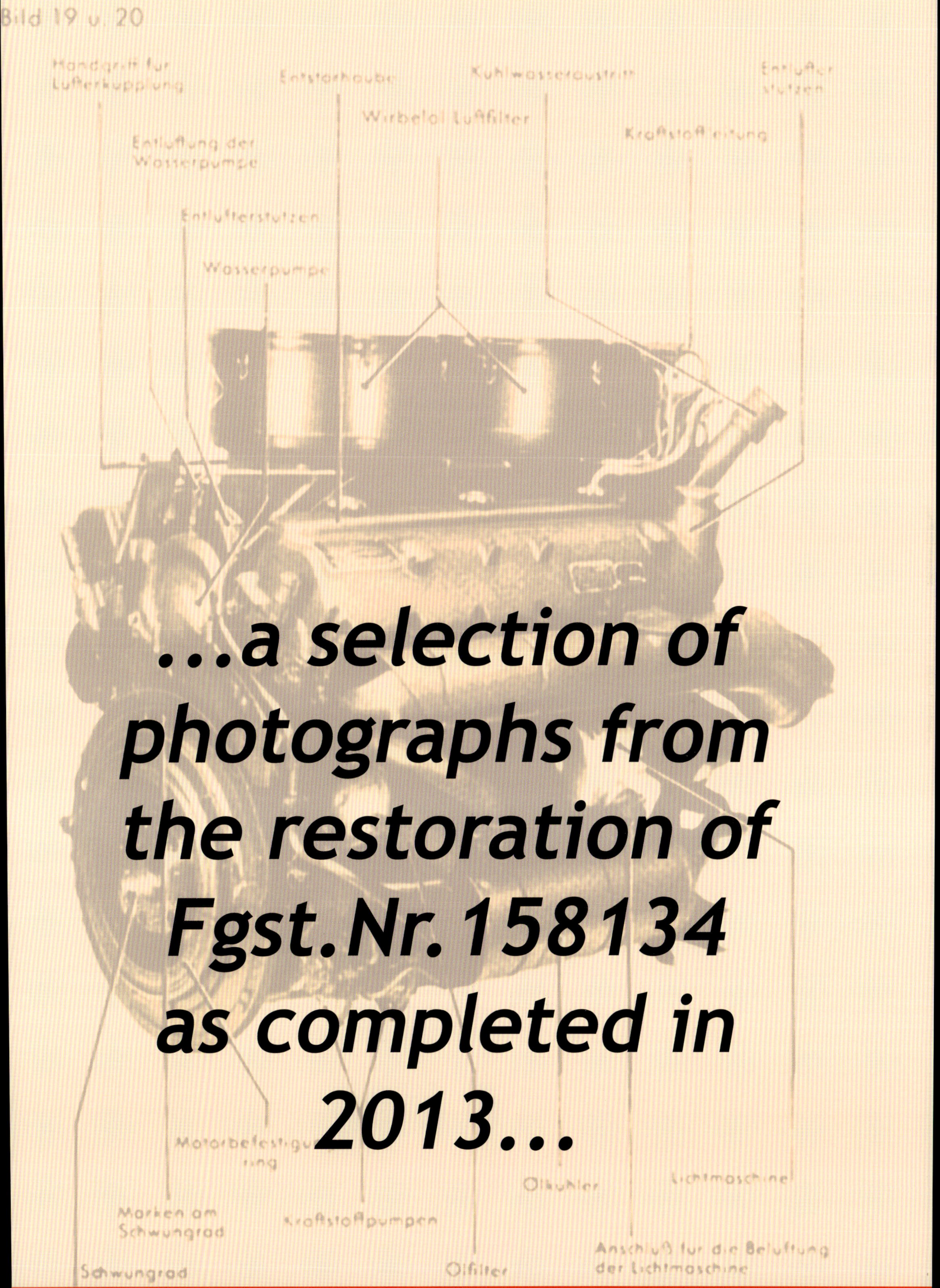

...a selection of photographs from the restoration of Fgst.Nr.158134 as completed in 2013...

246-247: The Panther **Ausf. A** was essentially comprised of an **Ausf. D** hull but with a new turret design. One of the most significant changes to the external turret appearance was the introduction of a new Commanders cupola that was cast as a single piece and was in places up to 100mm in thickness.

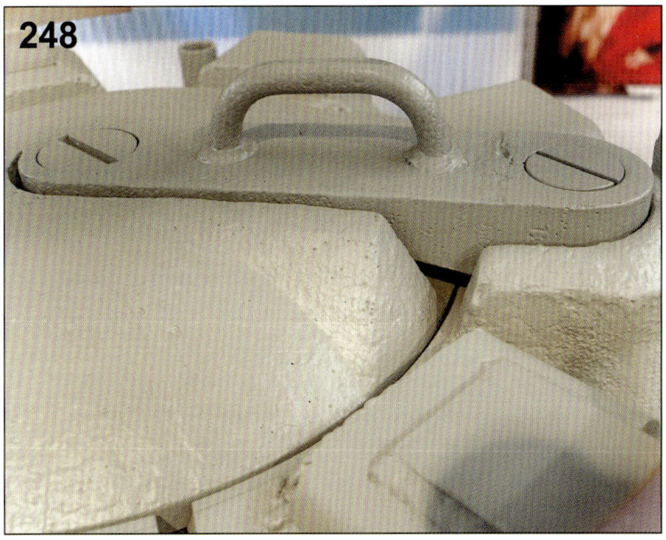

248: A look down on the top of the Commanders cupola hatch. We can see the large connecting arm that was secured in place with two large screw headed bolts to both the hatch centre and the hatch operating post.

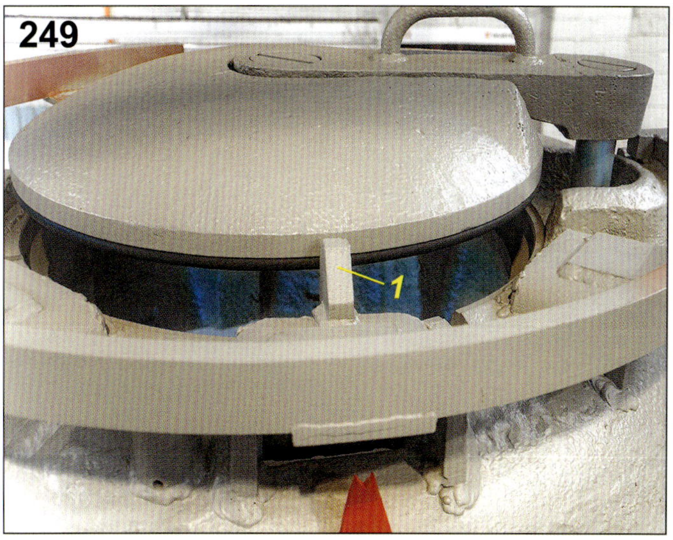

249: Here we can see how high the Commanders cupola hatch is raised when the operating handle is wound up, see page **81**, photos **269-271**. Note the bump stop at ***1*** designed to stop the hatch rotating clockwise and hitting the anti-aircraft ring mount.

250: A horizontal view of the hatch raised to its maximum height to show the clearance above the cupola casting. Note the large rubber seal, at ***1***, designed to prevent ingress of water into the turret when the hatch was closed.

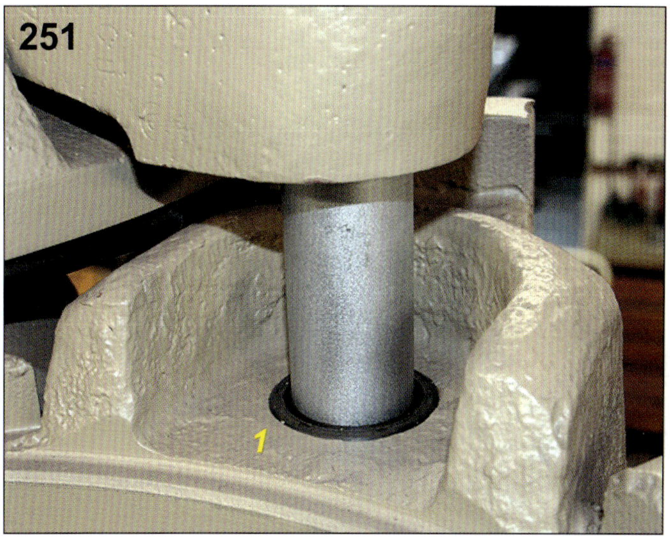

251: A close-up of the hatch operating post and the armoured casting that protected this post when the hatch was open. We also see here another rubber seal, at ***1***, again to prevent ingress of water into the turret.

252: The large hatch grab handle was designed to allow crew members to expose the hatch opening by horizontal rotation when the hatch was raised up to the open position. The hatch could not be fully closed from the outside of the tank.

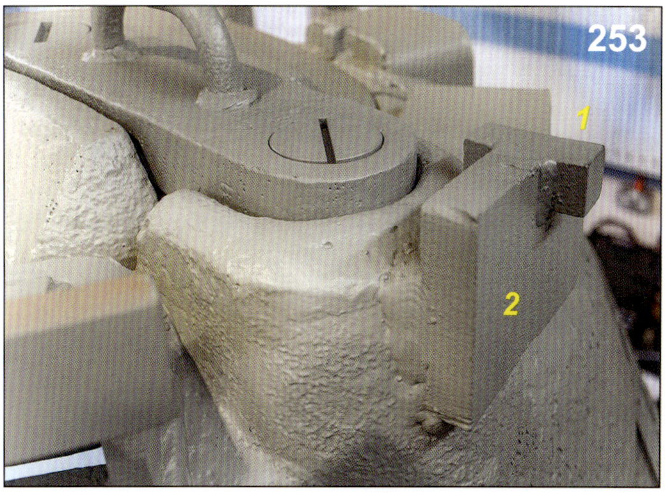

253: Here we see the bump stop designed to prevent the hatch from rotating too far in an anti-clockwise direction when opened, at ***1***. The block this bump stop is welded to, at **2**, provides double duty as a support for the hatch as well as being extra protection for the casting around the hatch operating post.

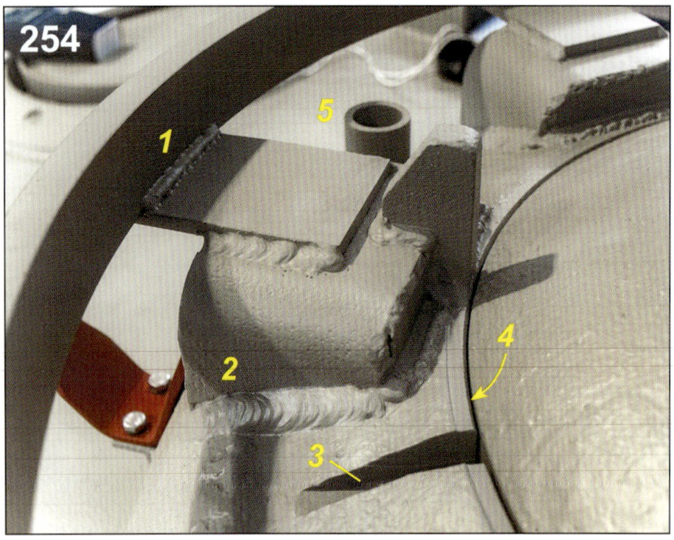

254: Here we see close-up details of different types of welding on the cupola. There is very neat welding on the anti-aircraft ring, at ***1***, while the welding on the armoured periscope cowlings is a lot heavier, at ***2***. Note the drain channel at ***3*** used to funnel away any water that may collect in the hatch rim, at ***4***.

255: In this photo we can see a small tube welded to the cupola, at ***1***. There is another of these at the opposite side of the cupola, at ***5***, photo **254**. These run along the centreline axis of the tank facing the 12 and 6 o'clock position on the cupola. They have small drain holes drilled in their bases, see ***1***, photo **258**. They do not appear to be for an awning for the Commander (the forward post would obscure his line of vision). Possibly they may have been for signal flags (we have seen no photographic examples of this). We would be interested on hearing from anyone who may be able to shed some light on what they are designed for.

256: Looking down between two of the armoured periscope cowlings. We can see the number **90** or **06** cast into the surface of the cupola. We have not been able to determine what this represents at present.

257: In front of the forward-facing episcope of the Commanders cupola was bolted a sighting vane. This was designed to give the Commander the ability to acquire targets of interest quickly and to pass that information on to the Gunner.

258: To sight on a target the Commander would look through the rear of the sighting vane and would adjust his view until he could see the single prong at the front of the vane centrally between the dual rear prongs.

259: Here we have a side profile view of the sighting vane and can see how it is bolted to a small bracket that has been welded to the front of the Commanders cupola.

260: A study of the rear turret crew hatch. The hinge mechanism for this was strengthened after issues reported on **Ausf. D** turrets [13]. Note the large rubber gasket used to create a watertight seal when the hatch was closed and locked.

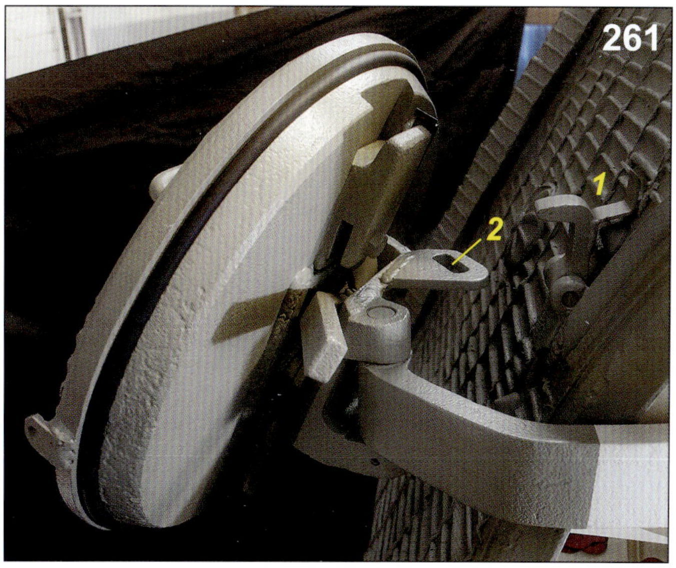

261: The rear turret crew hatch could be secured in the open position using the latch welded to the rear plate, at ***1***. The latch would drop down into the eyelet, at ***2***, locking the hatch in place.

262: Outside the turret looking towards the crew hatch from the 7 o'clock position. The grab handle welded to the outside of the hatch was a field modification often added by tank crews. Note the rain guard above the upper edge of the hatch, at ***1***.

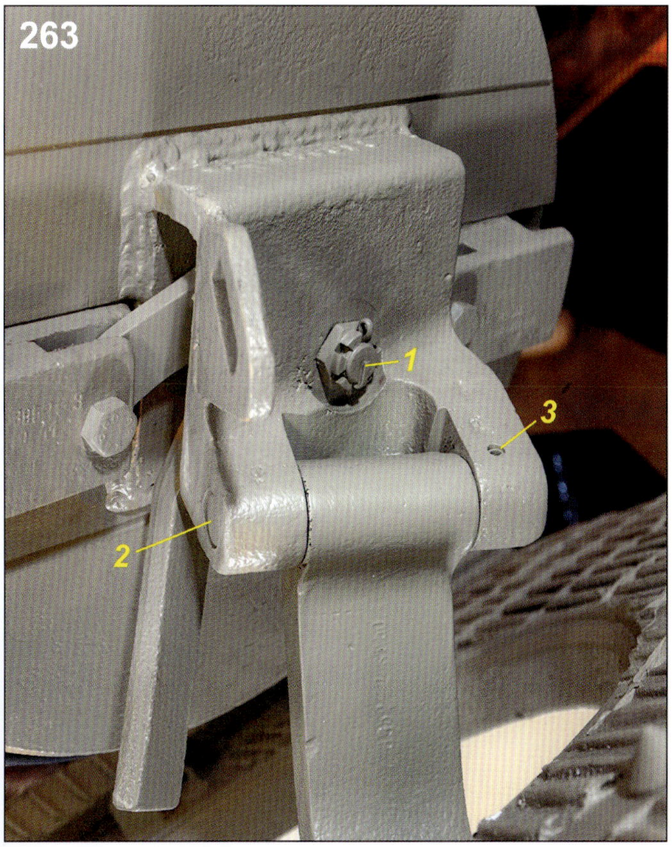

263: A close-up view of the hinge mechanism on the rear turret crew hatch. The handle that operates the cam for the locking levers pivots at ***1***. The hatch itself is secured to the hinge arm by the pin, at ***2***, which itself is secured by a cotter pin, at ***3***.

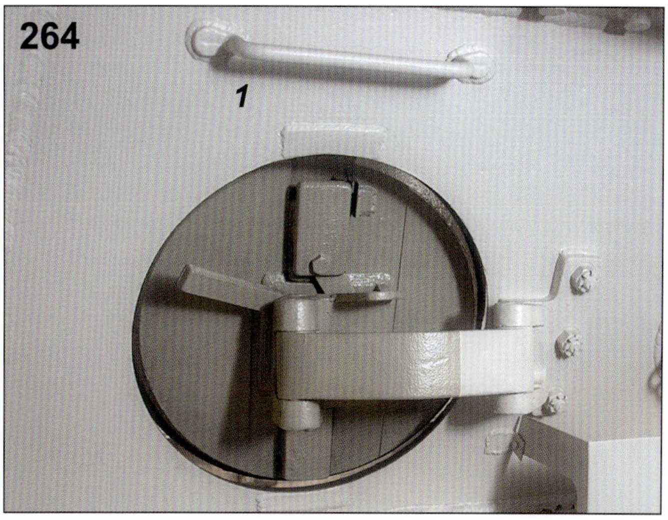

264: The grab handle, at ***1***, could be used by the turret crew to help evacuate the turret quickly in an emergency. Note the colour contrast of the turret **Elfenbein** against the **Dunkelgelb** of the crew hatch interior face.

265-266: The test fitting of the mantlet. A rubber seal was fitted at ***1***, photo **265**, to prevent ingress of water into the turret. Note the dual holes for the binocular gun sight, photo **266**. Old stocks of dual hole mantlets continued to be used until single hole units became available. In the meantime an armoured plug was welded into the LHS gun sight port to seal that mantlet opening, **2**, photo **266**.

267: A look up directly beneath the Commanders cupola. The mount for the Commanders periscope, **T.S.R.1 Sehstab**, was bolted to the positions marked by ***1***. The azimuth ring, installed in the cupola that rotated with the turret, is still to be fitted.

268: A close-up view of the vision block ports. The vision blocks were designed to be quickly replaceable in the event of damage and were retained in position using the projection lug at ***1***.

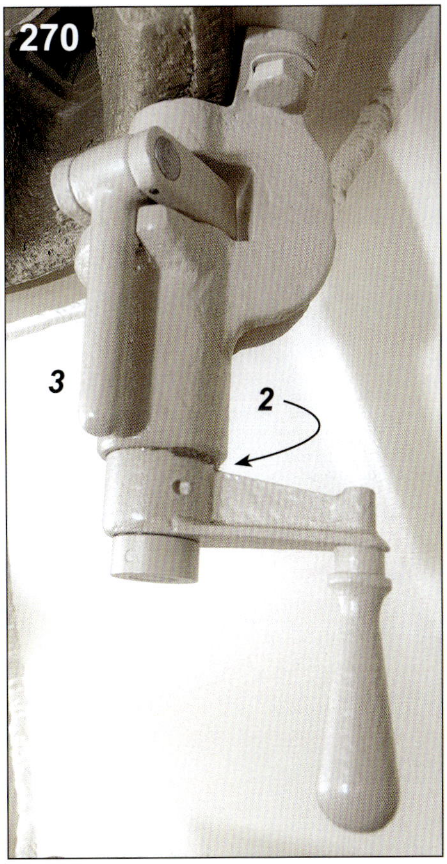

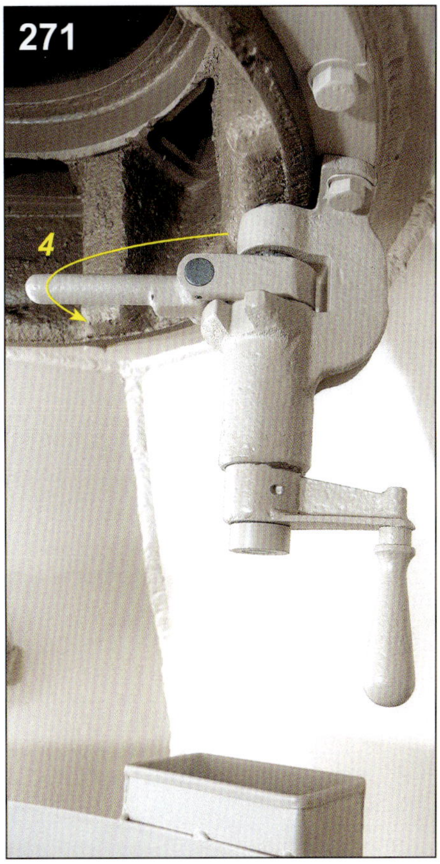

269-271: The operating lever for the Commanders cupola hatch. To open the hatch the winding handle, at ***1***, photo **269**, is turned clockwise until it butts up against the handle body housing, at **2**, photo **270**. This raises the hatch above the top of the armoured vision block cowlings, see page **77**, photo **249**. The lever, at **3**, photo **270**, is raised up to the horizontal position, at ***4***, photo **271**, and is then rotated anti-clockwise. This action rotates the hatch outwards so that it hangs over the LHS of the turret, page **76**, photo **247**.

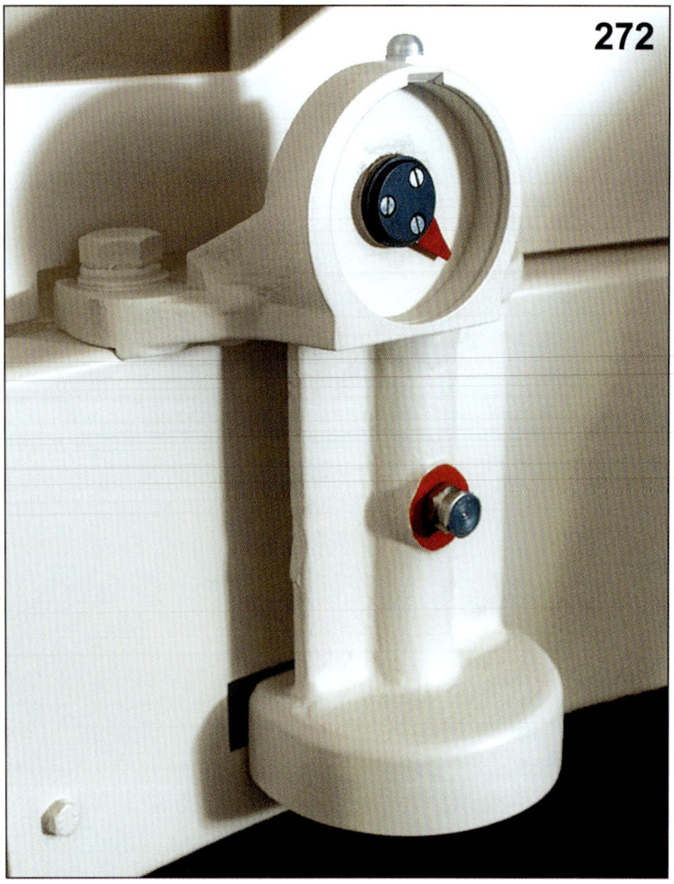

272: Fitting of the housing of the turret azimuth indicator. In the Panther **Ausf. A** this device had been simplified from a two-dial indicator device to the single dial type as shown here. The actual dial face has yet to be fitted.

273: An underside view of the turret azimuth indicator showing the single gear wheel that meshes with the primary gear race that is affixed to the hull roof inside the turret ring.

274: A general view of the inside of the rear turret hatch. This is painted in dunkelgelb on the inside face so that it will blend in against the turret rear wall when open.

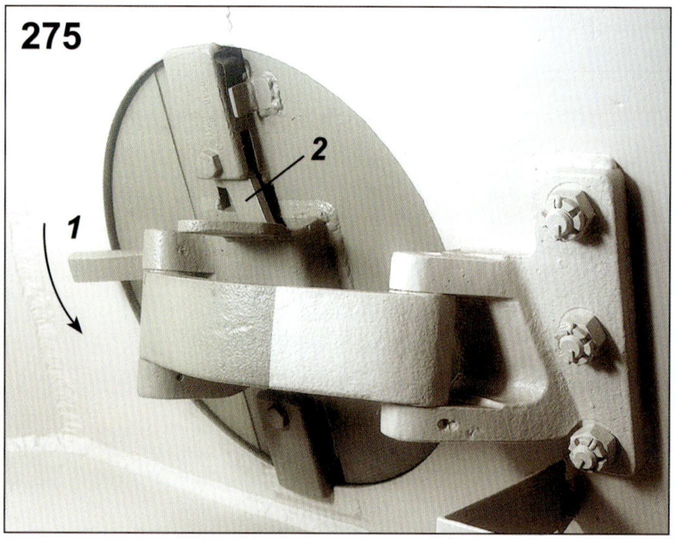

275: When the hatch locking lever is rotated anti-clockwise, at ***1***, the vertical bars, at ***2***, acting against a cam move the locking blocks outwards thus securing the hatch.

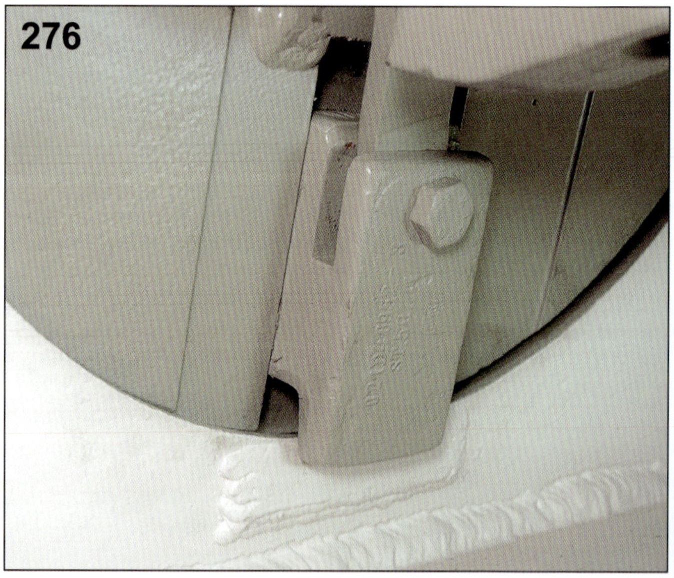

276: Here we have a close-up of the bottom hatch locking block. We can see a section of weld that had been laid down to ensure that when the hatch is locked the block is secured tight against the inner surface of the turret rear plate.

277: On this page we have a series of photos looking at the gun carriage box frame onto which the main gun and mantlet will be installed. The trunnions on which the main gun pivots are part of this frame. The trunnions sit in two large blocks, see ***1***, page **150**, photo **411**, and ***1***, page **151**, photo **412**, and are secured in place each with two large bolts, for example at ***1***, photo **280**.

279: In the large tube at ***1*** is fitted the main gun recoil cylinder. In the channel at **2** is bolted the elevation quadrant, see ***1***, page **179**, photo **466**.

281: In the smaller port to the right of the recoil cylinder is fitted the coaxially mounted **M.G.34**, at ***1***. Note also the upper section of the frame, at **2**, that fits in between the main gun carriage and the mantlet and to which the turret mantlet seals are secured.

278: Here we have a view into the channel in which the main gun is mounted. A seal to prevent the ingress of water would be fitted at ***1***. The return cylinder for the main gun would be fitted at **2**. Note also the plug in the mantlet, at **3**, that blanks off one of the holes drilled in the mantlet that was used originally to be used for the binocular **T.F.Z.12** gunsight.

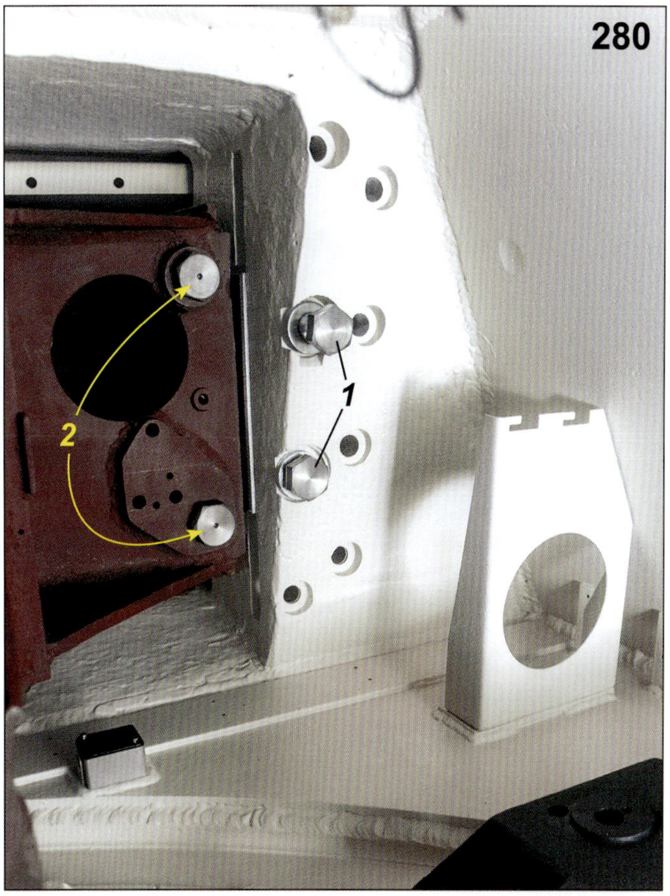

280: The two large bolts, at **2**, protrude out through the front of the main gun carriage and will screw into the mantlet once it has been lifted into position. We can see these bolts at **2** and **3**, page **151**, photo **412**.

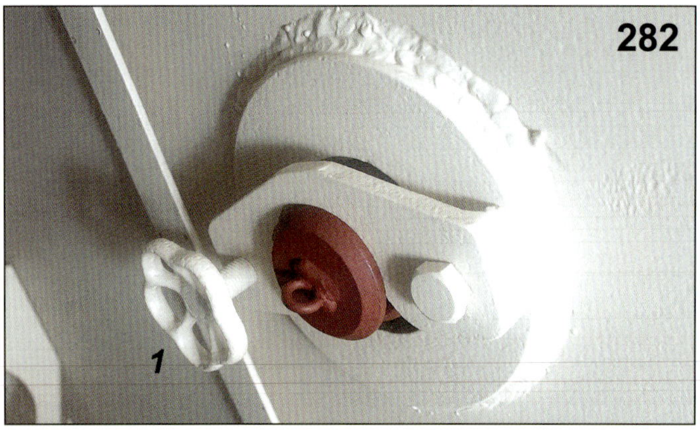

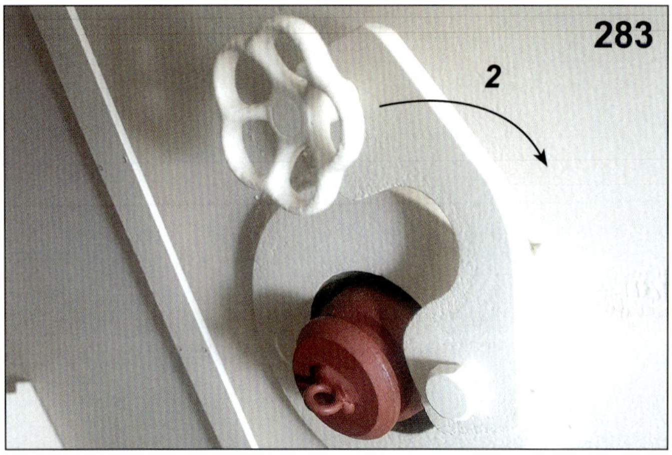

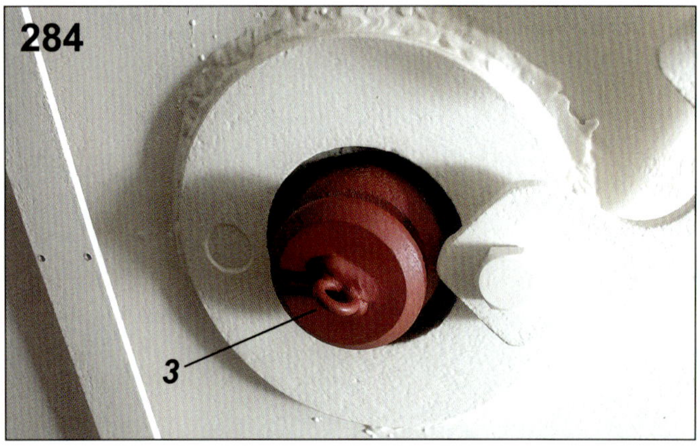

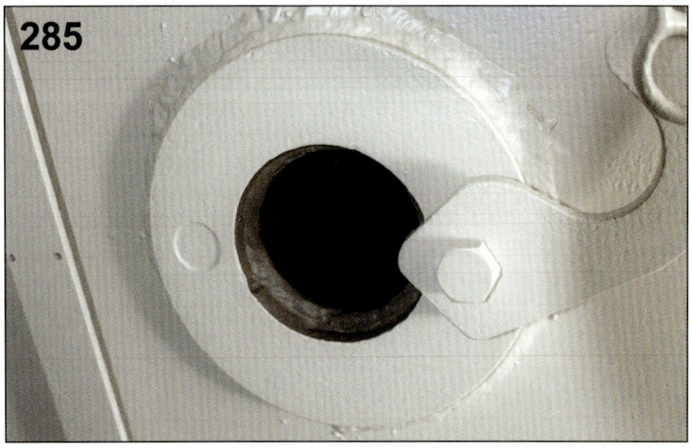

282-285: The pistol port on the RHS of the turret. To use this port simply unscrew the spigot handle, at ***1***, photo **282**, and rotate the locking bar to the right, at ***2***, photo **283**. The pistol plug is then pushed out of the port. To stop the pistol plug being lost a retraining chain would be fitted to the loop at ***3***, photo **284**. These chains can be seen, still to be fitted, at ***1***, page **160**, photo **427**.

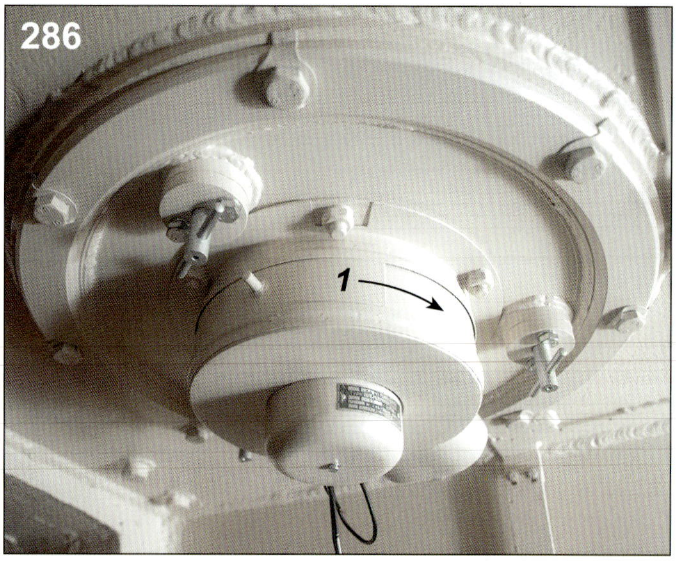

286: Here we have the roof mounted exhaust fan, **Lüfter**, before being wired into the electrical circuit of the tank. When the fan was running and the sliding grate, at ***1***, was open, air that was contaminated with spent main gun round powder gases would be drawn out through the fan from around the breech area.

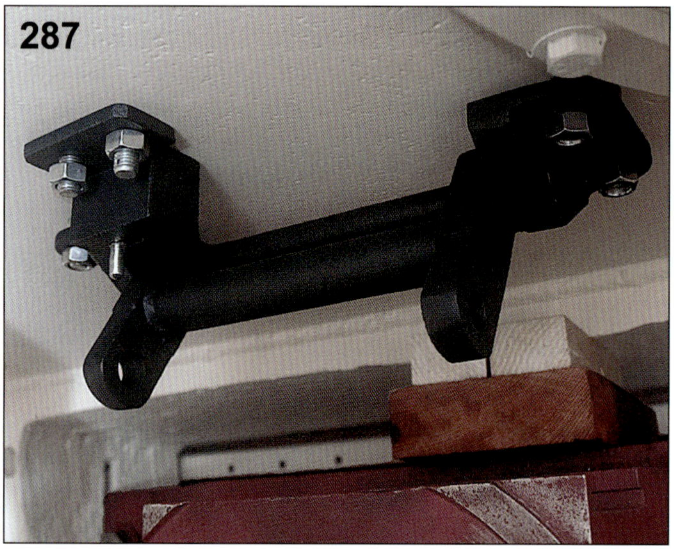

287: Mounted on the centreline of the turret roof, above the main gun, is the travel lock, **Rohrzurrung**, used to secure the main gun when the tank was in travel but not combat mode.

288: The port in the RHS of the turret roof is designed to hold the periscope, **Winkelspiegel**, for the Loader.

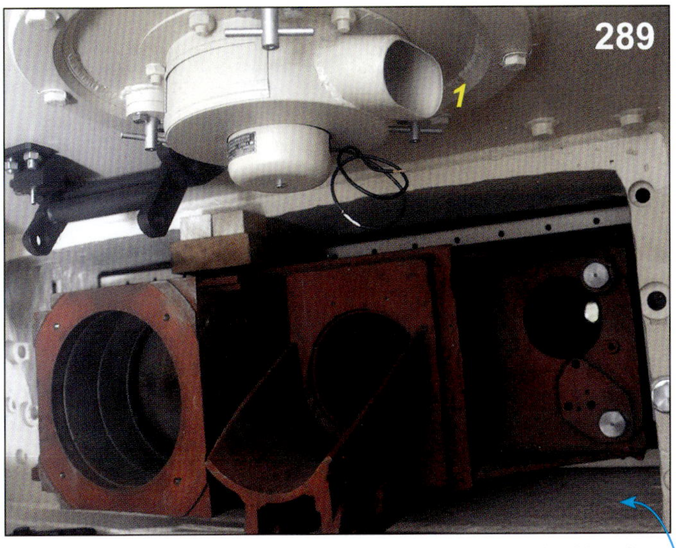

289: Here we have a study of the main gun carriage looking from the Loaders position. The port to which the flexible metal tube, **Absaugleitung**, that connects from the turret extractor fan to the front of the spent shell basket case is seen at ***1***.

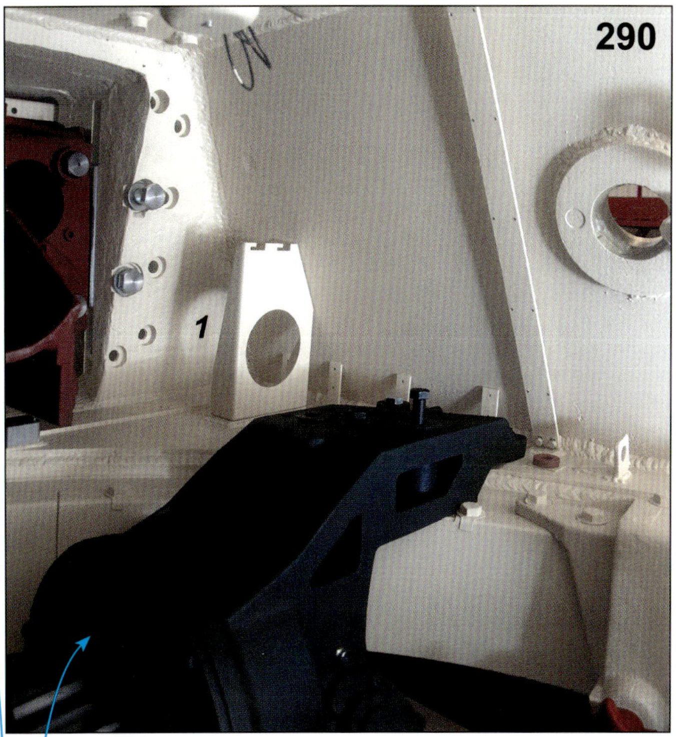

290: A look to the 1 o'clock position inside the turret from the Loaders station. At ***1*** is the receptacle into which is placed an ammunition pouch holding belted ammunition for the coaxially mounted **M.G.34**.

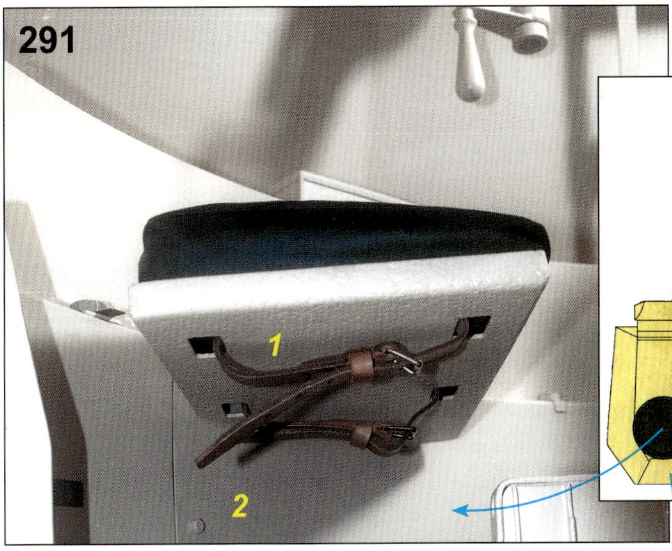

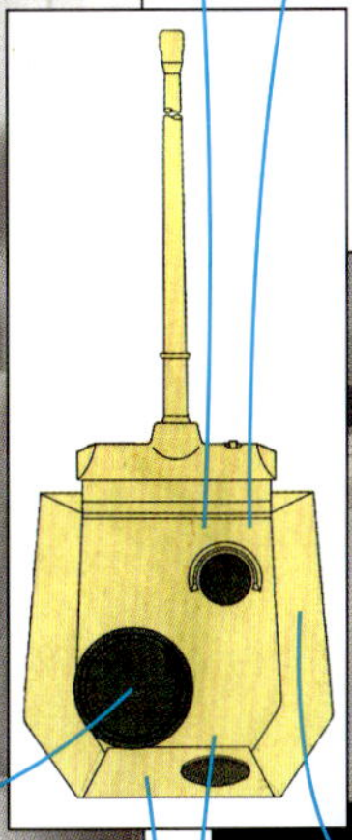

291: A view underneath the Commanders seat. The seat plate had four holes through which were fed leather straps that were secured to the underside of the Commanders seat cushion. The straps were belted together under the seat, at ***1***, to prevent the Commanders cushion from moving. Note that the Gunners seat cushion was also strapped in place, see ***1***, page **186**, photo **488**, whilst the Loaders seat was not, page **183**, photo **483**.

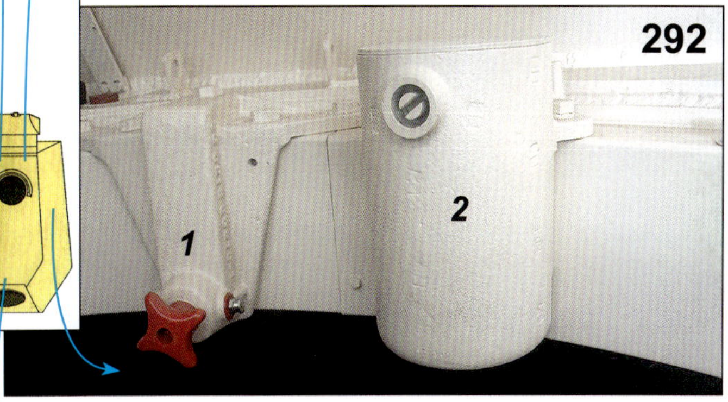

292: At the RHS of the turret ring we have the turret traverse lock, **Turmzurrung**, at ***1***. When this was screwed in a toothed section was engaged into the turret gear ring thus preventing the turret from rotating. At **2**, we can see the turret auxiliary manual traverse, **Hilfsantrieb**.

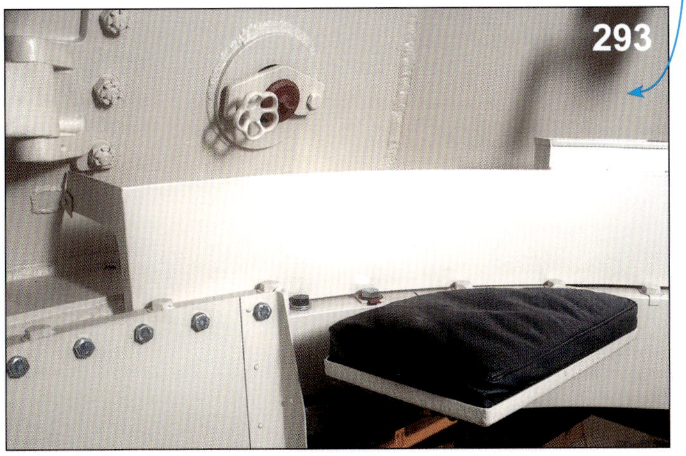

293: A look across at the Commanders seat from the Loaders station. The Commanders seat is bolted to the turret ring using two large bolts, see **2**, page **160**, photo **427**.

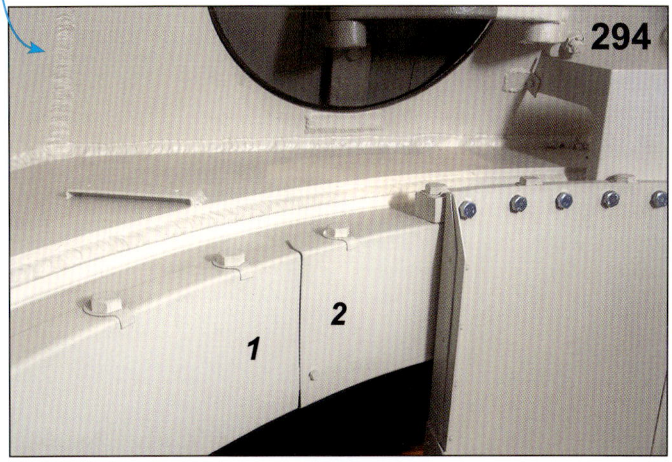

294: The turret crew were protected from the mechanisms of the turret traverse and associated equipment by a set of protective panels. We see two of these panels, at ***1*** and **2**, at the rear RHS corner of the turret. Another of these panels is at **2**, photo **291**.

295-298: On this page are four views of the turret traverse mechanism, **Turmschwenkwerk**. This unit enabled both power assisted or manual activation of turret traversal. Inside the main body of the traverse housing, at ***1***, photo **298**, is a vertical shaft on which are mounted three large gears. The upper gear on this shaft is connected via a bevel gear, at ***1***, photo **295**, to the Gunners manual traverse handwheel, at ***1***, photo **296**. The central gear is connected via a worm gear in the housing at ***2***, photo **298**, to a bevel gear, at ***3***, photo **298**, and then via a cardan shaft, at ***4***, photo **298**. The cardan shaft is mechanically driven from the power take off transfer box, **Flüssigkeitsgetriebe**, mounted centrally on the turret basket floor, at ***1***, page **88**, photo **305**.

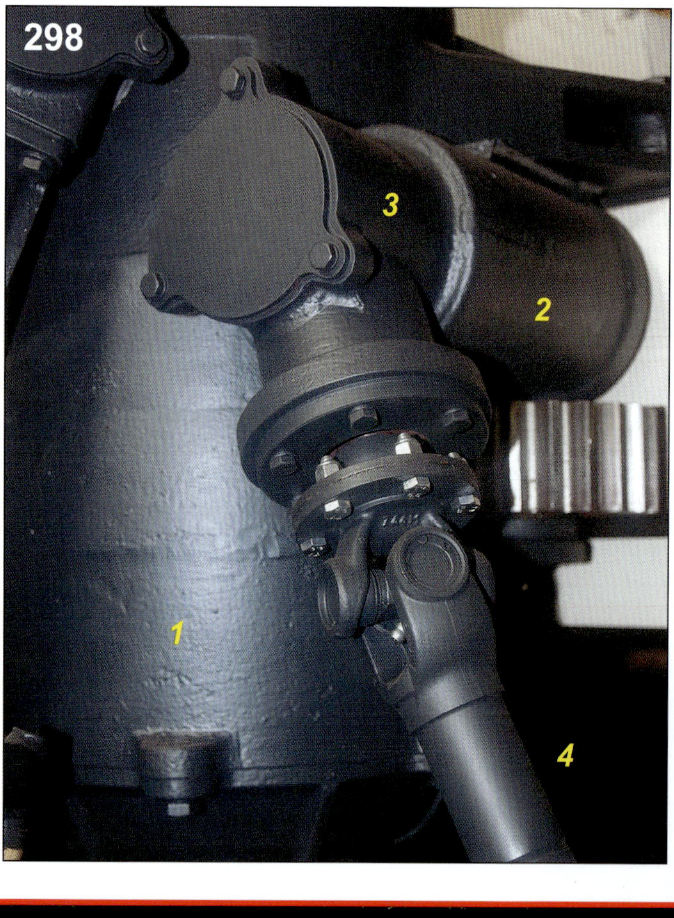

299-300: Bolted to the turret ring in front of the loader is the main gun elevation mechanism, **Höhenrichtmaschine**, photo **299**. A large gear quadrant was bolted to the main gun carriage, at ***1***, photo **299**, and meshed with the large pinion gear, at ***1***, photo **300**.

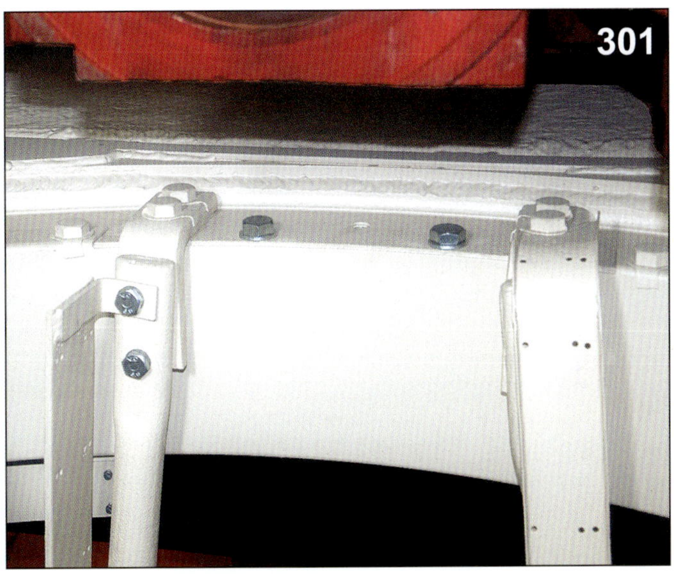

301-302: Here we see the two stanchions that are bolted to the front of the turret ring, photo **301**, and down to the front section of the turret basket floor, photo **302**. These stanchions provide both structural strength and a frame for equipment to be mounted upon.

303-304: The **Kasten Pz. Nr. 5c** was the primary fuse box of the Panther tank and was mounted on the RHS stanchion bolted to the front of the turret ring. This box was connected via a cable from ***1***, photo **304**, to the slip ring transformer, **Schleifringübertrager**, and from there to the **Kasten Pz. Nr. 20** in the fighting compartment, page **65**, photo **202**. Both the Commanders and Gunners intercom boxes were connected to this unit.

305: A general view of the LHS of the turret basket. Issues had been reported in the **Ausf. D** that the turret basket very easily became damaged [13]. In November 1943 a new design of turret basket floor was introduced that was significantly strengthened due to the employment of a tubular steel frame. This new frame design can be seen clearly on page **90**, photos **314** and **315**.

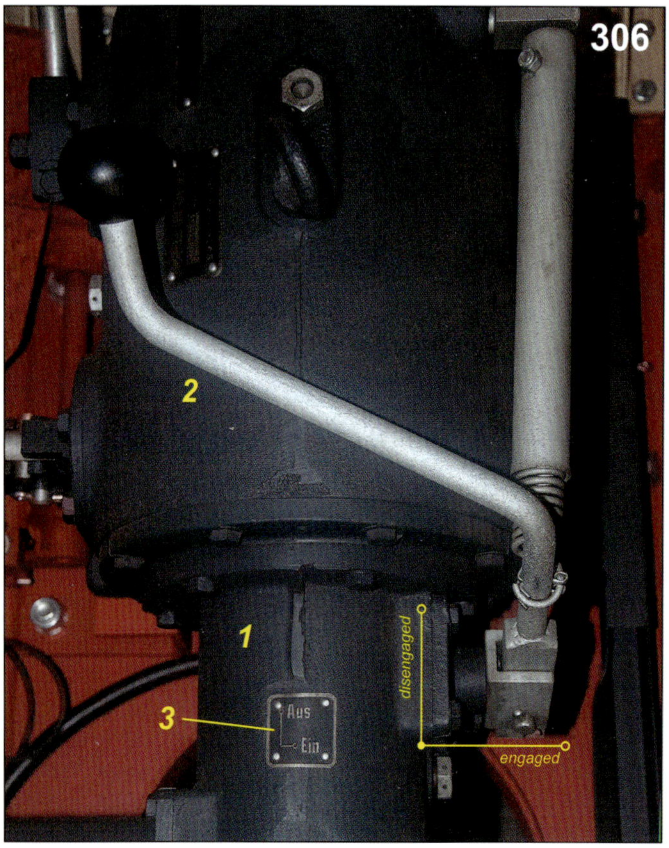

306: The power take-off transfer box. Drive via the splined shaft on top of the power take off mechanism on the hull floor, at ***2***, page **61**, photo **179**, feeds into the transfer box housing at ***1***. The lever at ***2*** engages or disengages the take-off drive.

307: The return spring, at ***1***, ensures that when the lever for the engagement of the turret drive is not in operation it is held in the forward disengaged position, see the operational data plate at ***3***, photo **306**, **Aus** = *disengaged*, **Ein** = *engaged*.

308: At the front end of the power take off transfer box is the housing, at ***1***, within which is a bevel gear that is connected to a cardan shaft, at ***2***. This cardan shaft is connected to the turret traverse unit, see ***4***, page **86**, photo **298**.

309: At the rear of the power transfer take off box, on the LHS, is a pulley wheel. This drives a belt, at ***1***, that operates the bore evacuator compressor. Note the guard, at ***2***, above the pulley wheel used to prevent either the Gunner or Commander coming into contact with moving equipment.

310: At the LHS of the spent shell basket is the bore evacuator. This compressor operated at **1500rpm** at an engine speed of **1150rpm**. A centrifugal clutch disengaged the compressor from the engine when the engine speed exceeded **1300rpm**.

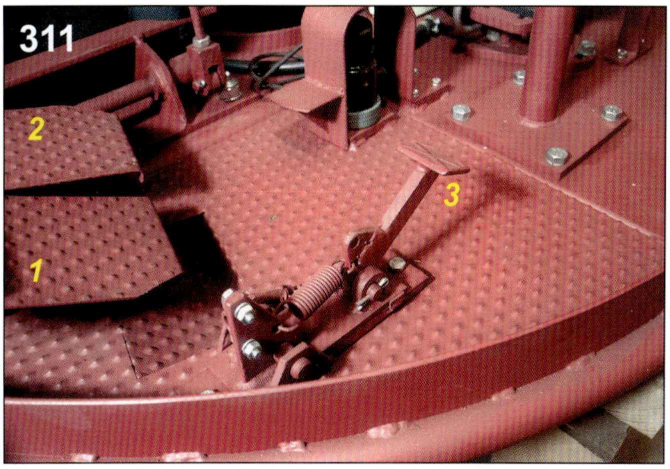

311: On the turret basket floor, in front of the Gunners station, are two pedals used for power assisted traversal of the turret. The pedal at ***1*** traverses the turret left and at ***2*** to the right. The foot pedal, at ***3***, controls the firing of the coaxially mounted **M.G.34**.

312: The underside of the turret traverse mechanism. There is a grease nipple, at ***1***, for lubrication of the internal gearing. Note how the traverse gearing meshes with the turret ring.

313: On the turret basket floor in front of the Gunners station was the emergency main gun firing switch, **Notabfeuerung**. In the event of a failure of the main gun firing circuit the Gunner would flip up the cover at ***1***, and step on the actuation switch, at ***2***.

2013 - Turret Basket Underside

314: A view underneath the floor of the turret basket. The turret is suspended in a frame that holds the turret basket about twelve inches above the workshop floor thus making it difficult to take photographs without perspective issues. The reference arrow points towards the front of the turret. The rear of the spent shell basket can be seen at ***1***.

315: In this photo of the underside of the turret basket the reference arrow points towards the front of the turret. At ***1*** and ***2*** are the two floor panels that can be raised to allow access to the three main gun rounds stored under the floor, see ***1***, page **138**, photo **394**, or for general maintenance duties that do not require turret removal.

...a selection of photographs from the restoration of Fgst.Nr. 158134 as completed in 2017...

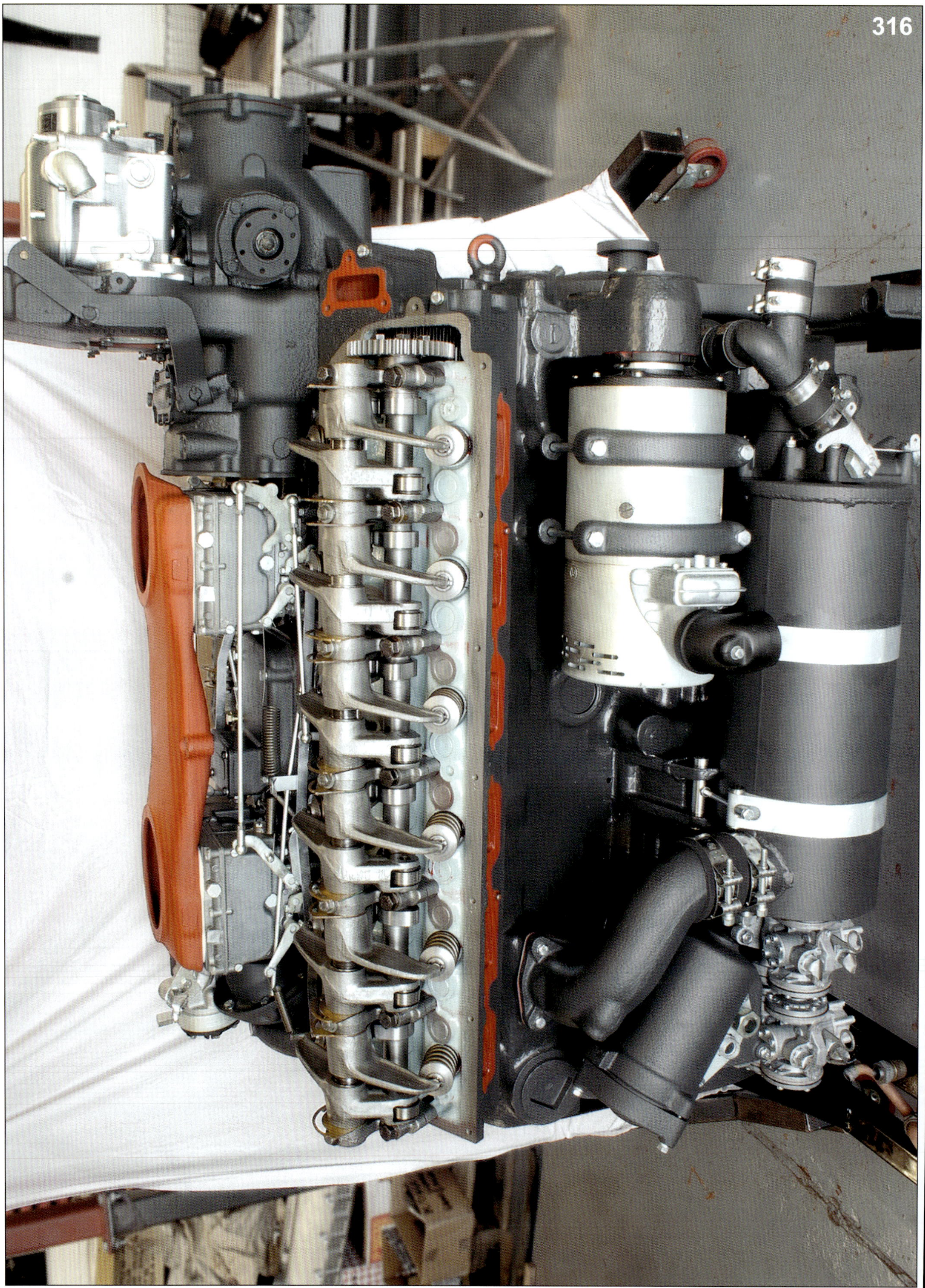

316: By 2017 all work on the engine was essentially completed. The engine had been run up and was operating perfectly. Over the next twenty-four pages we show the engine as we were able to document the build just before the final components were added.

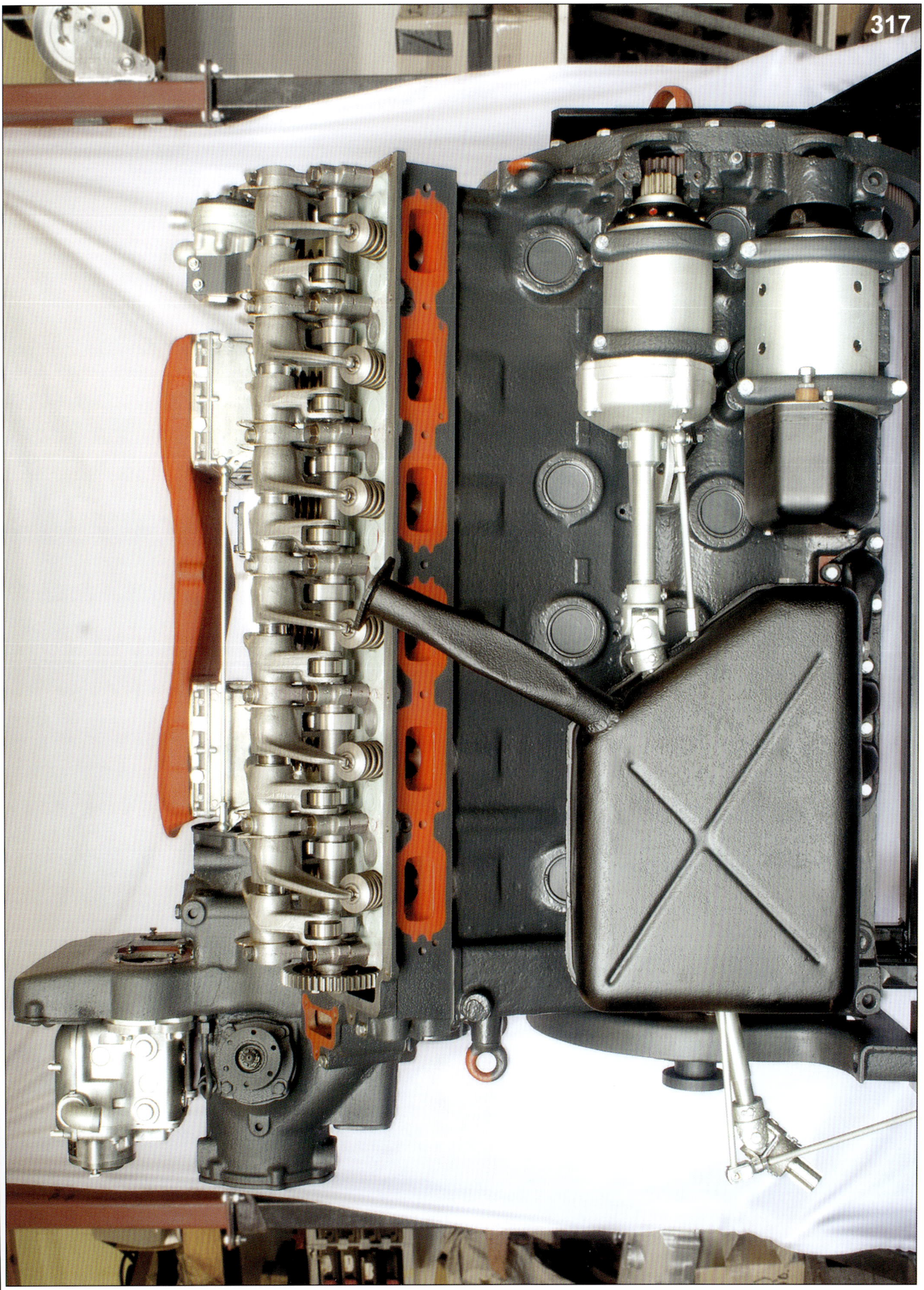

317: Here we see an overall side profile of the RHS of the engine. The sheet in the background was being used to provide some contrast for us to photograph against.

318

318: A full view of the rear of the engine. Note the gear wheels on the end of the camshafts and the timing markings on those gears in red, at ***1*** and ***2***.

319

319: Looking obliquely along the LHS of the engine. Here we have a very nice profile of the LHS rocker gear. Note the double springs, inner and outer as seen on both inlet and exhaust valves.

320

320-321: The two photos here again show the engine just before the fitting of the cylinder heads as seen on the previous two pages. The head gasket, made by **Reinzolit**, and in conjunction with the use of copper compression gaskets, see page **27**, illustration 22, were used to prevent blown head gaskets that were a common problem on early **Maybach HL230 P30** engines.

321

322

322: A view along the LHS of the engine showing the control and linkages as connected to the carburettors. The **Maybach HL230 P30** employed four **Solex JFF 2-2V2046** carburettors that were each twin jet downdraft/choke units. These carburettors fed the two inlet manifolds, one per cylinder block, on each side of the engine.

323-324: In photo **323** and page **99**. photo **325**, we are essentially looking at a side profile of how the air intake manifold was mated to the carburettors. Note also inside the manifold the mesh grills designed to prevent foreign objects entering the carburettor bores.

325-326: The air filters (not shown) were designed by **Feifel**. They were cyclone filters with no moving parts and other than checking the oil level in the oil bath were maintenance free. At maximum engine rpm the filters had a **99%** dust separation efficiency [14].

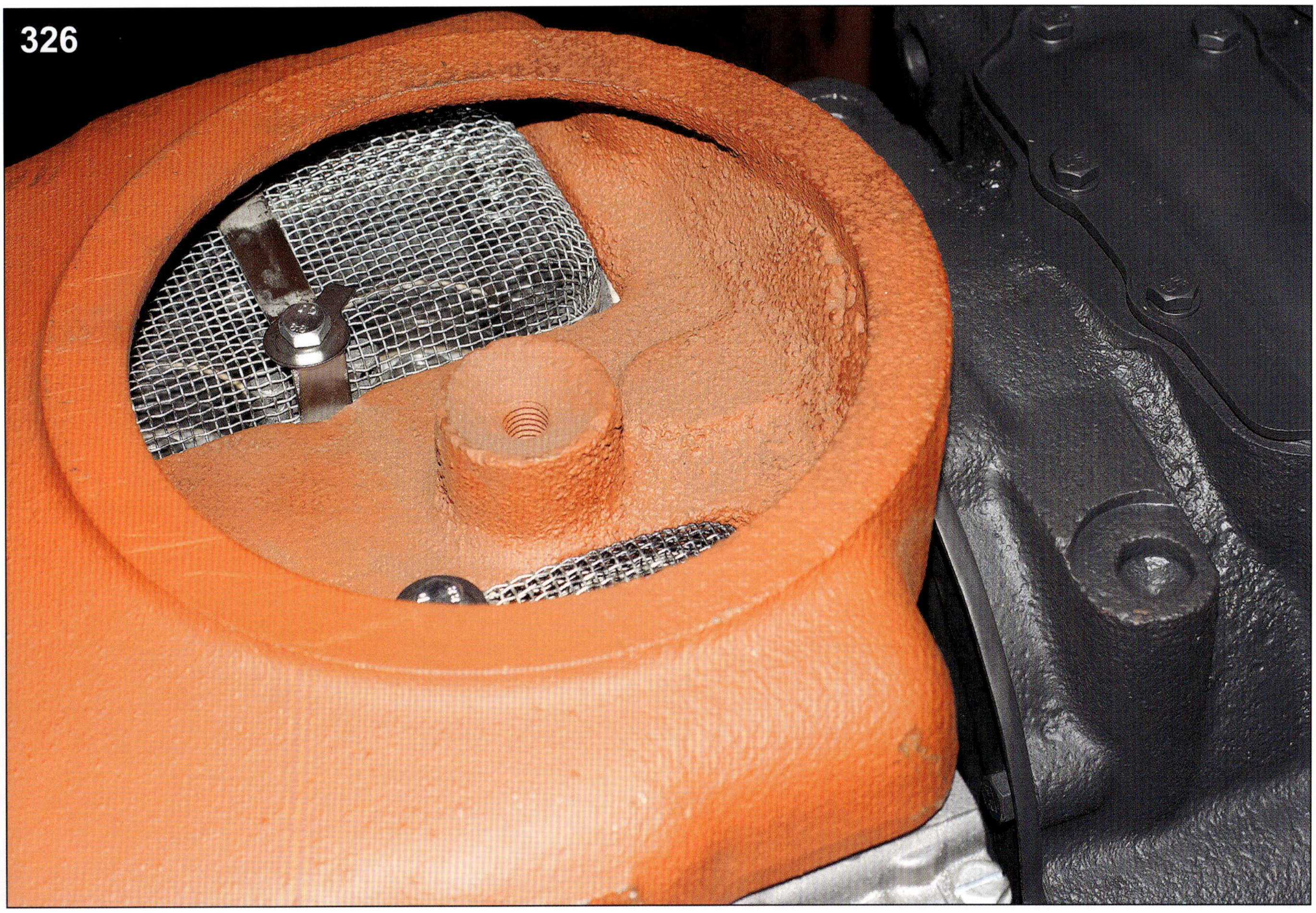

327

327-328: On these two pages we see a montage of images of the twin **Bosch** magnetos. These magnetos were driven by the gear, at ***1***, page **36**, photo **61**, via a spur gear, at ***1***, page **104**, photo **335**, and also seen at ***3***, page **105**, illustration **339**. This large upper gear was driven by the crankshaft, at ***2***, page **105**, illustration **339**.

328

329

329-330: The **Bosch** magnetos were automatically compensated for advance and retard through the use of internal rotating magnets. The engine was rated at **700hp** at **3000rpm** but due to a number of failures, starting in November 1943, the engine governor was preset to run at a maximum of **2500rpm** under full load [13].

330

331: Here we see the rear top section of the magneto drive housing to which the **Bosch** magnetos were mounted. The rear cover plates have been removed to allow the gear wheels of the magnetos to be timed to the spur gear, at ***1***, page **104**, photo **355**.

332: A side view of a **Bosch** magneto at the LHS of the engine. A tube holding the six shielded spark plugs would be secured onto the curved pipe section at ***1***. This can be seen on the completed engine at **2**, page **116**, photo **356**.

333

333: The fuel cut-off valve as bolted to the front top of the engine. If the oil pressure of the engine drops or the oil pump fails while the engine is running, the valve in the fuel cut-off body will close and stop the fuel supply to the carburettors, thus halting the engine.

334

334: To perform an emergency engine start, before sufficient oil pressure was reached, the lever, at ***1***, could be depressed. This would bypass the oil pressure cut-off valve allowing fuel directly into the carburettors, see also page **34**, photo **55**.

335

335: The rear end of the engine. The camshaft and all auxiliary units are driven by straight spur timing gears from the opposite end of the crankshaft to the flywheel. A torsional oscillation damper is fitted at the timing end of the crankshaft outside of the crank case.

336

336: A close-up view of a spur gear on the LHS of the engine, meshed with the auxiliary gearing from the crankshaft, that is used to drive the camshafts, see ***1*** and ***2***, page **94**, photo **318**. The bearings for these intermediate timing gears ran on fixed stub shafts. There was little clearance in this area so the gears could not be manufactured wide enough to use shoulders with bearing retaining circlips. The solution was to rivet bearing retaining rings to either side of the gear for the inner and outer race of the bearing, seen at ***3*** and ***4***. Effectively then the bearing was the same width as the gear itself. This spur gear is object ***1*** on page **105**, illustration 339.

337-338: In photo **337** is the opposite side of the spur gear seen on page **104**, photo **336**. We can see the primary spur gear that is driven directly from the crankshaft, see **2**, illustration **339**. In photo **338** is a close-up view of the gears seen in photo **337**. The port, at ***1***, photo **338**, is for coolant circulation.

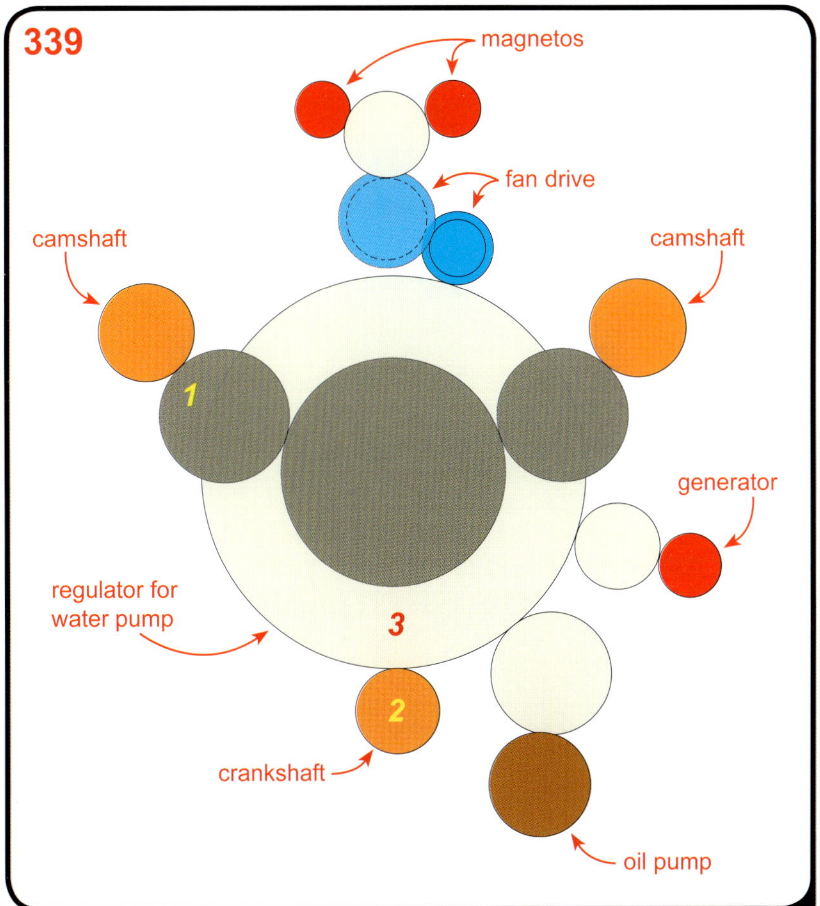

339: A schematic diagram of the spur and timing gearing as driven from the flywheel at the rear of the engine [20].

340: A partial view into the LHS inlet manifold. In each inlet manifold there was a longitudinal shaft controlled by the engine governor. Each shaft held butterfly valves opposing each of the carburettor butterflies. This allowed the governor to override the Drivers throttle as required. Each inlet manifold also had drain holes to vent excess wet fuel.

341: Here we see the crank and the electrical starter. At ***1*** we can see how when engaged the pinion of the crank starter would mesh with the flywheel. The hand crank, turned from outside the tank, would transmit kinetic energy through a spur reduction gear. A series of plates within the crank starter body would start turning and these plates would only lock once the pinion was fully meshed with the flywheel. Once a certain rpm was achieved the plates would slip and a return spring would pull the pinion out of mesh [14].

342: The reduction spur gear in the crank starter is in the body, at ***1,*** with the slip plates in the forward section, at ***2***. The crank starter could be operated by three means: **a)** hand cranked by two crew members, **a)** by a 2-stroke engine unit that could be bolted to the rear armour plate of the tank, **c)** by a reduction gearbox unit that was connected to the engine of a **Kübelwagen**.

343: Here we see the engine again this time essentially in the completed state. Note the protective plate fixed, at ***1***, over the opening in the bell housing over the crank starter pinion and the power cable connected to electrical starter motor at ***2***.

344

344: Here we can see a modern type of braided fuel line connected to the **Solex** fuel filters. The reported instances of fires in the engine compartment of initial production vehicles were often caused by fuel leaking from poorly fitting fuel pipe unions. This problem was partially solved by using improved types of fuel lines, as well as creating a low-pressure environment in the engine compartment by having air being drawn into the fan drive boxes, thus reducing the amount of vapourised fuel in the atmosphere.

345: In this photo we are primarily interested in the operation of the cold engine starting mechanism as connected to the oil cooler. The lever, at ***1***, by default is in the **OFF** position for cold starting. Two butterfly valves are fixed to the shaft at ***2***. Each of these valves are mounted at **90°** to each other. One valve is in the pipe at ***3***, the other is in the housing at ***4***. In the **OFF** position the valve at ***4*** is open. When the lever is operated, in the direction of the arrow at ***5***, the valve at ***3*** is opened and the valve at ***4*** is closed. Cold engine starting is then **ON**. In this configuration hot oil will only flow through the oil cooler and the engine block and not the oil cooler radiator. The cold starting oil flow configuration is seen clearly in the technical illustration, page **199**.

346: The **Bosch 12V** generator could operate at very high temperatures and so to aid in cooling cold air from a vent in the engine compartment firewall, see ***1***, page **66**, photo **206**, was drawn through a flexible hose, at ***1***, and into the generator body.

347: Another view of the front LHS of the engine just before the installation of the oil cooler. The routing of the water pipe from the oil cooler to the water pump was changed in only a minor way from the original design of the **Maybach HL210 P30**.

348: Here the oil cooler has now been installed and awaits the oil pipes to be fitted. Note that the oil cooler is secured to the engine using metal straps, at ***1*** and ***2,*** as opposed to the large c-clamps as employed by the generator and starter mechanisms.

349: The cold engine starting lever, at ***1***, is seen before the return spring has been fitted, see ***6***, page **109**, photo **345**. A Bowden cable was connected to the eyelet at ***2*** and ran forward to the Drivers station. The operating switch for cold engine starting was mounted on the flange seen at ***1***, page **71**, photo **230**.

350

350-351: The **Bosch GILN 700/12/1500/B1 1** generator was driven from the engine via a spur gear, see page **105**, illustration 339. This generator incorporated a current governor designed to ensure that a constant voltage was always supplied irrespective of the engine speed. When voltage fell to a low level an automatic switch-off device would activate thus disabling the battery charging.

351

352: The oil filter housing. The oil filter, once the oil was drained from the engine, could be changed by removing the three bolts on the filter housing cap, at ***1***. This filter was accessed from the fighting compartment through the removable panel on the LHS of the engine firewall in the fighting compartment, see ***2***, page **135**, photo **391**. The oil filter housing is angled at about 45° and gave easy access through the access panel for the changing of the actual filter unit itself.

353-354: Heat from the exhaust manifolds in the engine compartment contributed to an already high temperature environment. Both exhaust manifolds were therefore enclosed by sheet metal sleeves. Cold air, via ducting from the fan compartments, was forced into the sleeves. At ***1***, page **116**, photo **356**, is a port to which the duct from the fan compartment would be connected.

355: A final study of the twin **Solex** fuel filters before being connected up to their appropriate fuel lines. The levers seen on each filter, at ***1*** and ***2***, are designed to aid in bleeding the system before first use, after a filter change for example, to ensure that all air is removed from the system before the engine is turned over.

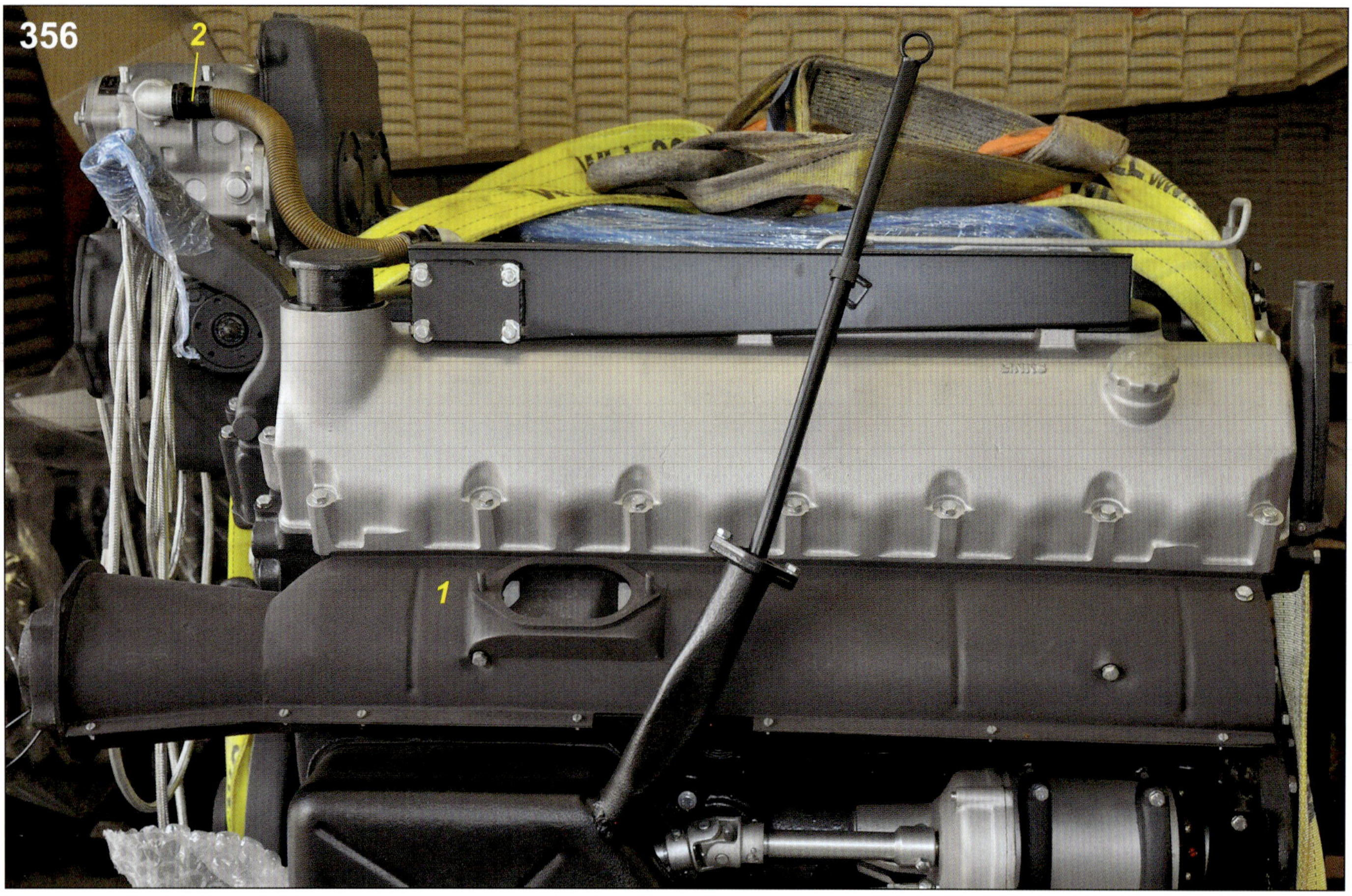

356-357: The two photographs on this page show the restored Maybach engine in the completed state. These views were taken just before this engine was successfully started up and run for the first time in over sixty years. This was a significant achievement for the restoration team. The engine is now ready to be placed into the tank.

358

358: A frontal view of the Panther. From this standpoint you can see how effective the design of the sloped armour was. Both the glacis and the lower hull nose were **60mm** thick angled at **55°** from the vertical position. This gave the front armour, when measured horizontally, an apparent thickness of **~95mm**.

359-360: The tracks fitted to a Panther had the designation listed by both Jentz and Spielberger as **Kgs. 64/660/150** [13][14]. Trojca however states Panther tracks are **Kgs. 64/660/160** [21]. The **150/160** relates to the measurement between the track pin centres, see *1*, photo **360**. We measured this distance (on these new tracks) and found it to be exactly **150mm** on every sample taken.

361-362: Views along the LHS of the Panther. In July 1943 the requirement for mounting two headlights was dropped with only a single light, manufactured by **Bosch**, being mounted now above the LHS track fender, at ***1***, photo **361**. Note under the Panther, at ***2***, photo **362**, the armoured air intake cover.

363-364: Views along the RHS of the Panther. Of interest here are the hangers welded under the sponsons that held brackets for the side skirts, **Schürzen**, at ***1***, photo **363**. Note also the engine under wraps as seen in both photos. This is the restored engine which by this point has been run up and tested and is awaiting fitting into the tank.

365-366: Two views of the rear armour plate of the Panther. In November 1943 at the **Demag** manufacturing works several Panthers were fitted with a low mounted towing coupling of the same type as was fitted to the Bergepanther. This practice was discontinued quite soon after introduction because this coupling reduced the overall ground clearance.

367-368: Here we have two views looking towards both the front and rear of the tank showing the current state of completed work. As all rear hull deck plates are now in place, air intake grills, fan drives plates etc. we can see extra detail being added, for example at *1*, photo **367**, we have the aerial mount, **Antennenfuß Nr.1**, and at *2* and *3*, photo **368** the brackets used to hang spare track links on.

369

369: Due to restricted space in the workshop has always meant it has been difficult to take unobstructed photographs. By standing on top of the turret we were able to take this photograph looking along the full length of the RHS of the hull.

370: Here we see the main gun travel lock, **Rohrstütze**. This was designed to support the main gun during travel operations, where combat was not expected to occur, in order to prevent movement of the gun and thus possible damage to the gun trunnions and other associated equipment. When in combat the travel lock would be folded down against the hull deck roof, see page **52**, photo **144**.

371: When the tank was in transit mode the gun barrel would sit in the holder, at ***1***, with the chain, **Spannkette**, over the top of the barrel. The chain was secured into place under tension by locking the handle in the notched bar at ***2***. In combat the chain was secured under tension using the notched bar on the side of the travel lock, see ***4***, page **52**, photo **144**.

2017 - Hull Crew Hatches

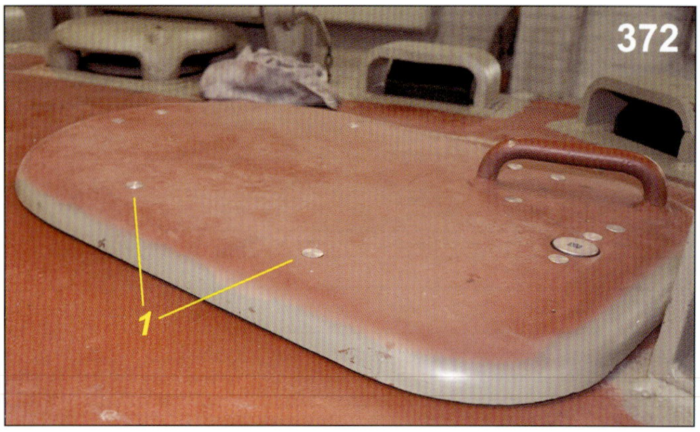

372: The crew hatch above the Radio Operators station. The various countersunk bolts, at ***1***, all join to retaining strips used to hold the waterproof rubber seal of the hatch in place. These can be seen on the original crew hatch photographs on page **20**.

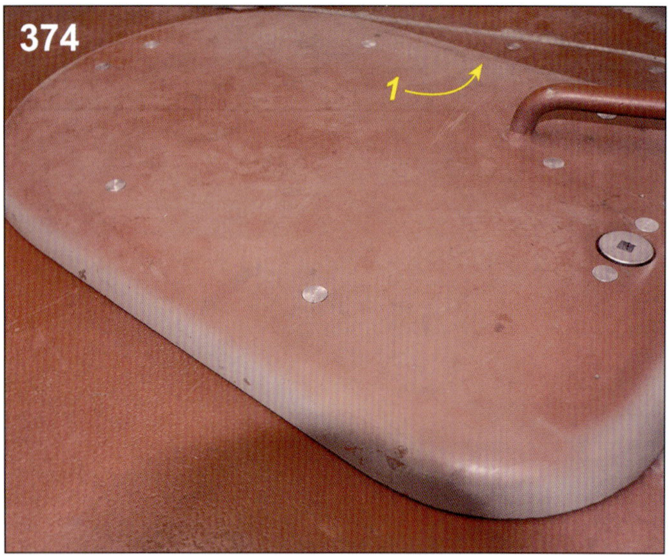

374: This design of the crew hatch on the Panther **Ausf. D** and **A** had a tendency to jam when damaged, leading to crews going into combat with the hatches open to allow for easy egress in the event of an emergency [13]. Jettisonable crew hatches were designed for the **Ausf. G**.

376: The Radio Operators hatch retainer operated as follows. The hatch would be swung open. The edge of the hatch, at ***1***, photo **374**, would catch in the jaws and under spring tension would be retained in place. To release the hatch the handle would be pushed down, at ***1***, releasing the spring tension and allowing the hatch to be rotated free out of the retainer jaws.

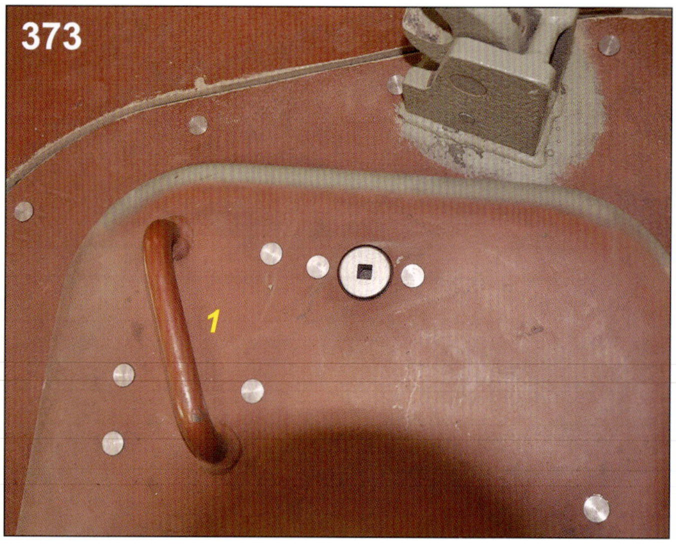

373: The crew hatch could be opened from the outside using a square head key. Once unlocked the crew member would pull up on the handle at ***1***, raising the hatch up on its piston, see page **52**, photo **143**, and swing the hatch horizontally out towards the front of the tank.

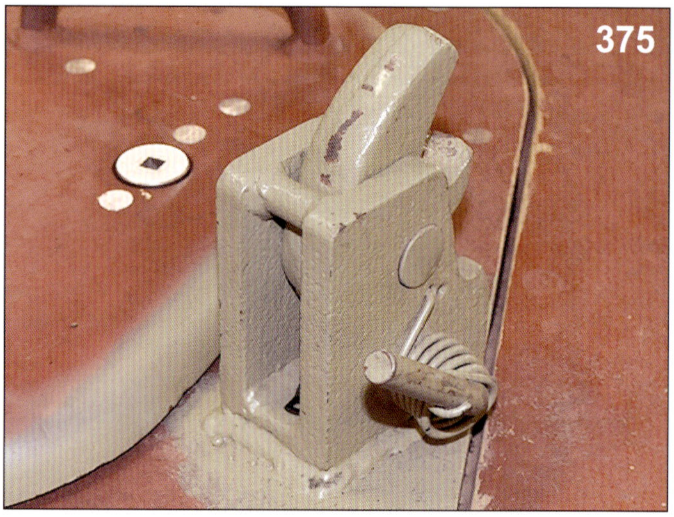

375: A rear side view of a crew hatch retainer that was designed to stop the hatch from swinging loose when the hatch was in the open position. All three photos here on page **126** show the hatch retainer of the Radio Operator.

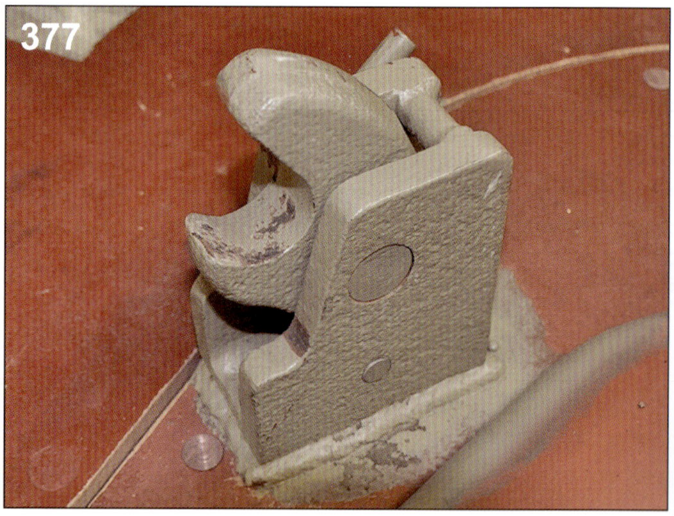

377: A view from the other side of the crew hatch retainer. Note that the Drivers hatch retainer had the spring release lever on the opposite side of the retainer body. This can be seen on page **52**, photo **141**.

378-379: As the engine compartment and general hull interior were covered very comprehensively in **Vol. 1** of this restoration project by **The Research Squad** all we show here is the current condition of the engine compartment as it awaits the fitting of the engine. All fan drives, radiators and armoured cowlings as can be seen are now in place.

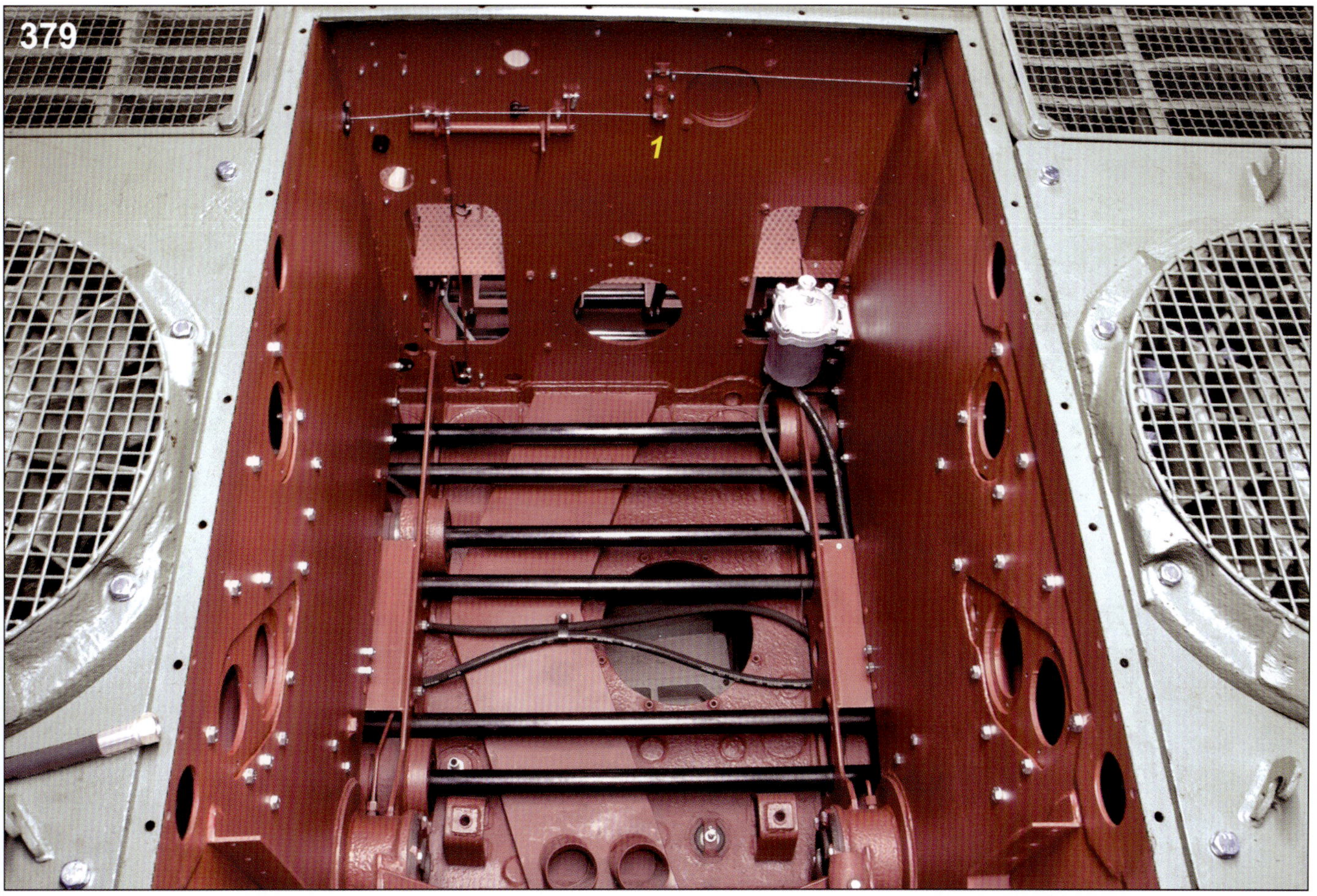

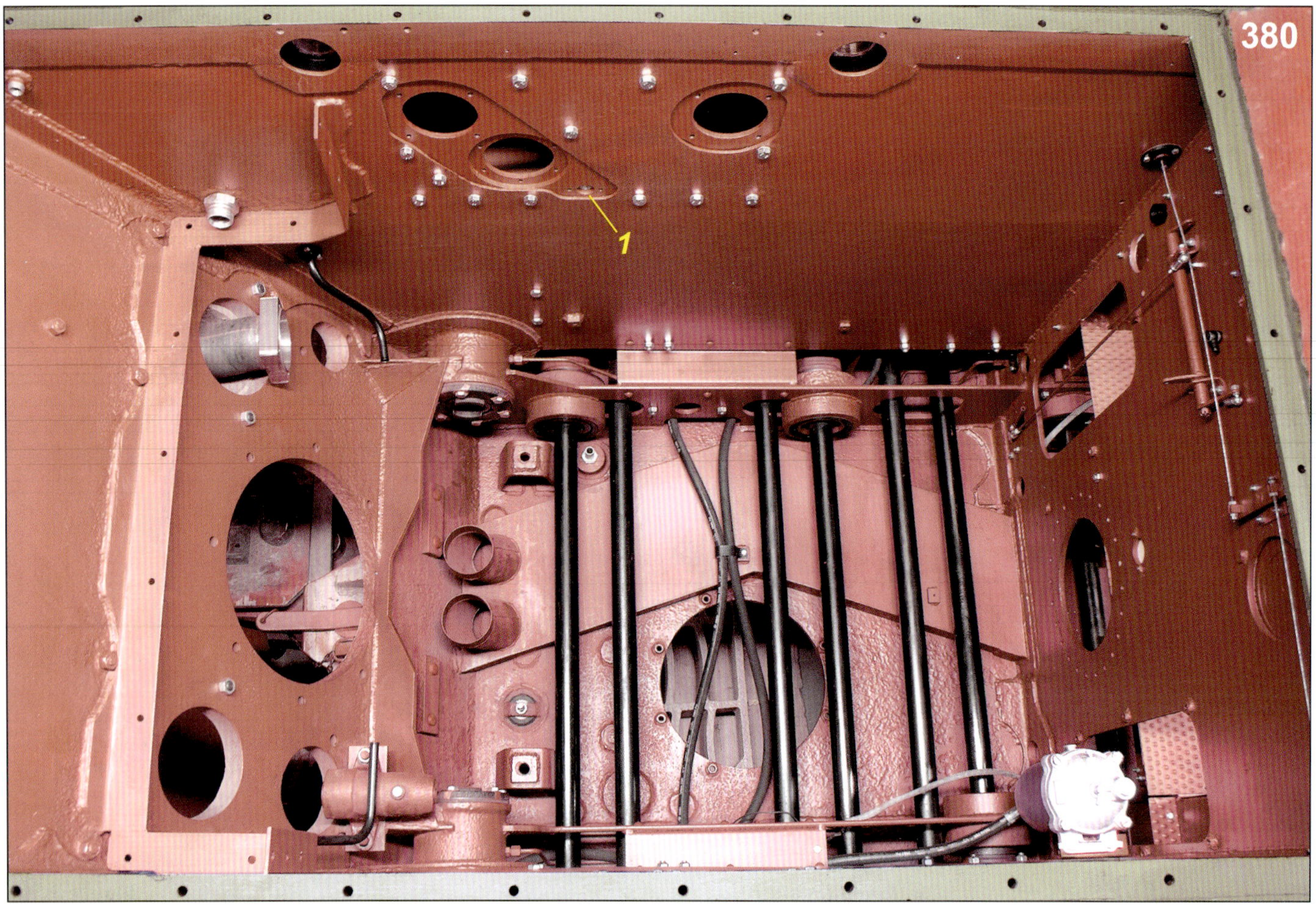

380-381: Again here we see overall views of the engine compartment. This time we are looking from RHS to LHS and vice versa. All other engine components will be fitted once the engine is installed.

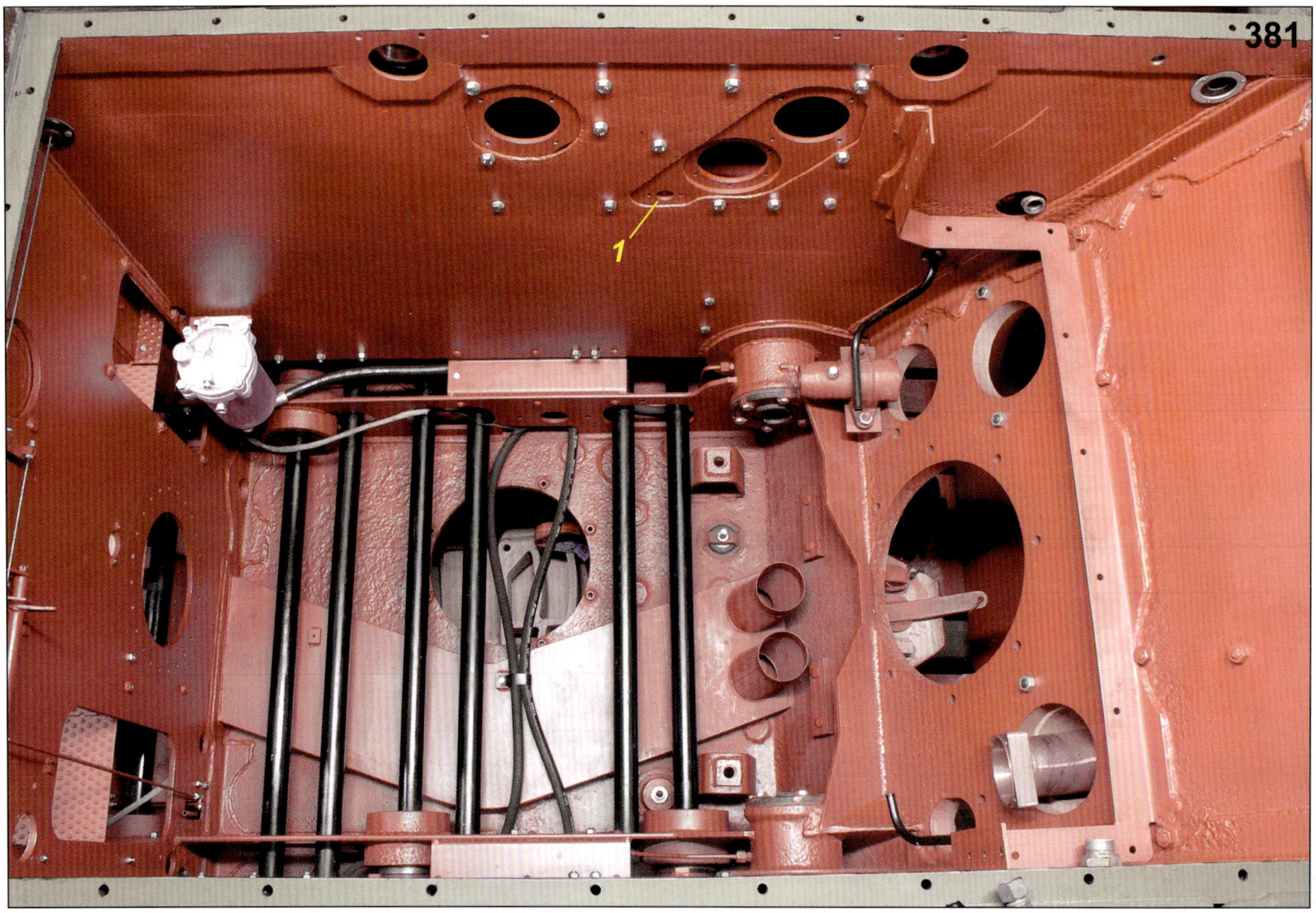

382: A look down over the fan drive and radiator units. Three deck sections make up this area. Two armoured plates, ***1*** and ***2***, with semi-circular cut-outs that fit around the fan drive while a large circular cast fan cowling sat over the fan drive, ***3***. These were all bolted together and typically would be removed as one piece using the lifting hooks at ***4***, ***5*** and ***6***.

383: Here we see the forward set of radiator louvres in front of the forward RHS oil cooler and water radiator. To aid engine warming in cold temperatures these louvres could be closed to prevent the flow of cold air over the radiators. These louvres were closed using the Bowden cable connected at ***1*** and to the rear of the engine compartment firewall at ***1***, page **127**, photo **379**.

384: The rear set of fan louvres in front of the rear RHS radiator. The Bowden cable for operating the opening and closing of this set of louvres can be partially seen at ***1*** and is connected through to the junction seen at ***2***, photo **383**.

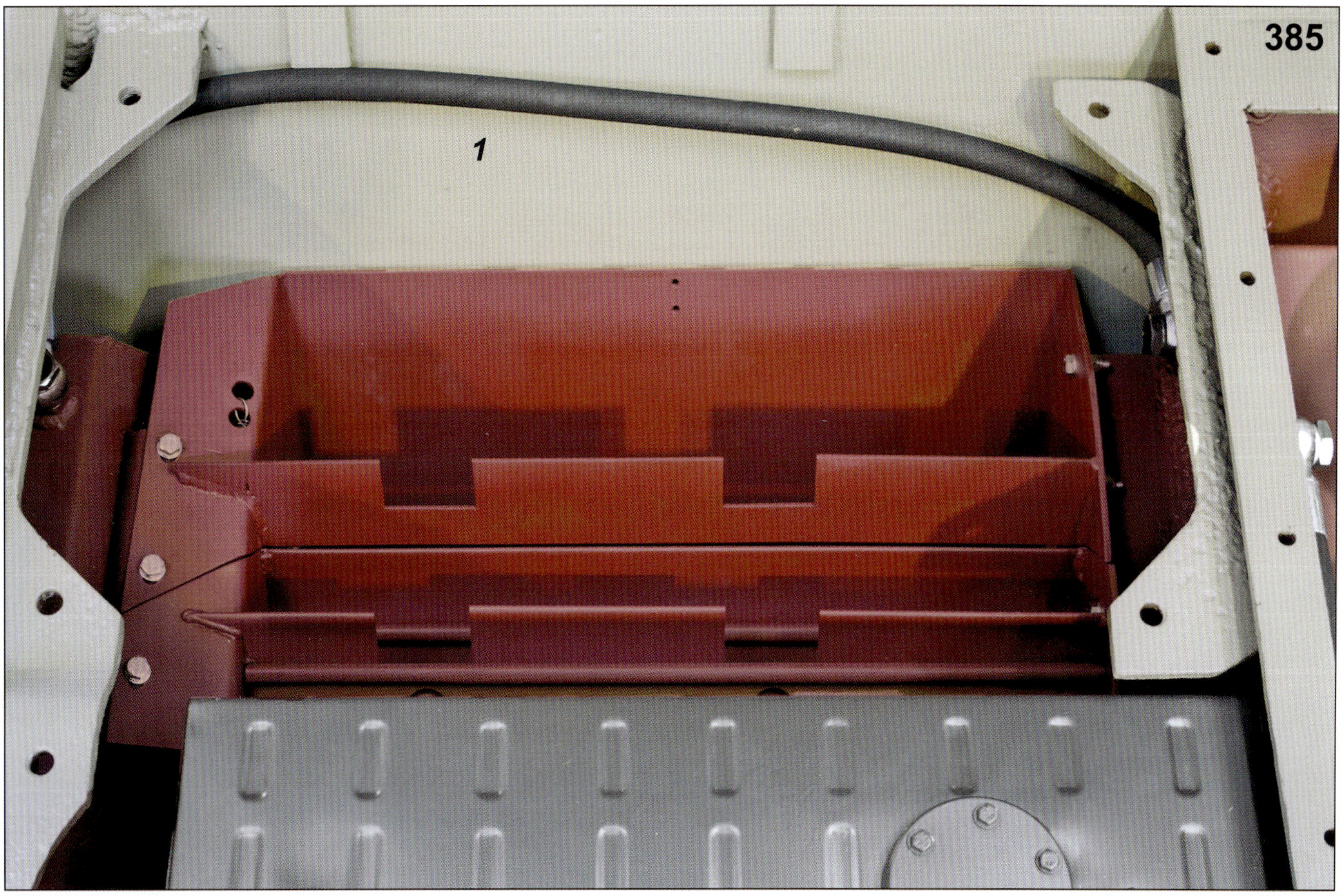

385: Another view of the rear fan louvres at the RHS of the tank, this time looking towards the rear of the tank. Note now that all the radiators have been painted grey.

386: Once all the radiators and fan louvres were mounted and plumbed into place the armoured cowlings above the louvres were fitted. These are large one-piece cast items. Note that the mesh grill used to prevent the ingress of foreign objects sits in a flat frame that is bolted to the top of the louvre cowling.

387: A top down view incorporating the complete RHS fan drive, water and oil radiators and the radiator louvres before fitting of the deck plates and cowlings. Note the overflow piping connecting the two water radiators together, at ***1***.

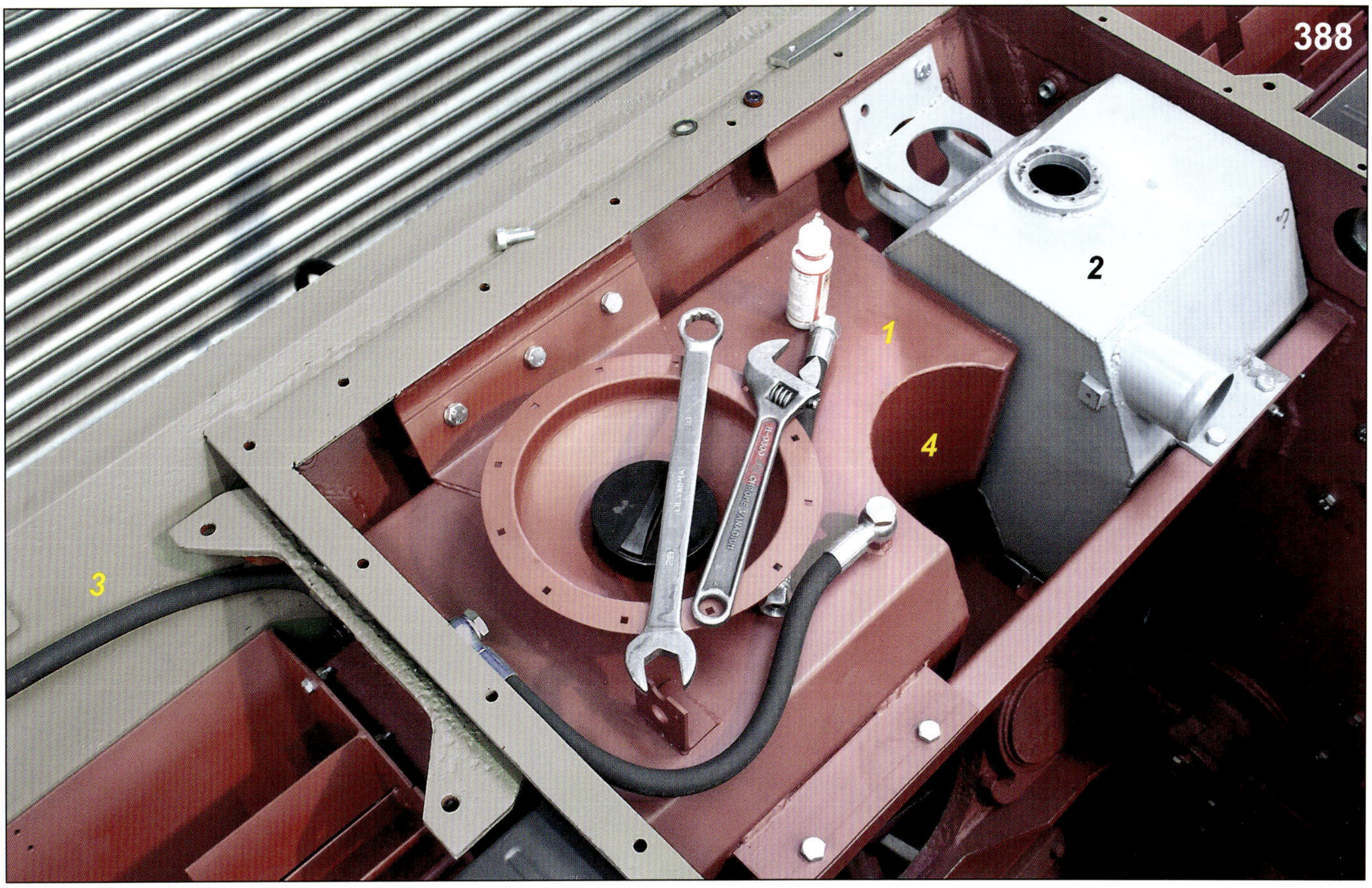

388: At the rear upper section of the engine compartment are located both the fuel filler tank and the coolant header tank, at ***1*** and ***2*** respectively. The flexible pipe, at ***3*** is connected to the overflow pipe union at the rear top of the fuel tank in the upper RHS sponson, page **55**, photo **158**. The circular cut-out section, at ***4*** is where the deep wading snorkel tubing would be located.

389: Here we see one of the two large ventilation caps, **Lufteintritt**, as are fitted to the engine hatch located on the hull deck. This is locked in place by fitting the cap and turning in place until the lugs lock home, see ***1***.

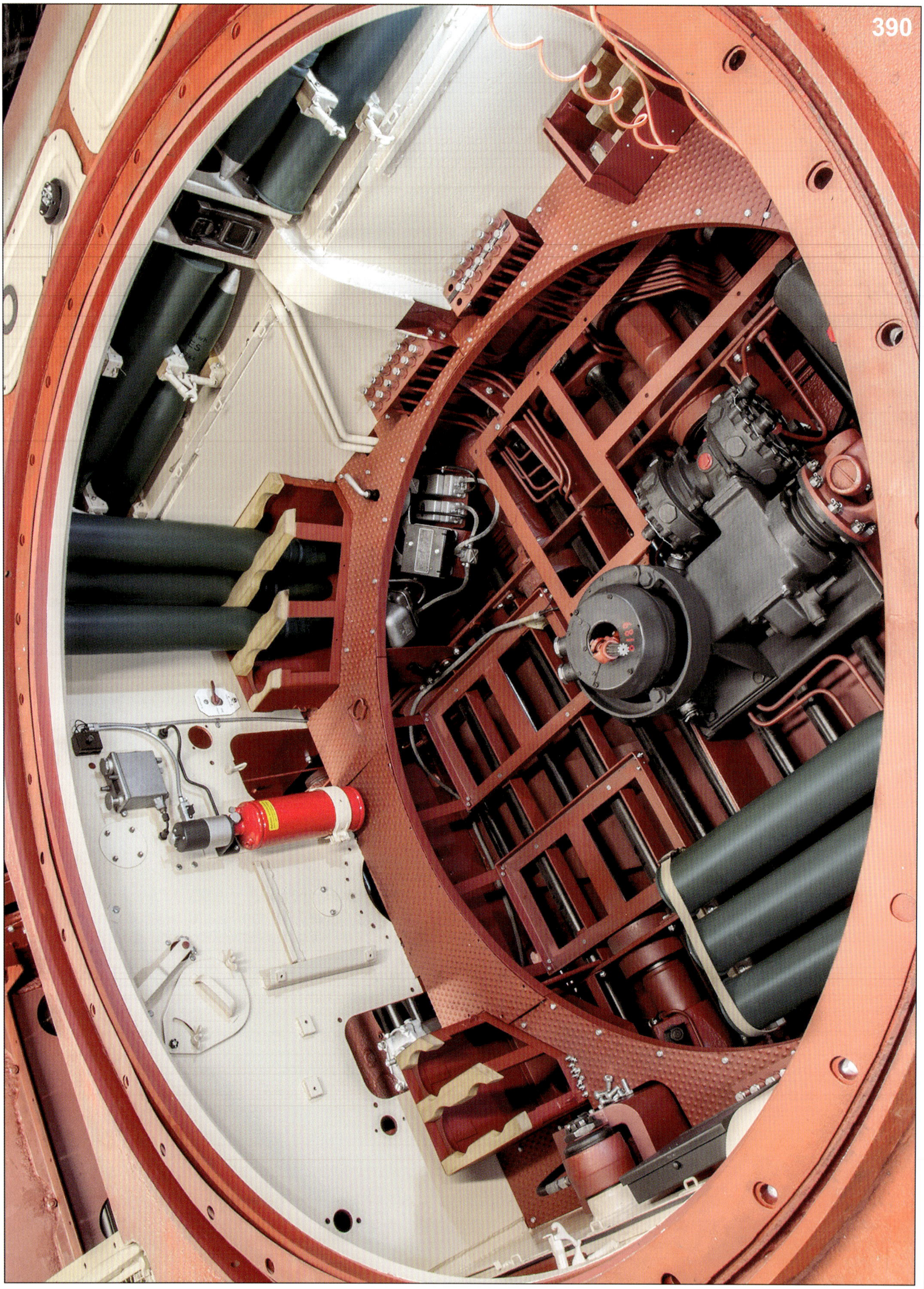

390: Over the next six pages we present a series of look downs into the fighting compartment from the hull deck. In this photo we are looking at the 7 o'clock position towards the rear of the tank.

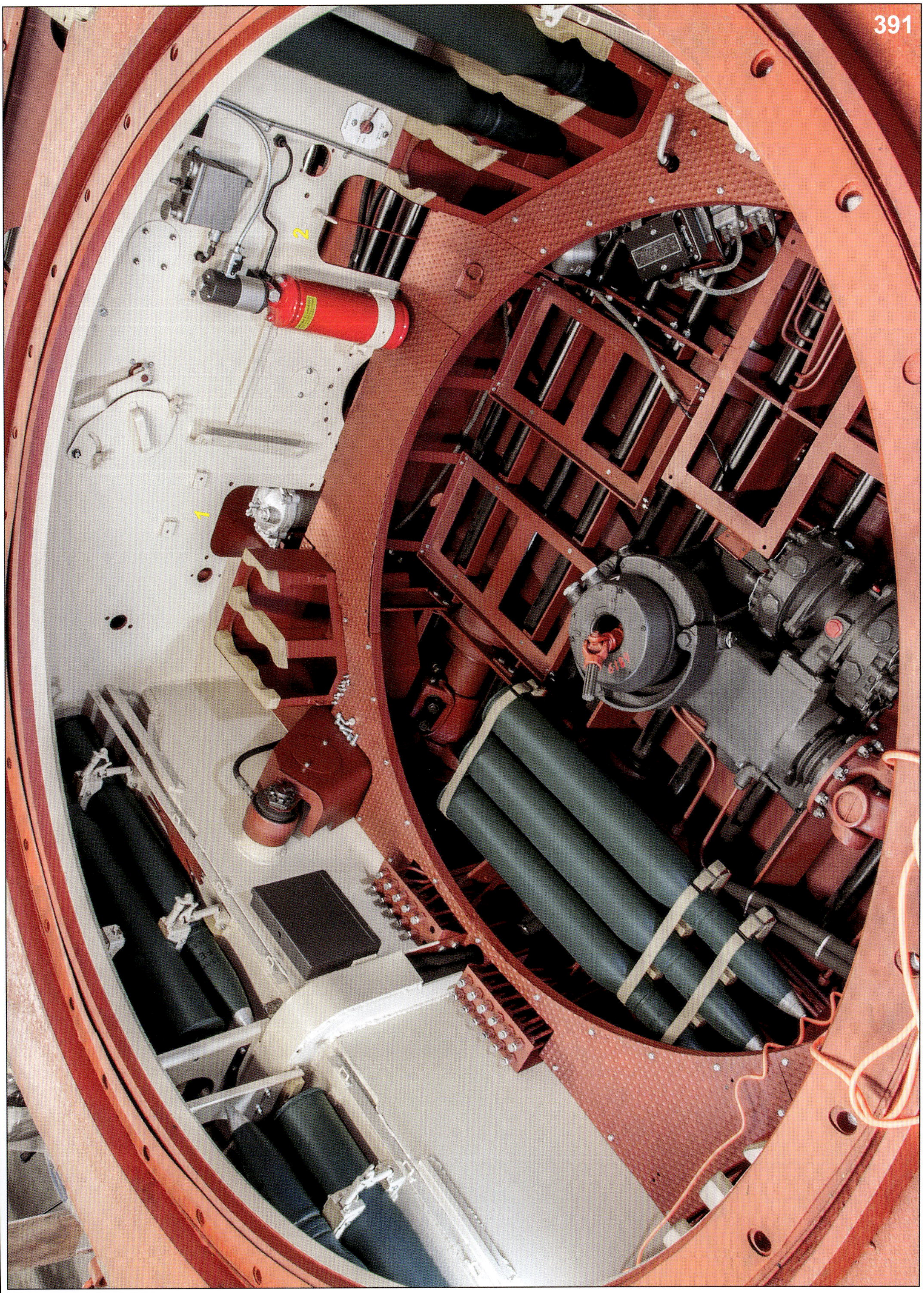

391: Here we are looking toward the 5 o'clock position. The cover plates, at ***1*** and ***2***, giving access to the engine compartment are still to be fitted.

392

392: Looking directly toward the rear of the tank at the 6 o'clock position. One of the access plates, referenced at ***1*** and ***2***, page **135**, photo **391**, can be seen lying on the hull deck, at ***1***.

393: We now swing around 180° and look directly towards the front of the tank at the 12 o'clock position. We can see how the forward ammunition panniers, when holding a full complement of main gun rounds, completely fills this space.

394: Moving our view slightly we now turn towards the 1 o'clock position. The sponson ammunition panniers on both sides of the tank are loaded to capacity with main gun rounds.

395: Finally we move our view to the 11 o'clock position. Note that as of yet none of the main gun rounds in the sponson panniers are locked in place using the spring-loaded retainers.

396

397

398

396-398: From the centre of the hull floor we look forward towards the Driver and the Radio Operators stations. We can see here the main gun rounds stored vertically, nose down, in the ammunition panniers directly behind the crew seats in the forward hull compartment as well as at the front of the fighting compartment. A combined total of **27** main gun rounds would be stored in these locations. With all ammunition in place it was a very tight squeeze for either the Driver or the Radio Operator to be able evacuate their station by climbing into the fighting compartment for egress out through the turret.

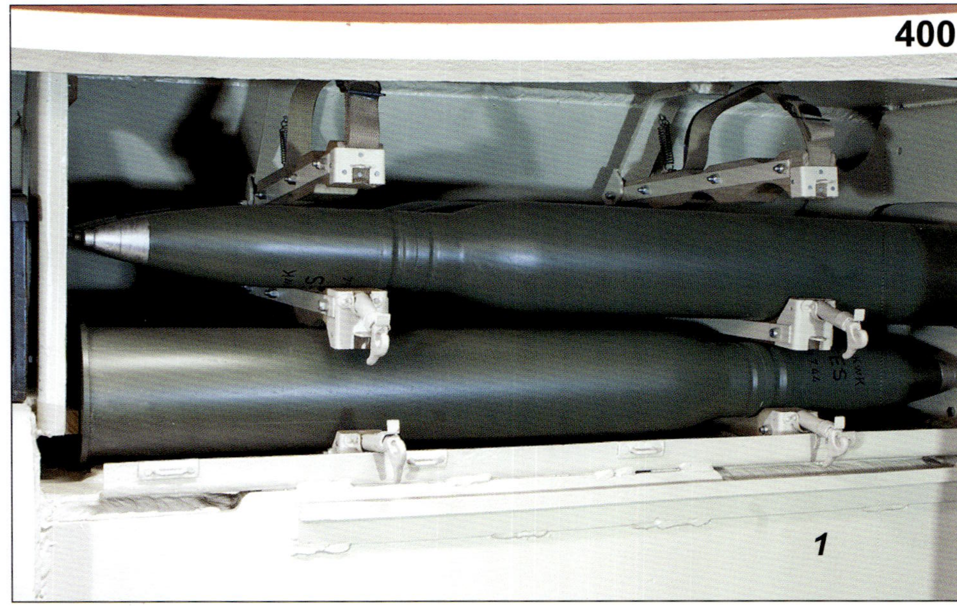

399-402: A look at the four ammunition panniers in the LHS and RHS hull sponsons in the fighting compartment. The Panther **Ausf.A** carried a total of **79** main gun rounds. Each pannier held a total of nine rounds stacked horizontally. In general, applicable to the combat situation, the main gun ammunition would be split 50-50 high explosive to armour piercing rounds. The main gun rounds here are reproductions, made from mild steel, and of course carry no explosive charges of any sort. They are replications of the **Sprgr.42** high explosive rounds. **M.G.34** ammunition would also be stored in the fighting compartment. On the rail at ***1***, photo **400**, under the LHS forward sponson pannier were stored six bags, **Gurtsäcke**, of **M.G.34** ammunition. On the rail at **2**, photo **401**, under the RHS forward sponson pannier were stored four bags and lastly, at ***3***, photo **402**, at the RHS rear sponson pannier were stored three bags.

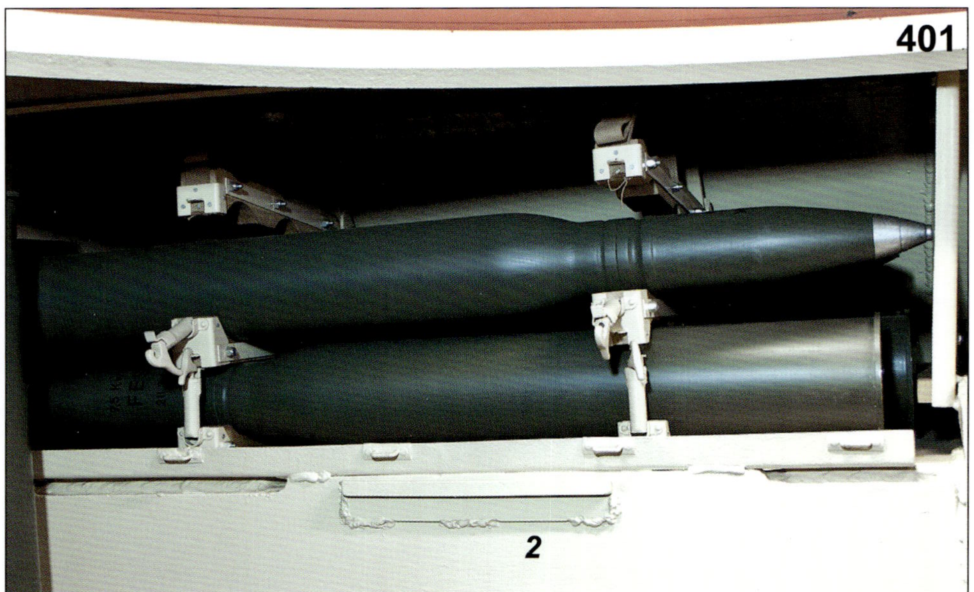

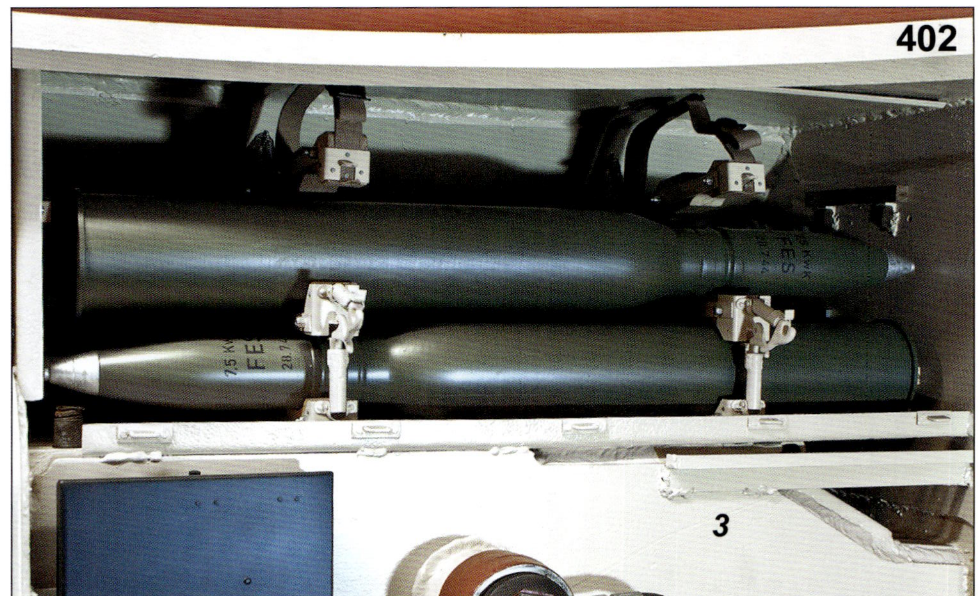

403: A study of the RHS of the turret. Note the pattern of the zimmerit on the pistol port plug. We can also see the tank aerial lying across the turret roof.

404: A close-up view of the 4 o'clock position of the RHS of the turret. The zimmerit has been replicated accurately and a description of how the restoration engineers achieved this result is described on page **194**.

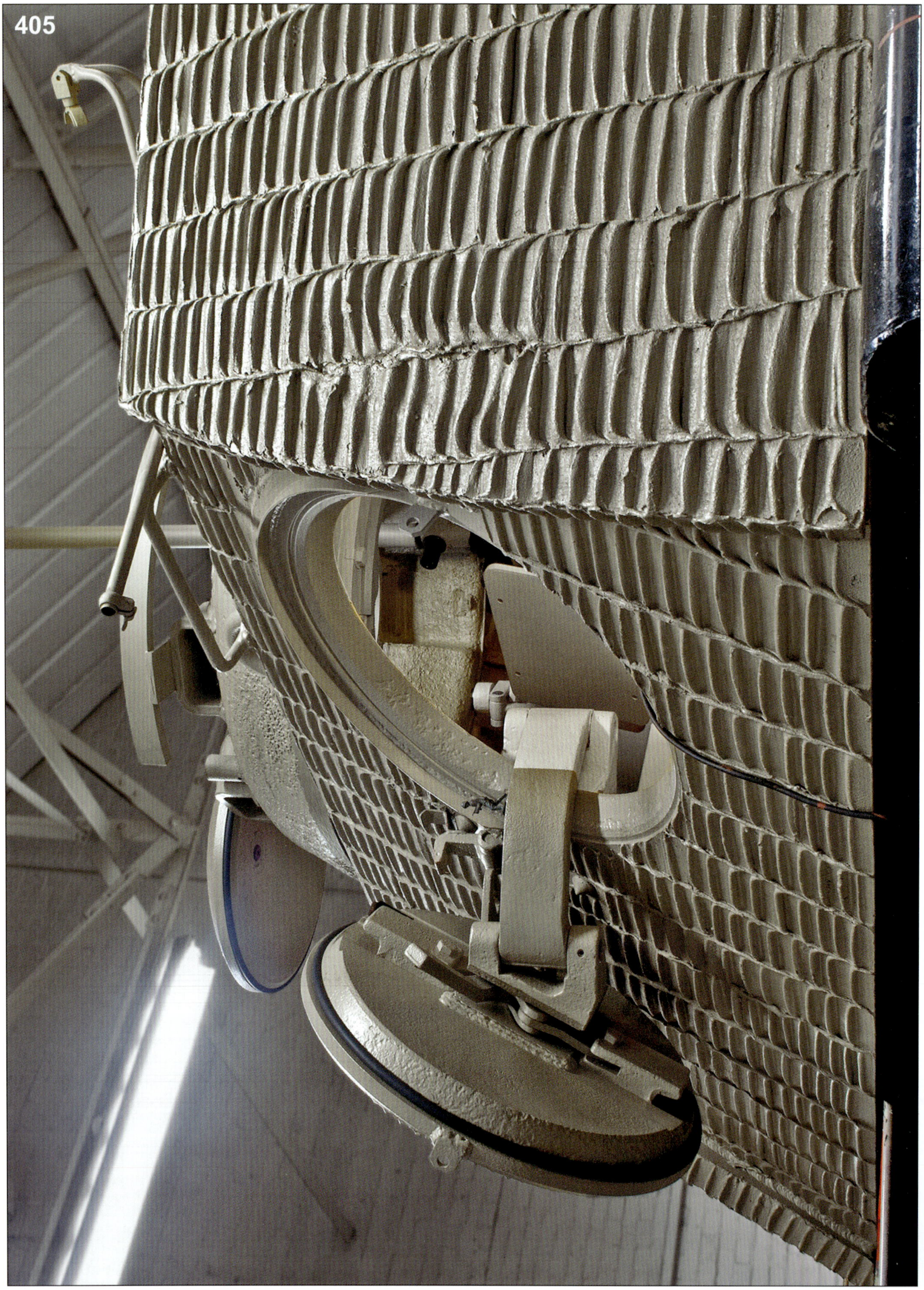

405: The rear of turret showing the crew hatch opened to the fullest extent. This hatch was painted dunkelgelb on the inside face and also on the hatch arm.

406

406: The rear of the turret from the 7 o'clock position that includes a view into the turret through the crew hatch. Note the turret lifting ring welded to the turret roof behind the Commanders cupola, at ***1***.

407: A view of the turret from the 7 o'clock position. Note that even though the Commander cupola is bolted in place, see page **81**, photo **267**, there is still a slight gap between the base of the cupola and the turret roof.

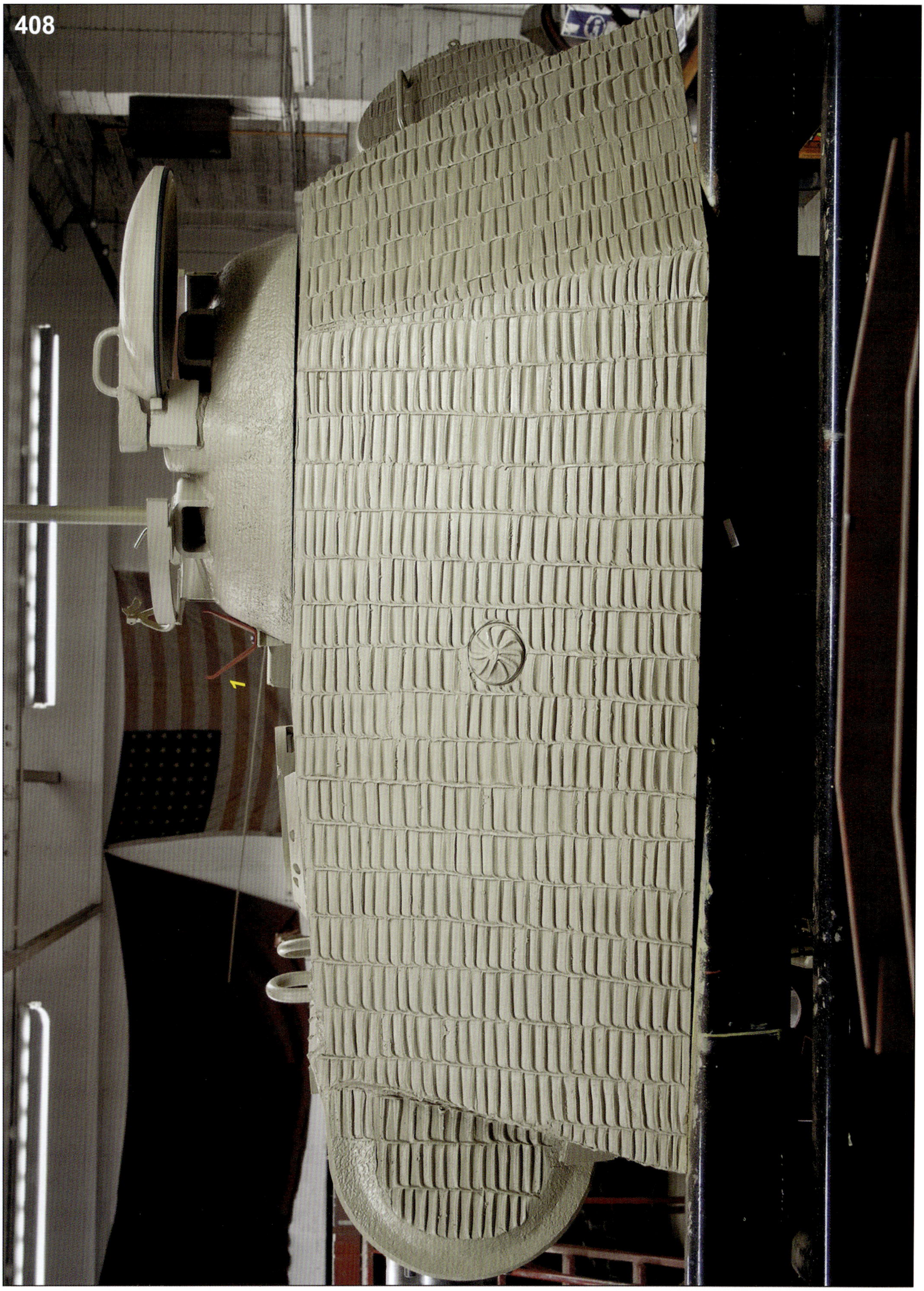

408: A study of the turret LHS from the 9 o'clock position. Again we can see a very clean and tidy application of the zimmerit here along with a good side profile view of the Commanders sighting vane, at ***1***.

409: Looking along the roof towards the front of the tank from the Commanders cupola. We can see the mantlet elevation bump stop at ***1*** and the forward turret lifting rings at ***2*** & ***3***. Note the bullet splash guard in front of the armoured cover of the turret roof fan.

410: Looking towards the rear of the turret roof. Of interest is the anti-aircraft gun mount, **Fliegerbeschußgerät**. The **M.G.34** located in the turret could be removed and fitted to this mount when a weapon was required for an anti-aircraft defence role.

411

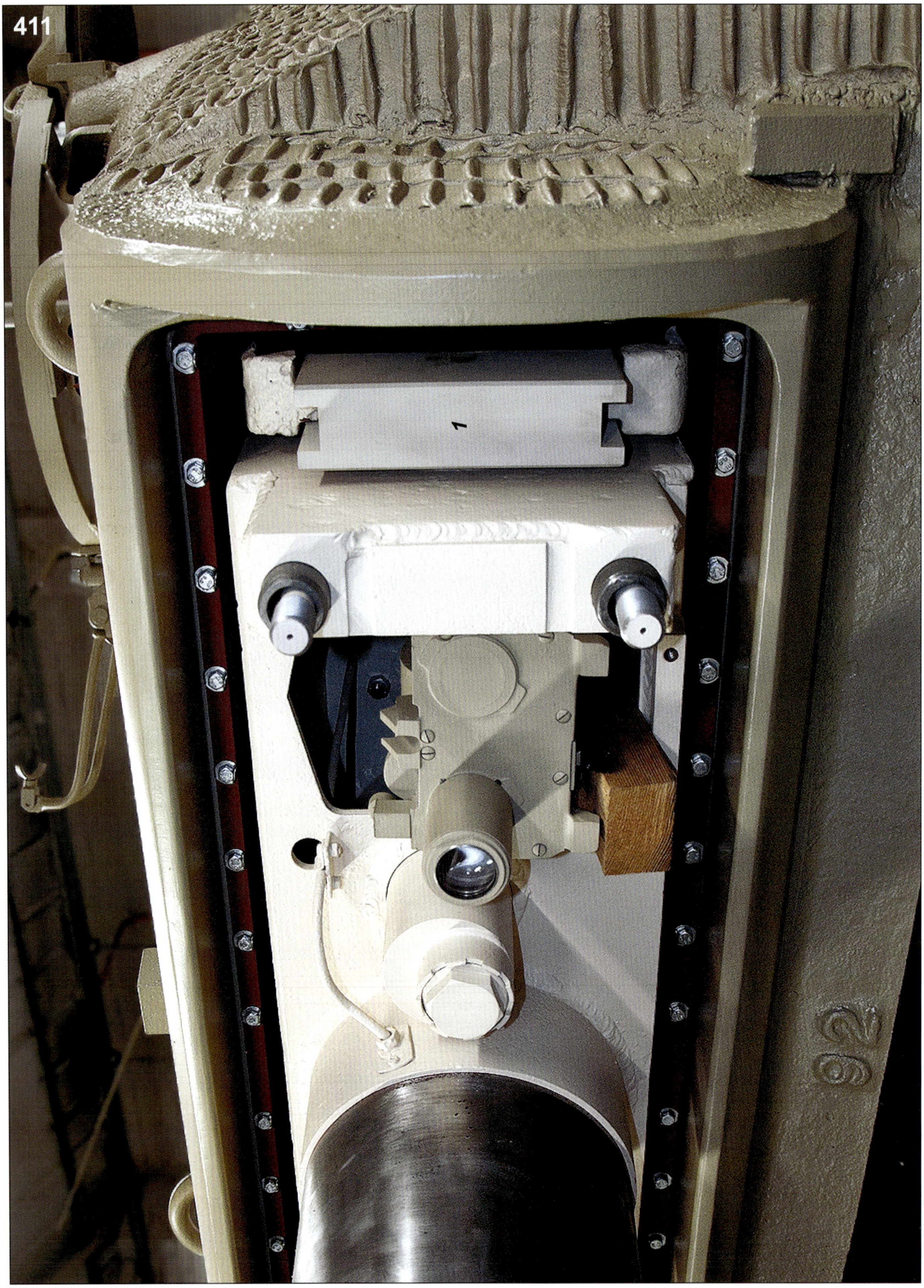

411: Over the next eight pages we have a series of photos showing the front of the turret, with all equipment in place including the main gun, but excluding the mantlet.

412: At ***1*** we see the large block that fits over the trunnion on the main gun carriage and so acts as the pivot point for the elevation and declination of the main gun.

413-414: Here we are looking at the RHS of the front of the turret showing views above and below the main gun carriage. Note how the **M.G.34** protrudes through the front of this carriage. The forward end of the recoil cylinder is seen at ***1***, photo **414**.

415-416: The LHS of the turret front again from a viewpoint of just above and below the main gun carriage. The wooden block under the **T.Z.F.12a** gun sight is a temporary support because the gun sight frame, **Turmzielfernrohrlagerung**, has not yet been fitted.

417-418: Here we have a close-up view of the recoil cylinder. The recoil cylinder was locked in place in the main gun carriage by a block that dropped down into a slot on the top of the gun carriage and which was then bolted into place, see ***1***, page **171**, photo **451** and ***1***, page **173**, photo **458**.

419

419-420: At ***1***, photo **420**, we have the forward end of the recuperator that was designed to return the gun to the ready position. If the forward lens of the **T.Z.F.12a** gun sight became occluded, with dirt for example, the Gunner had no other option than to disconnect the gun sight, withdraw the sight back into the turret and manually clean the lens.

420

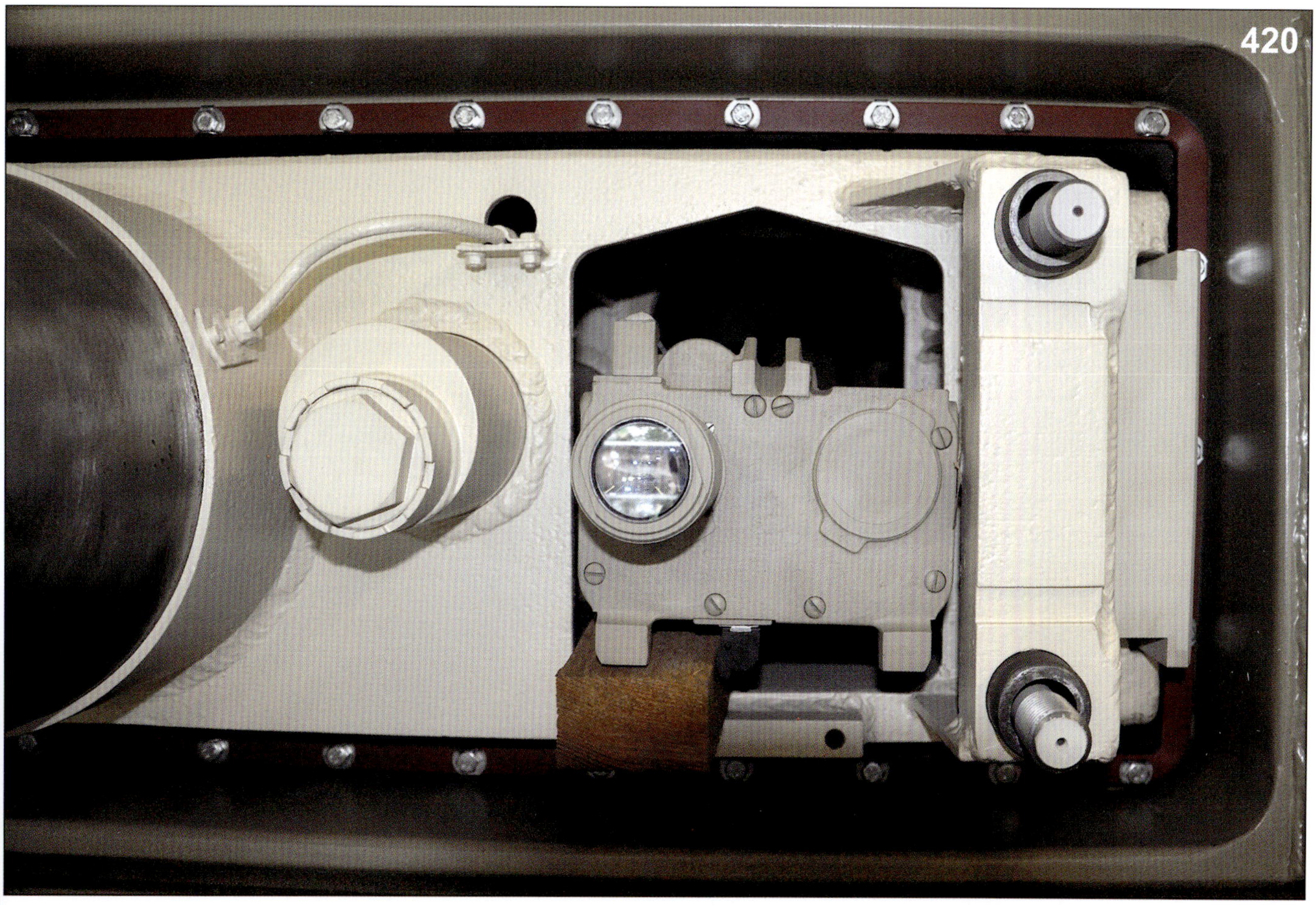

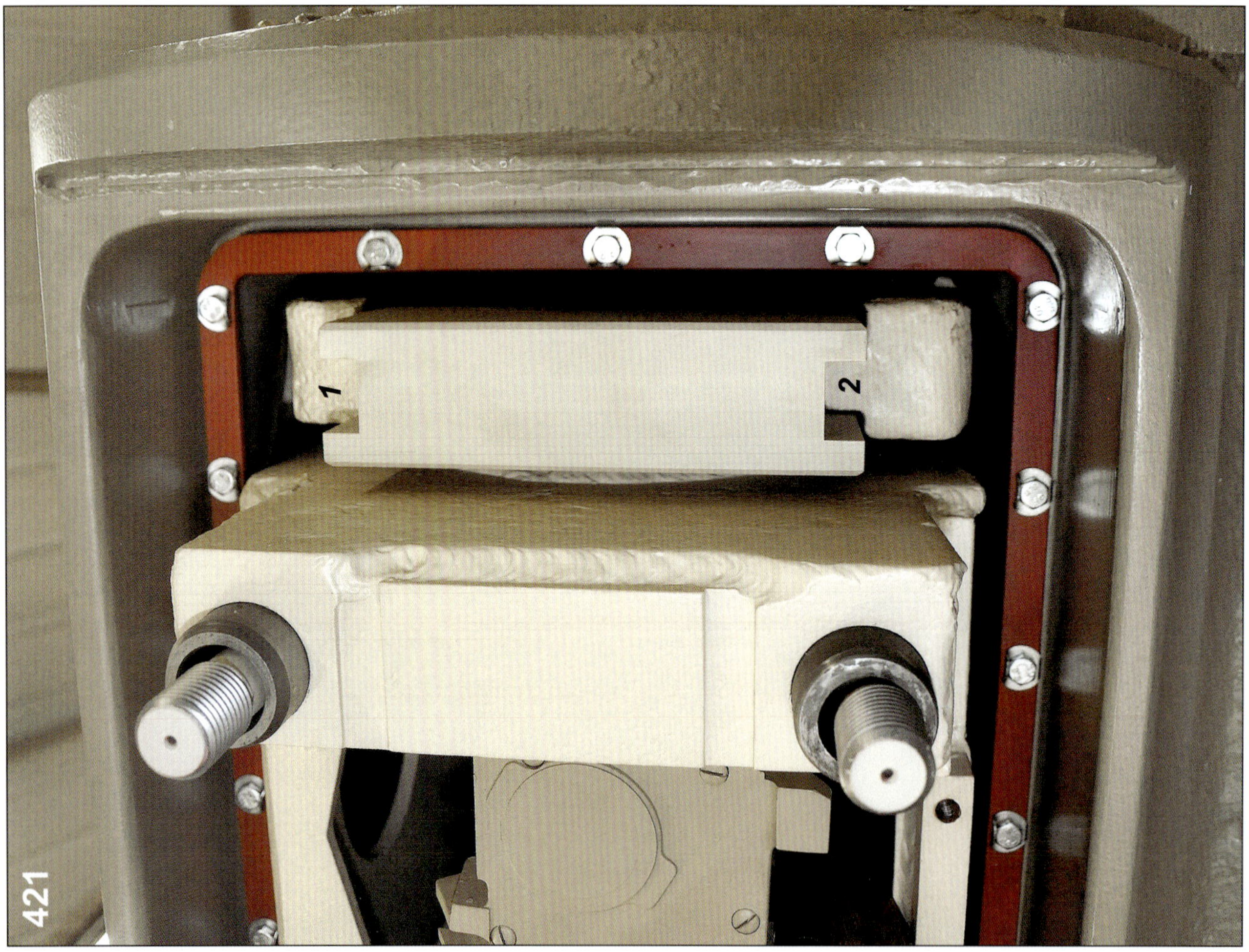

421: Here we have a close-up view of the trunnion block at the LHS front of the tank. These blocks have two slots, top and bottom of each block, that slide onto the rails that are cast into the front plate of the turret, at ***1*** and ***2***.

422: One of the distinctive features of the **Ausf. A** turret was the redesign of the turret front. This was manifest in the circular shape, with a taper towards the leading edge, of the cast section behind the mantlet, at ***1***.

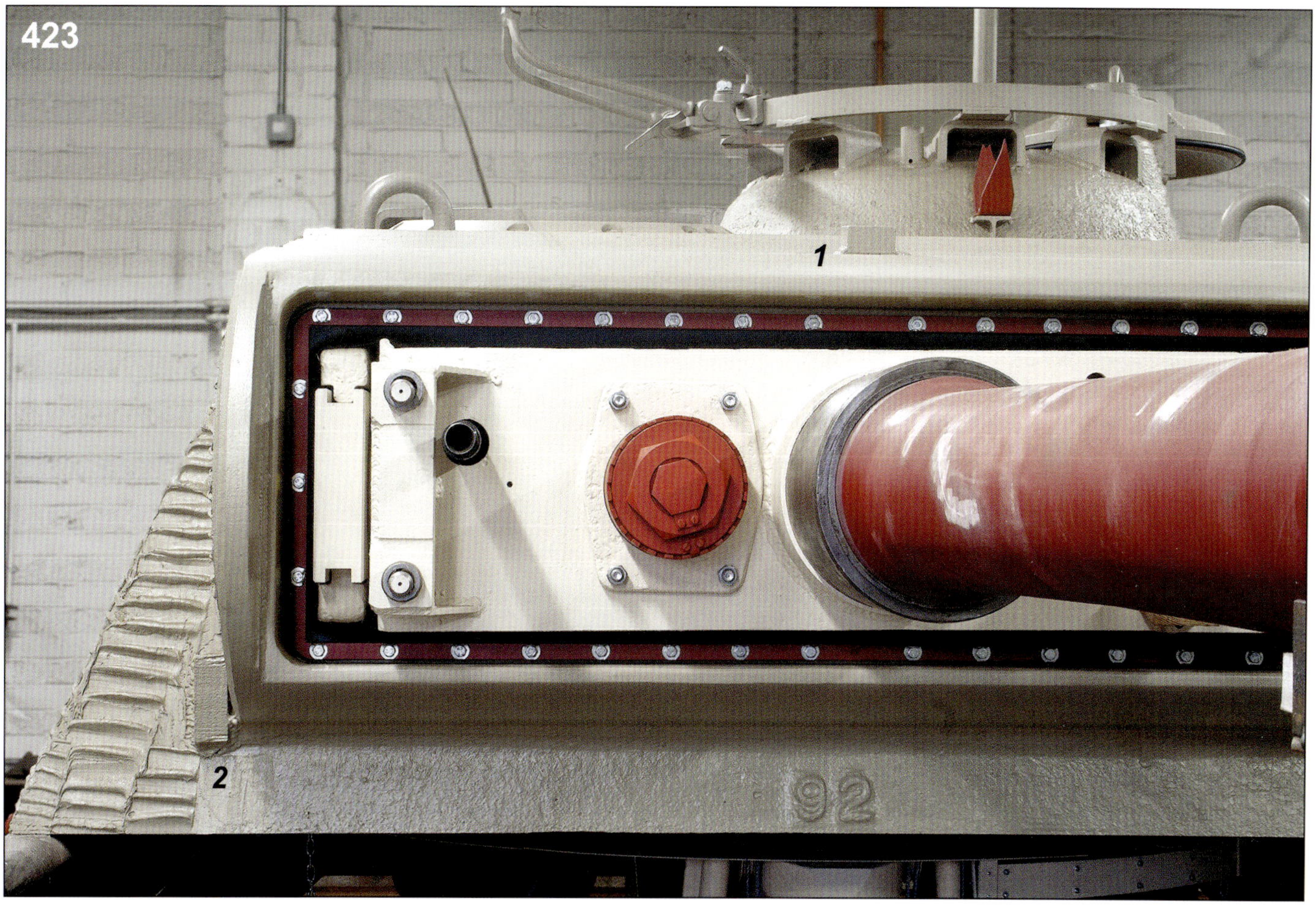

423-424: Two final studies looking directly towards the front of the main gun carriage. Note the bump stops that limited the maximum elevation and declination that could be traversed by the main gun at ***1*** and ***2***, photo **423**, and ***3***, photo **424**.

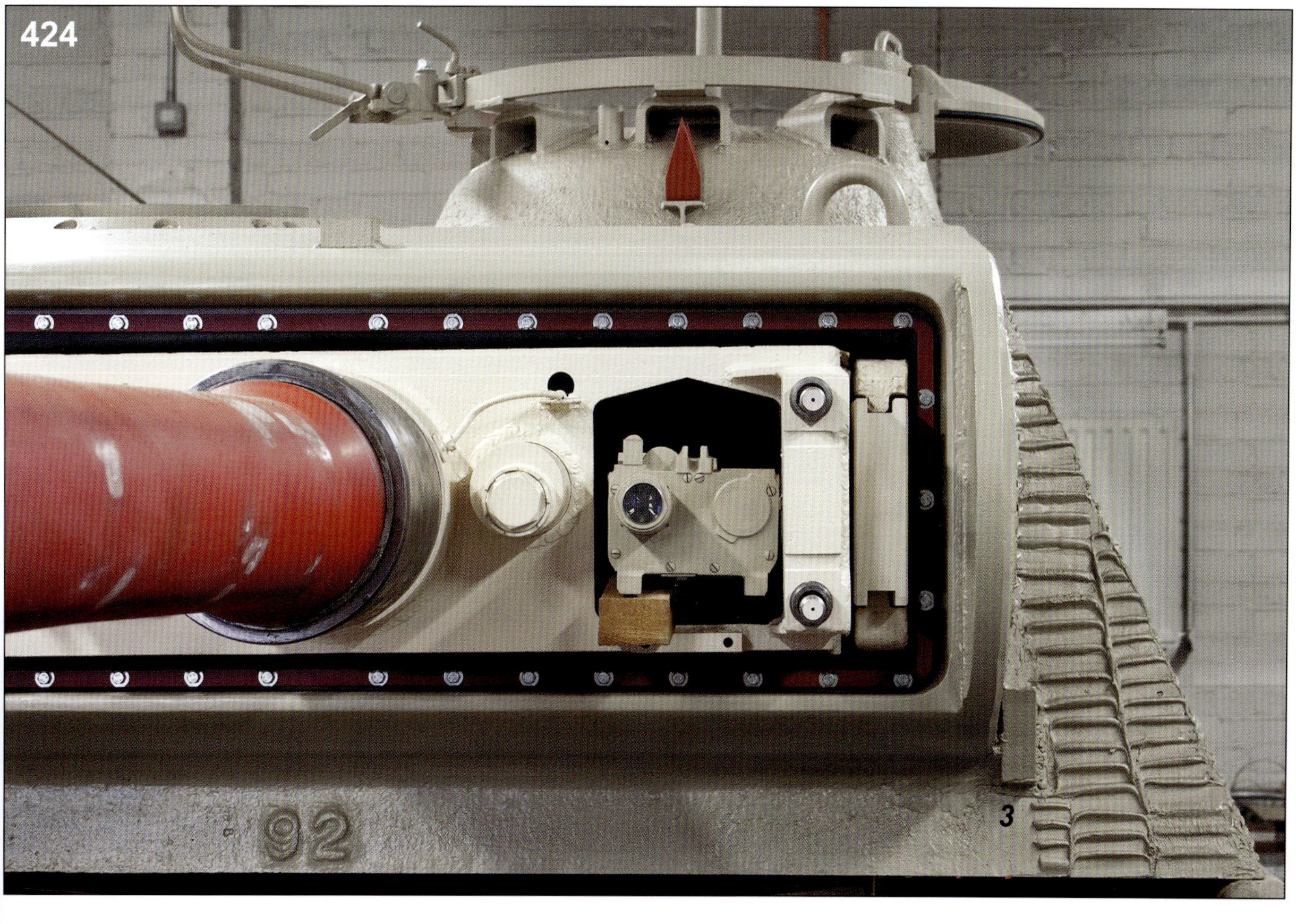

425: The muzzle brake screw thread is anti-clockwise (left-handed) and is known as a buttress or saw-tooth thread, **Sägegewinde**. On main gun firing the muzzle brake locking ring would compress the muzzle brake threads thus allowing a stress-free transfer of forces. A locking bolt, fitted vertically either at the top or bottom position, in this case at ***1***, prevented rotation of the muzzle brake.

426: The main gun on a Panther could not be fired without the use of a muzzle brake. The deflection of blast on the muzzle break baffles was reported to reduce barrel recoil by up to **~70%** [14].

...a final selection of photographs from the restoration of Fgst.Nr.158134 up to date as of 2018...

427-428: Here we are positioned directly above the Commanders cupola looking down directly into the tank at the Commanders and Gunners stations. The box, at ***3***, photo **427**, was used to store the Commanders headphones and throat microphone. In photo **428** we have a good view looking directly down into the main gun spent shell basket.

429: A look from the Commanders station to the LHS of the turret ring. We can see the Commanders intercom box, **Kasten Pz. Nr. 21 Ausf. B.**, is in place at ***1***. Behind the protective guard on the turret ring can be seen an original set of headphones, at ***2***.

430: In this view we look directly down to the Gunners station from the Commanders station. At ***1*** is a box used to store the Gunners headphones and throat microphone. An original throat microphone set can be seen at ***2***.

431: When not used the **T.S.R.1** periscope was stored at the LHS of the Commander. The bottom section of the tube sat in the holder, at ***1***, with the upper section held by the spring clip at ***2***.

432: From the Commanders station we are now looking towards the breech of the main gun. The deflector guard, **Abweiser**, was connected to the rear of the breech block and was retained in place using two pins, at ***1***, and at ***1***, page **185**, photo **487**.

433-434: Here we have the **T.S.R.1** Periscope, **Sehstab**. This was a vision device used by the Commander for when the tank was in a turret down position and the Commander still required visibility of the surrounding terrain. The periscope tube was about **1.5m** tall and the cupola hatch was required to be open when using this device, see page **149**, photo **410**.

435: The **T.S.R.1** periscope was mounted in a swing arm bolted to the underside of the Commanders cupola. The periscope sits in the block, at ***1***, and was secured in that block using the arm at ***2***. If the Commander had to change his point of view he would unclasp the periscope, rotate it in the block and retighten it again, as the field of view through this periscope was very narrow indeed.

436: The **T.S.R.1** periscope did not rotate in the base mounting block but could be rotated to some degree around the pivot point at ***1***. In inclement weather this could not have been a very useful tool to employ. In high winds there would be a lot of shake at the top of the periscope as the only fixed support was at the base clamp. In wet weather rain would likely enter the turret through the open cupola hatch. This may be part of why the use of this periscope was discontinued in July 1944.

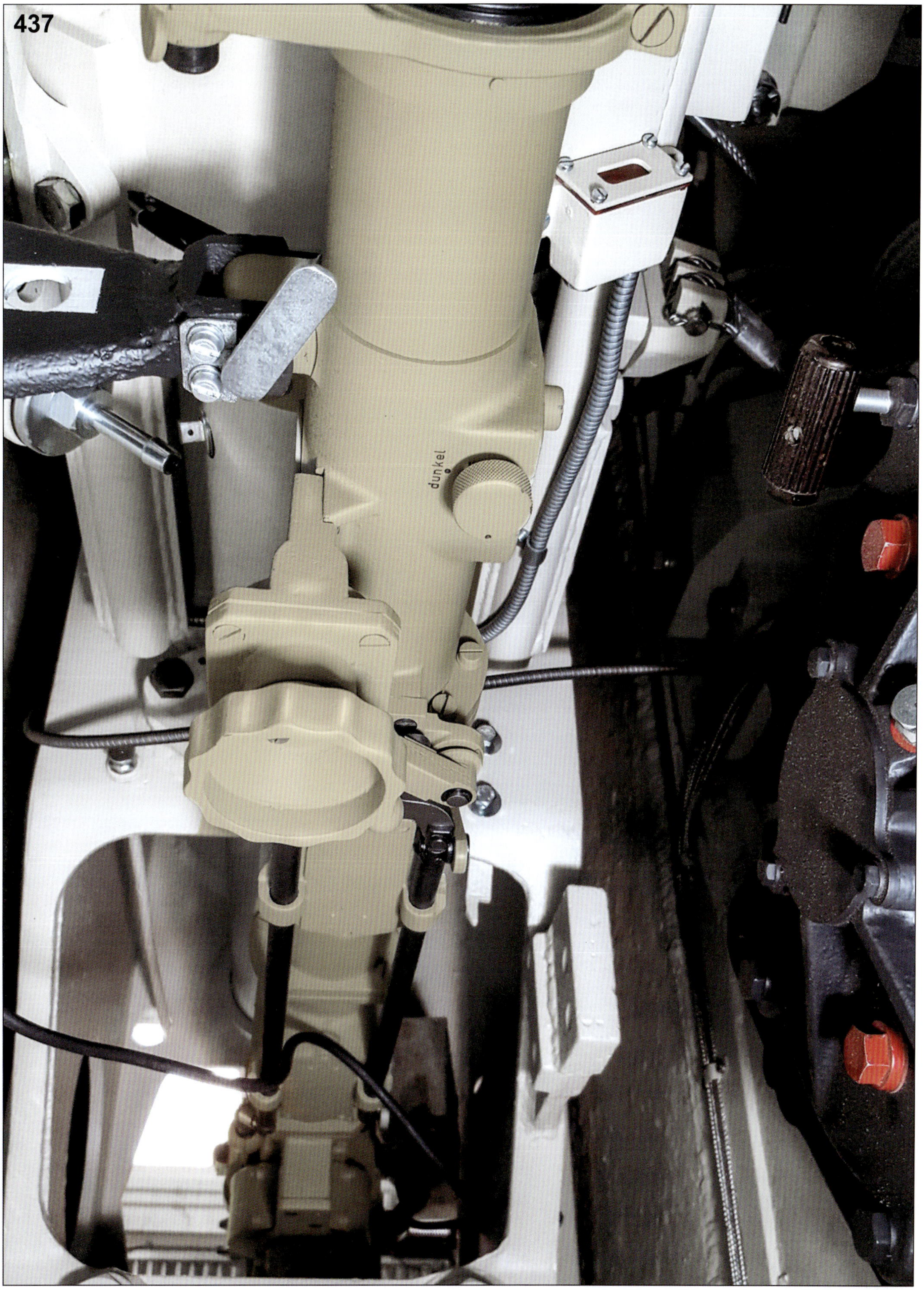

437: The Gunners station. In November 1943 the binocular **T.Z.F.12** gun sight was replaced with a monocular **T.Z.F.12a** gun sight. These gun sights were only manufactured by **Leitz**.

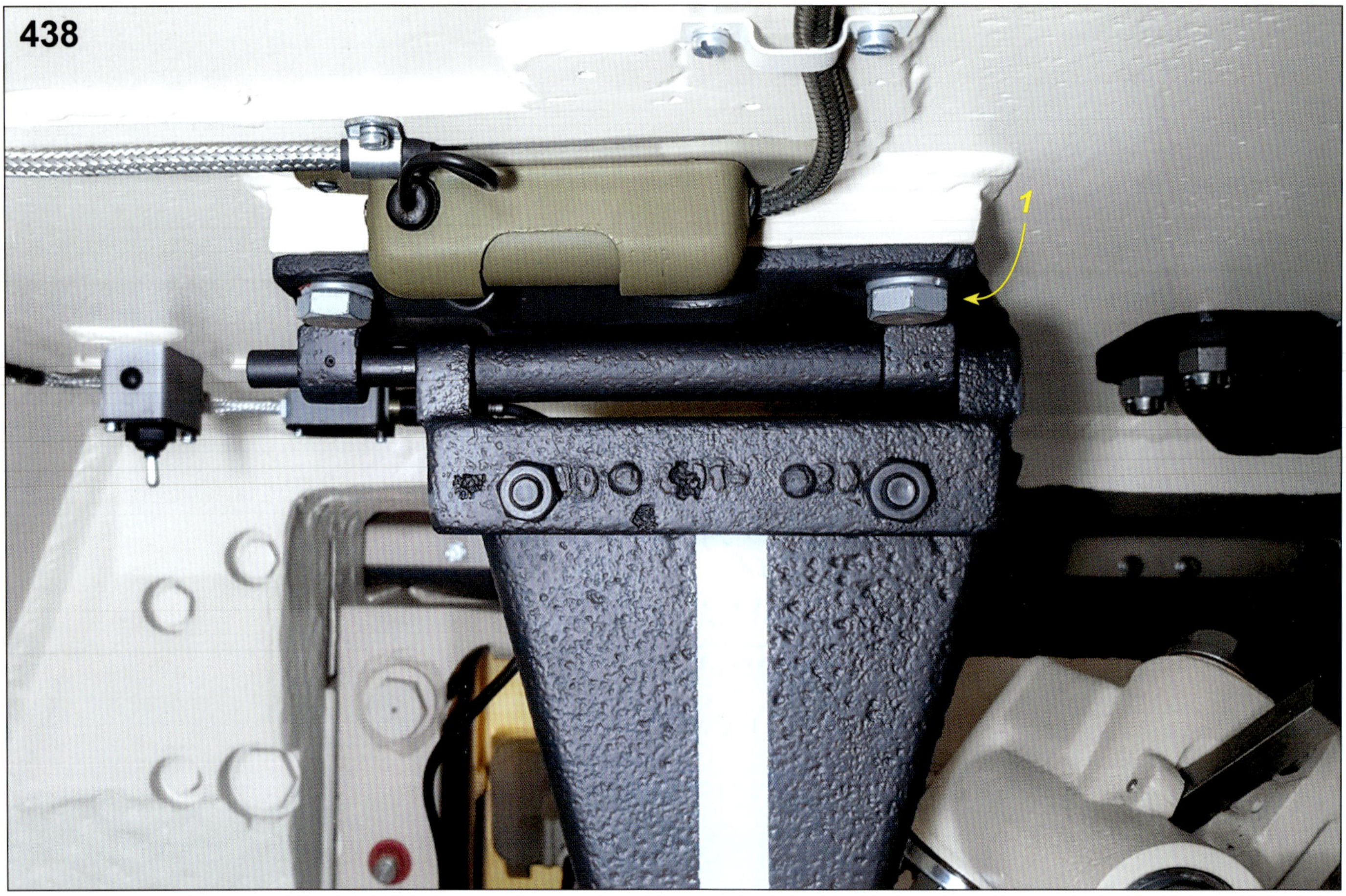

438-439: The **T.Z.F.12a** was mounted to a frame, **Turmzielfernrohrlagerung**, that was installed in the main gun carriage. This frame has not yet been fitted and so the gun sight is currently being supported in position using a wooden block, see **2**, page **165**, photo **441**. The rear section of the gun sight is connected to a swing bracket, **Dreieckträger**, that is bolted to the turret roof, at ***1***, photo **438**. This allows the sight to elevate and decline and thus stay in alignment with the main gun. Note the large rubber protective guard, at ***1***, photo **439**, used to provide a degree of protection for the Gunners head.

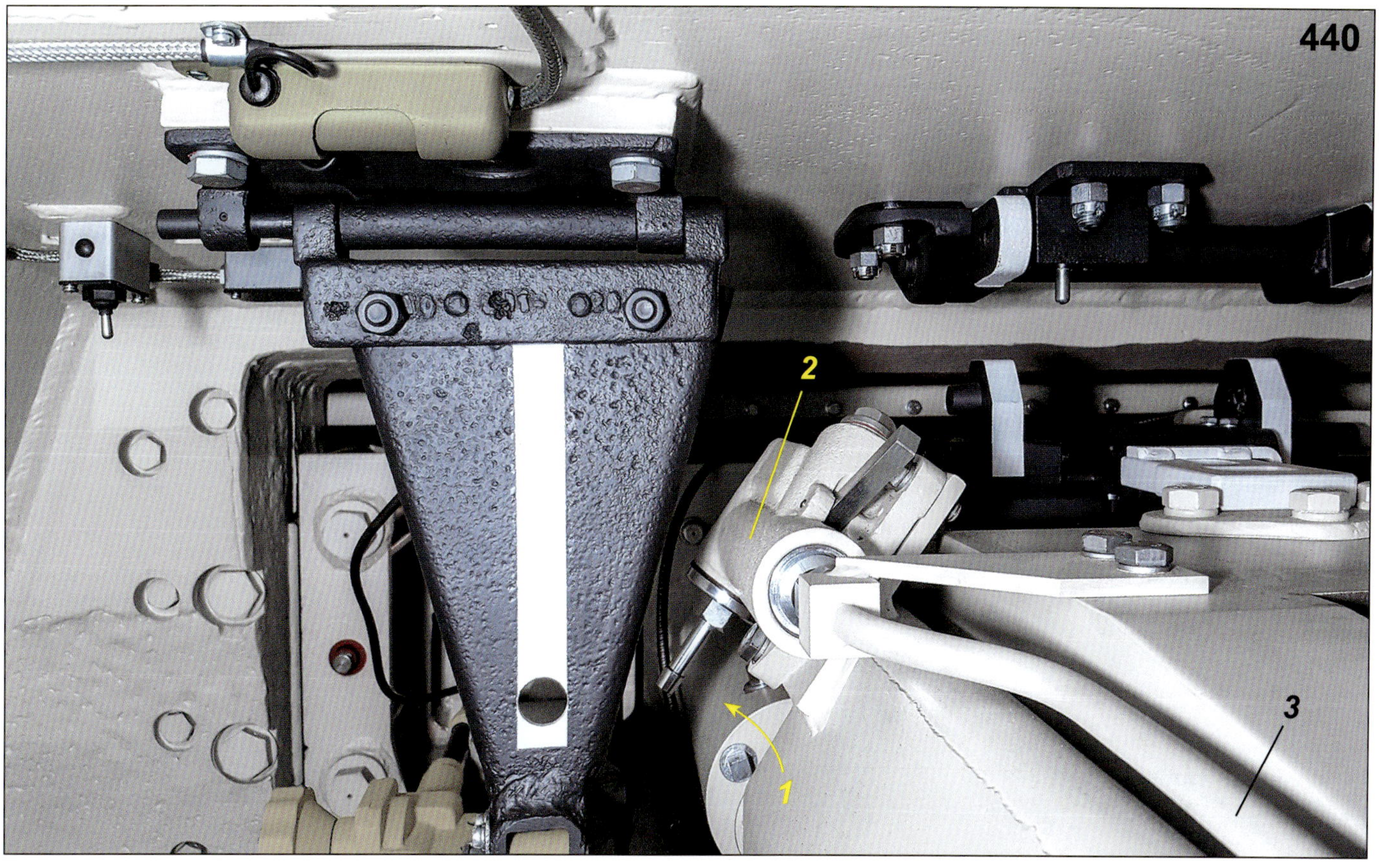

440: In this photo we can see the rear section of the recuperator cylinder, at ***1***, which was designed to return the main gun back to the firing position. This was a hydro-pneumatic unit that used **~2.3** litres of **Braunark** hydraulic fluid with the pneumatic chamber being compressed to **~55** atmospheres. At ***2*** we have the evacuator valve that is part of the bore evacuation mechanism. The pipe, at ***3***, is routed to the rear of the breech block and was used to carry compressed air to the breech ring, at ***1***, page **169**, photo **446**.

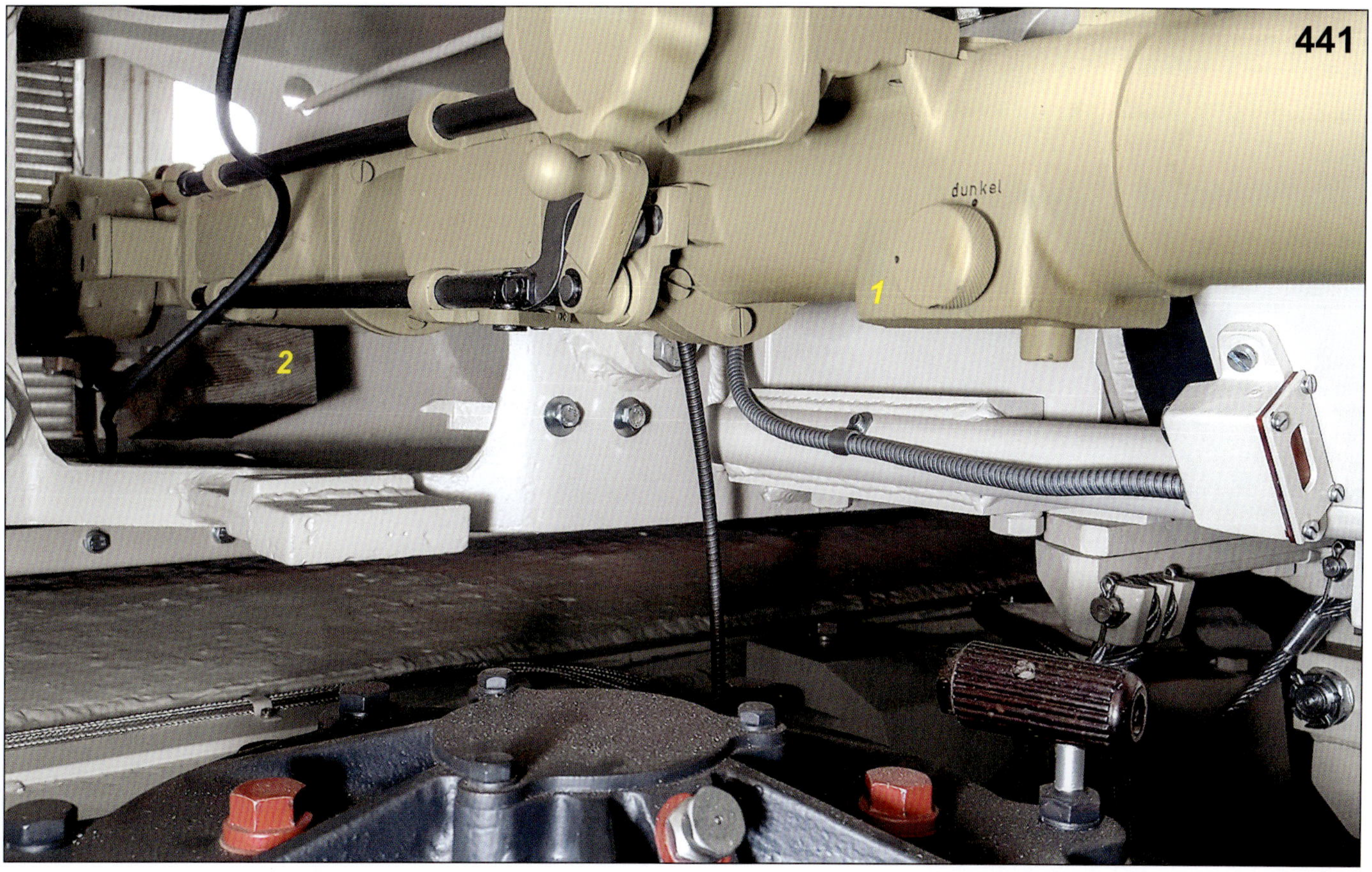

441: The **T.Z.F.12a** had a focal length of **1140mm** with the optical elements comprising of 20 lenses and 3 prisms [23]. Two degrees of magnification were available, with these being **2.5x** and **5x**. At the **2.5x** the field of view of the Gunner was **28°** that translated to **498m** at **1000m**. This magnification was commonly used for target acquisition and battle field monitoring. The **5x** magnification gave a view of **14°** translating to **249m** at **1000m**. This magnification was primarily used for precision gun laying.

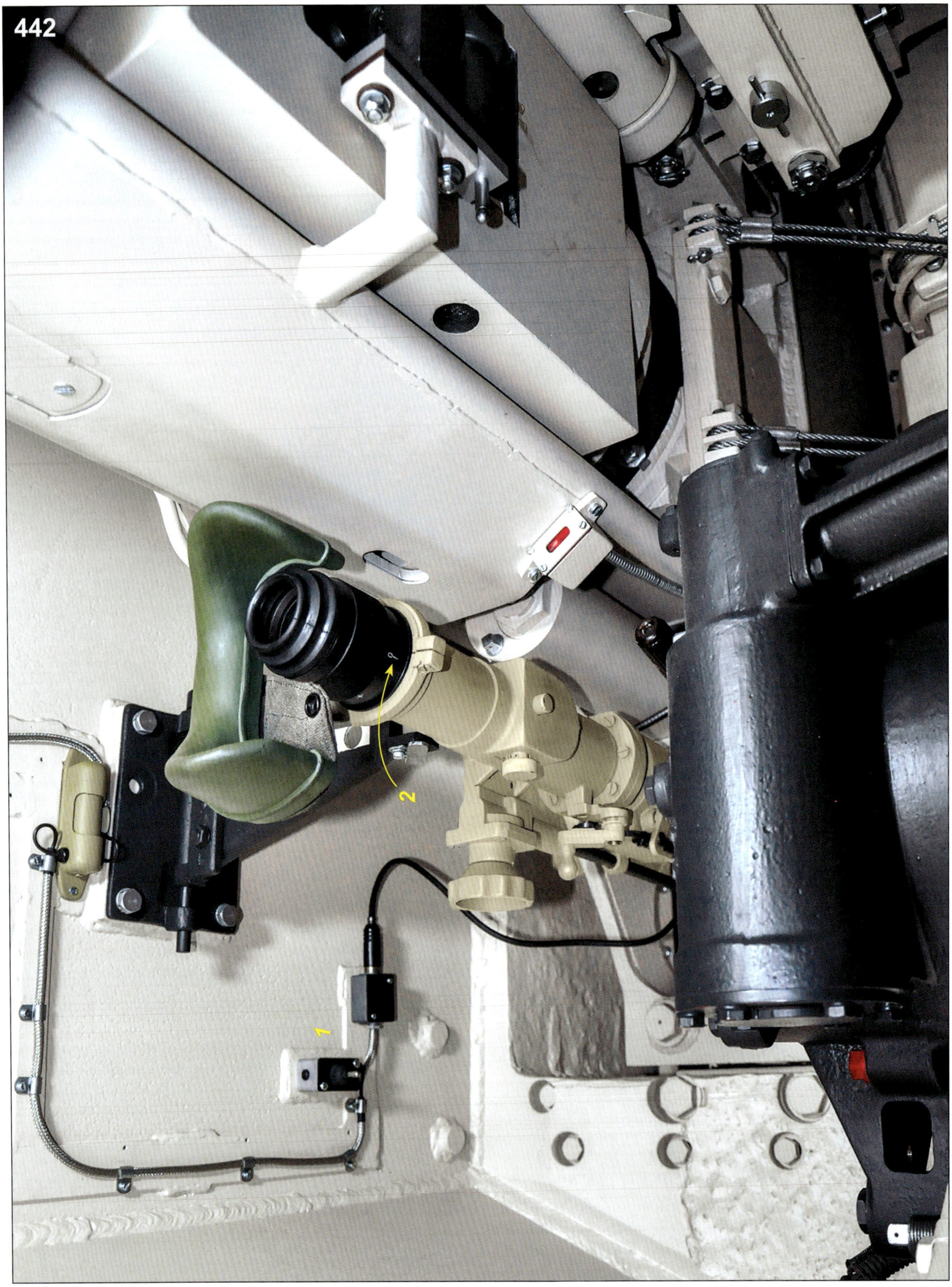

442: A general view looking up at the **T.Z.F.12a** gun sight. The electrical circuit, at ***1***, feeds to the front of the sight and was used to illuminate the internal reticule. The light intensity could be varied using the control knob at ***1***, page **165**, photo **441**. The monocular eyepiece could be adjusted to compensate for the Gunners eyesight, see the diopter graduations at ***2***. The **T.Z.F.12a** also employed optical filters to compensate for glare or contrast resolution.

443

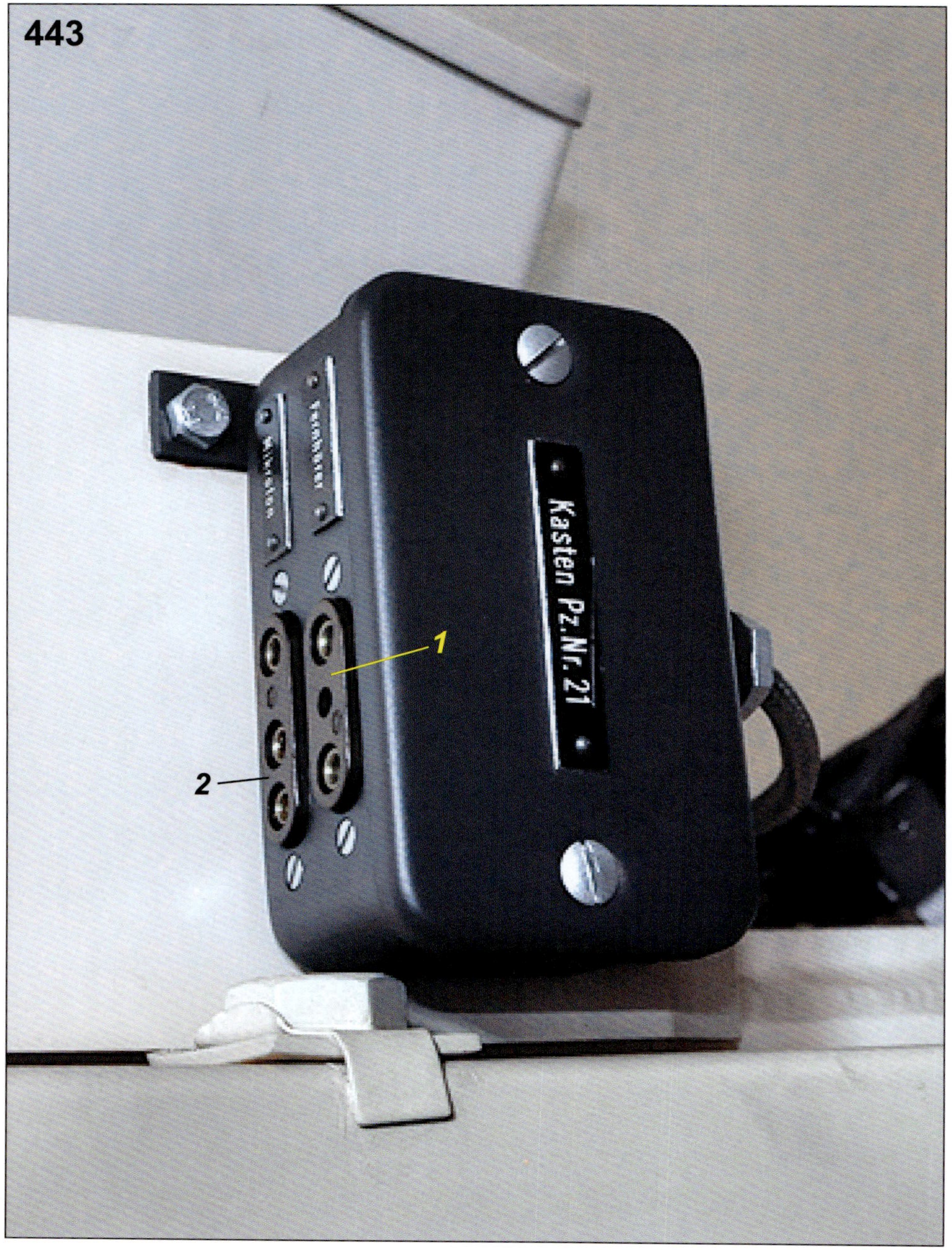

443: To the LHS of the Gunners station, bolted to the frame just above the turret ring, is the Gunners intercom box, **Kasten Pz. Nr. 21**. The Gunners headset would be plugged into the port, at ***1***, with his throat microphone being plugged into the port at ***2***.

444

444: Here we see the turret azimuth indicator has now had the both the dial and indicator pointer fitted. The two dials were designed to give a coarse or fine measurement of arc of the turret from the forward 12 o'clock position of the tank. The coarse inner disk graduations were used when platoon level firing, i.e. several vehicles at the same time, were ordered to lay down fire at a specific target. The fine outer disk was used for precision fire targeting.

445: Here we have a general view of the LHS of the main gun breech. The Panther mounted a **7.5cm Kampfwagenkanone 42 L/70** (**7.5cm KwK 42**) designed by **Rheinmetall**. The gun was semi-automatic and was electrically fired. The breech mechanism was of a falling wedge type block with the spent round ejection system being fully automatic.

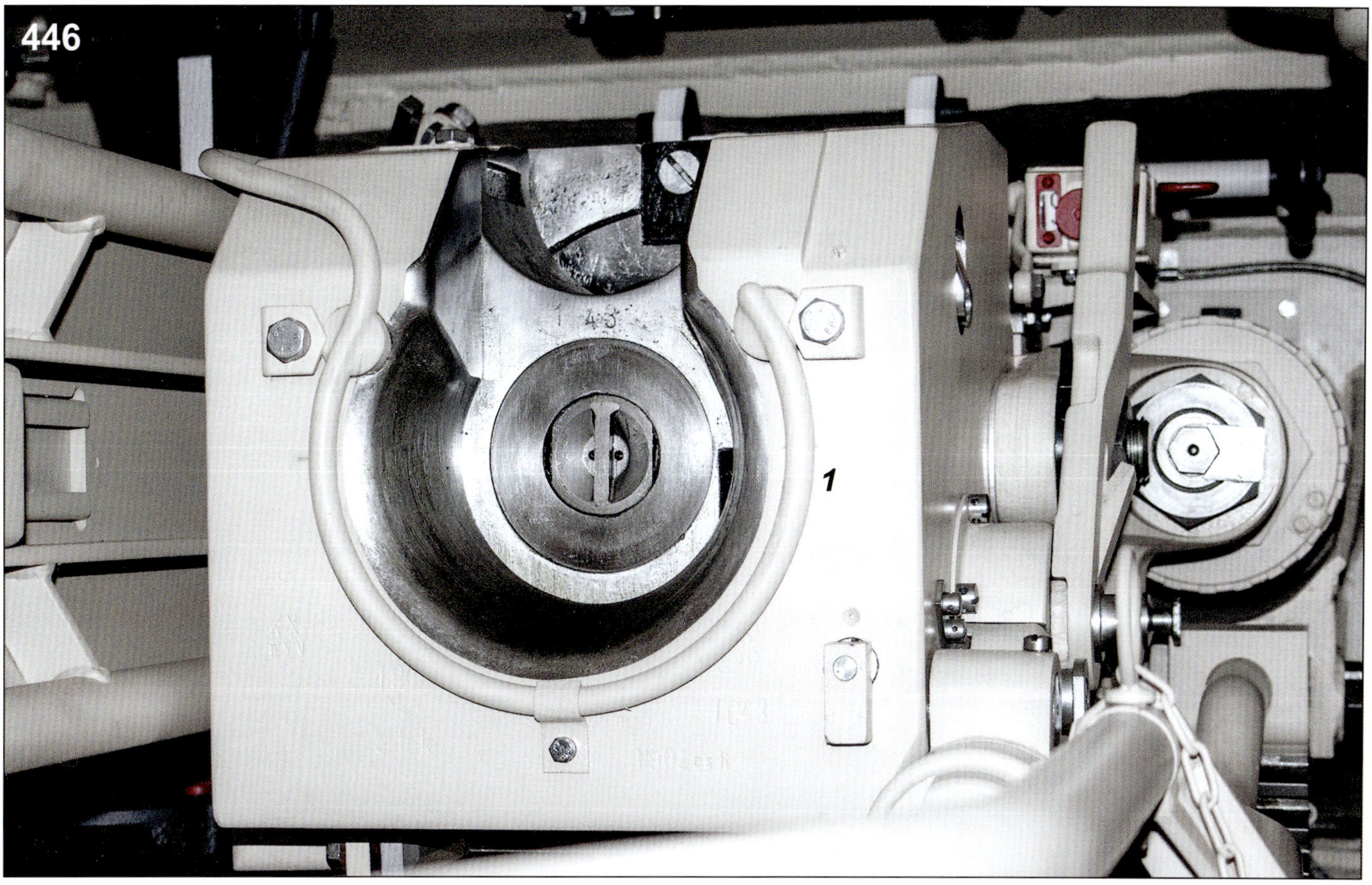

446-447: Two views of the rear of the breechblock. The pipe, at ***1***, photo **446**, fed compressed air from the bore evacuator valve, at ***2***, page **165**, photo **440**, into the rear of the breech at two points, ***2*** and ***3***, photo **447**. On activation of the ejection mechanism, after the ejection of a spent round, the bore evacuator valve would open and two blasts of air from ***2*** and ***3*** would enter the bore. The internal nozzles at ***2*** and ***3*** were set at an angle so the compressed air stream mixed along the bore axis. This process lasted for **~1** second with the injected air stream being at **~10** atmospheres. Note in photo **447** the year of manufacture of this gun, **1943**, at ***4***.

448-449: The **7.5cm KwK 42** fired three main types of ammunition: **i)** **7.5cm GrPatr. 42** (**High Explosive**), **ii)** **7.5cm PzGrPatr. 39/42** (**High Explosive Armour Piercing with Tracer**), **iii)** **7.5cm PzGrPatr. 40/42** (**Armour Piercing Composite, Rigid, tungsten cored with Tracer**) [23]. The latter type of ammunition was not commonly used as tungsten was a material that was often in short supply. The typical life of the **7.5cm KwK 42** was **~3000** rounds. When **7.5cm PzGrPatr. 40/42** ammunition was extensively used the bore life dropped to **~700** rounds.

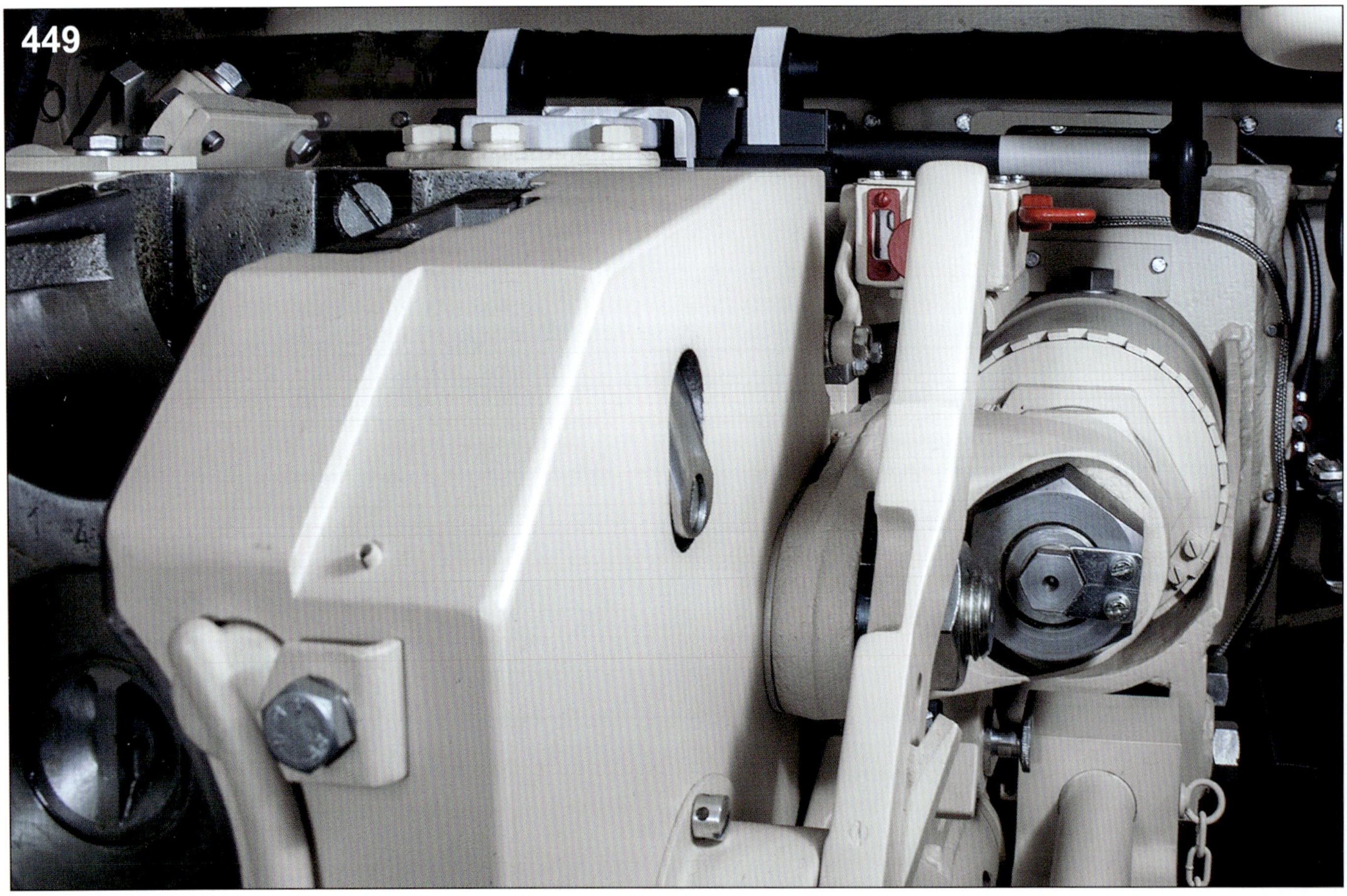

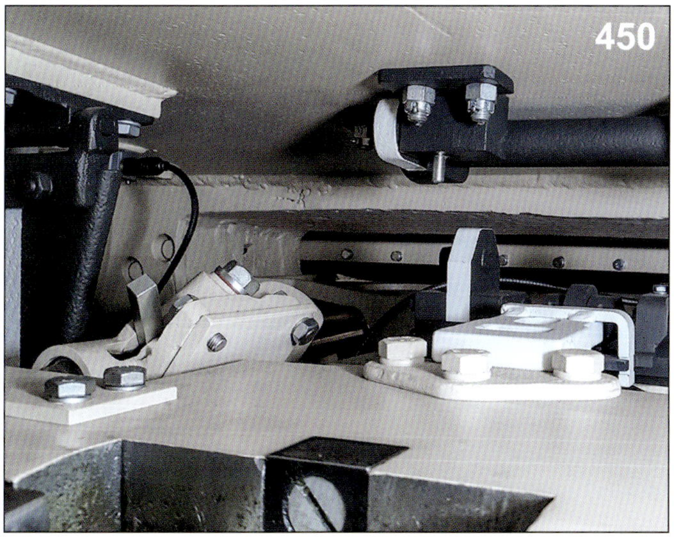

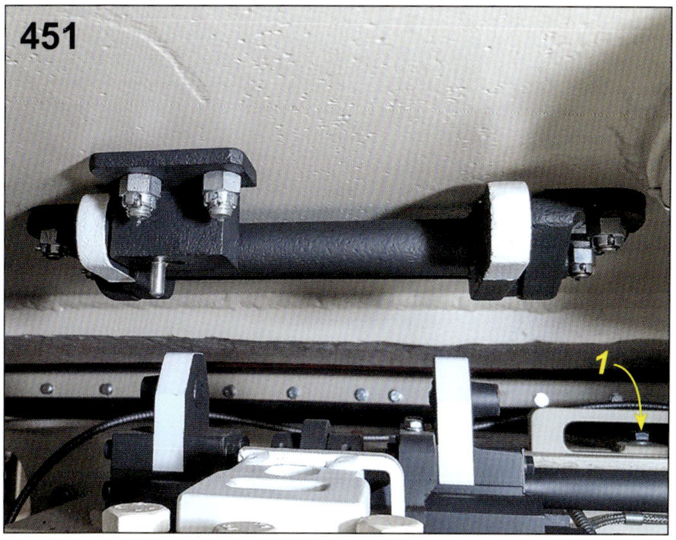

450-451: The images on this page all relate to the breech locking mechanism, also known as the travel lock, **Geschützzurrung**. This was used to prevent movement of the main gun and breech when the tank was undergoing non-combative movement. An H-shaped restraint block, see ***2***, page **177**, photo **462**, would be secured to the mount on the turret roof, photo **451**, and the mount on top of the breech block, photo **454**.

452-453: To lock the breech in place first the swing arm on the roof was released and allowed to hang vertically downwards. This was done by moving the lever, at ***1***, photo **452**, to the right thus allowing the swing arm to hang free. The restraint block, at ***2***, page **177**, photo **462**, was then connected to the swing arm by locating the ends of the bar, at ***3*** and ***4***, page **177**, photo **462** into the holes at the end of the swing arm, at ***1***, photo **453**. The shaft, at ***5***, page **177**, photo **462**, was then screwed out so the bar locked into the holes.

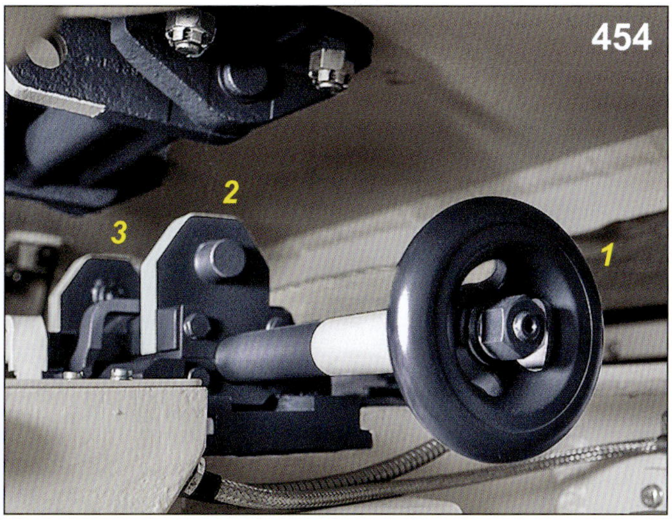

454-454: The restraint block would now be hanging down from the swing arm. The Loader would then turn the wheel, at ***1***, photo **454**, anti-clockwise. This moved two vertical bars with lugs, at ***2*** and ***3***, photo **454**, that were on a screw shaft towards each other. The arms of the restraint block would then be positioned over the lugs on the vertical bars and the wheel turned clockwise. This would separate the two vertical bars and their lugs would mate with the holes on the arms of the restraint block locking everything together.

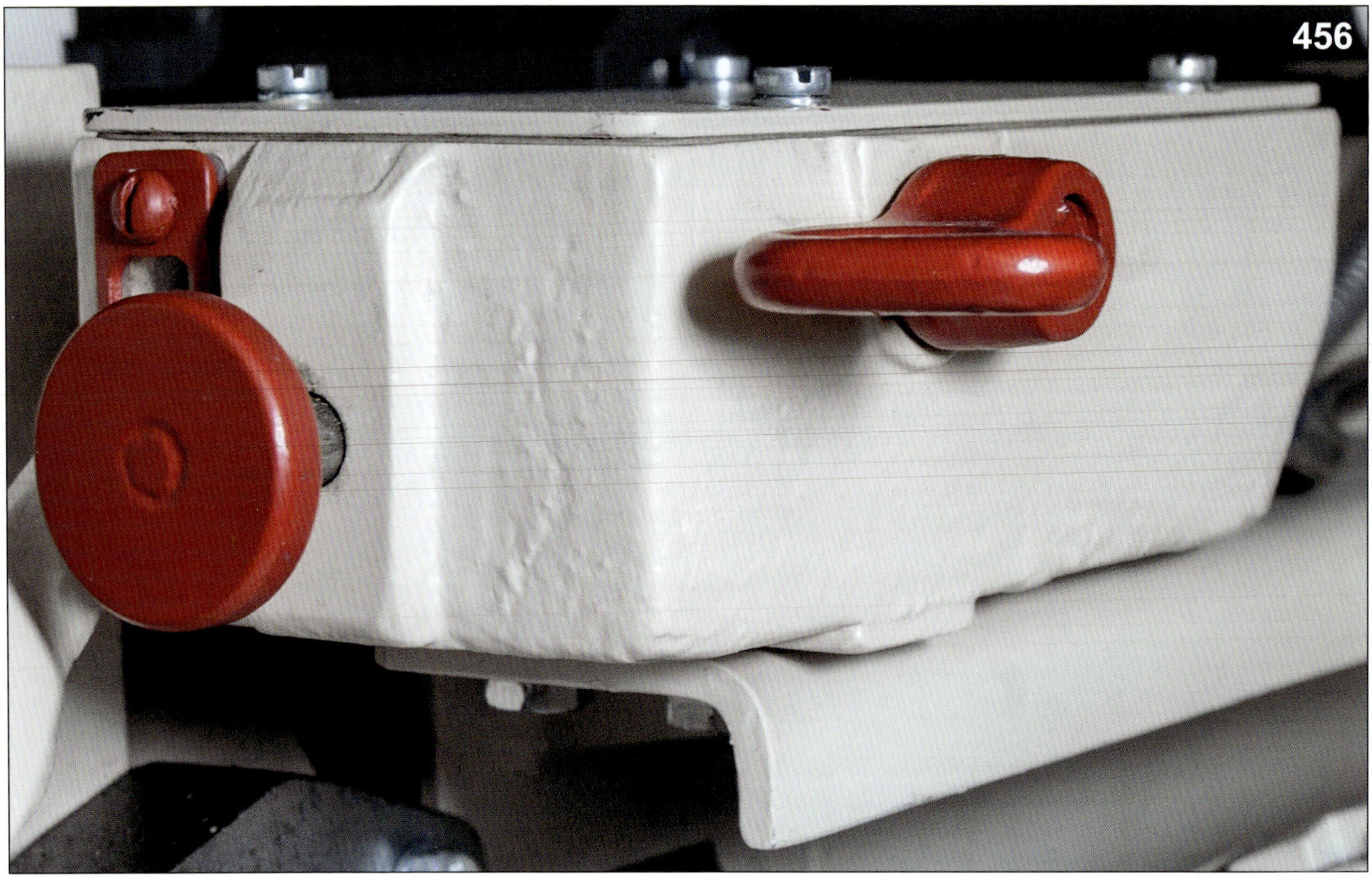

456-457: The main gun safety switch is seen in photo **456**. In the inset photo at **457** we can see the gun is currently set to **Sicher** = **Safe**. In the page from the **Pantherfiebel** we can see how the firing circuit of the **7.5cm KwK 42** was configured. After a shell had been inserted into the breech the Loader would switch the gun to live and the indicator light, at (B), would illuminate. The Gunner could then fire the main gun using the trigger on the elevation handwheel.

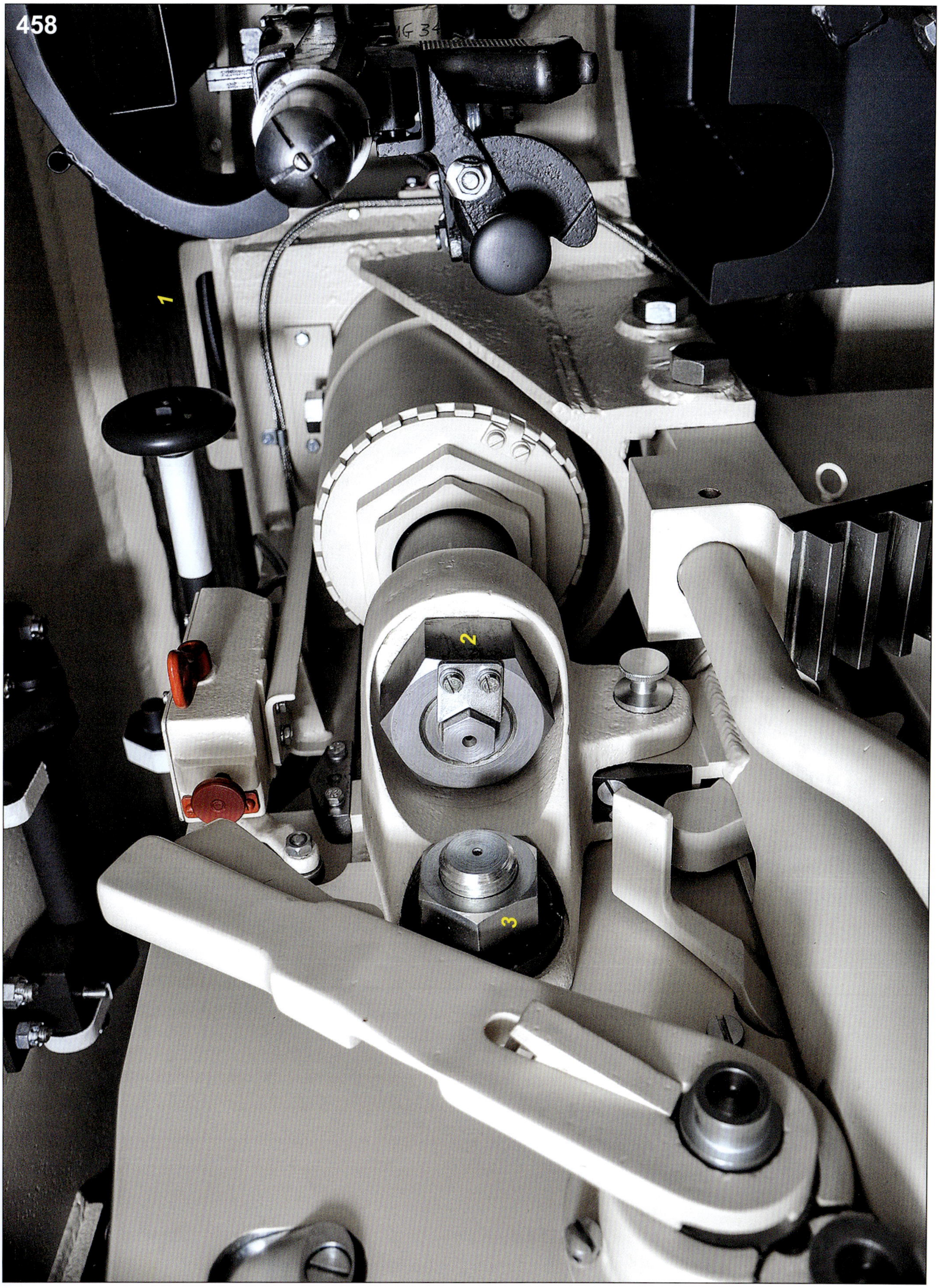

458: Our main point of interest in this image is the large recoil cylinder that is mounted the RHS of the main gun. This is secured using the large nut at the end of the recoil cylinder piston, at **2**, and to the breech block at ***3***. The recoil cylinder was designed to hydraulically brake the rearward motion of the main gun after firing. The cylinder was filled with **~9** litres of **Braunark** hydraulic fluid.

459

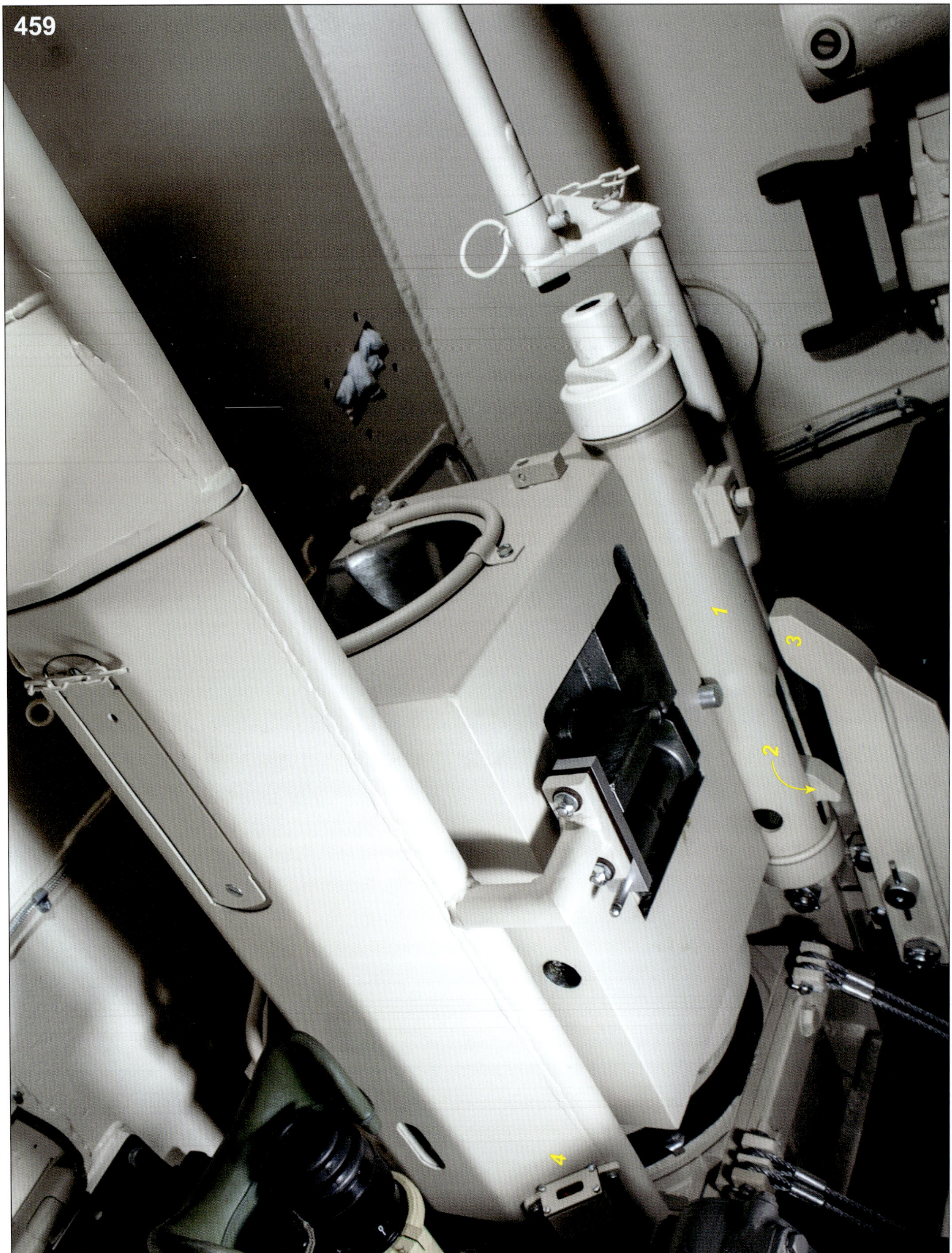

459: Looking up at the underside of the breech block of the **7.5cm KwK 42**. At ***1*** we can see part of the automatic ejector system. As the gun recoils on firing the lug, at ***2***, hits the arm at ***3*** and drops the breech block. The ejector mechanism in the breech then ejects the spent round. As the gun returns to the ready position the breech stays open allowing the loader to immediately insert a new round. The insertion of that new round will close the breech block. At that point the Loader can again set the safety switch, page **172**, photo **456**, to live so the Gunner can once again fire the main gun.

460: A closer view of the underside of the breech block. When the main gun had been loaded and the safety switch, page **172**, photo **456**, had been set to live the indicator light for ready to fire status would illuminate. This light is seen at ***4***, page **174**, photo **459**. The contact point for the electrical firing circuit is seen at ***1***. Note the oil drips at ***2*** from the lubrication of the breech mechanism.

461: Here we are looking at the underside of the **7.5cm KwK 42** as fitted into the main gun carriage. We can see the cables that are connected to the base of that carriage that form part of the equilibrator mechanism. These cables are under tension and significantly help to reduce oscillation of the main gun when being either elevated or depressed. The main body of the equilibrator can be seen at ***1***. The Gunners elevation handwheel, not yet fitted to the tank, on each full traverse of that handwheel gave **0.5°** of vertical elevation or declination of the main gun.

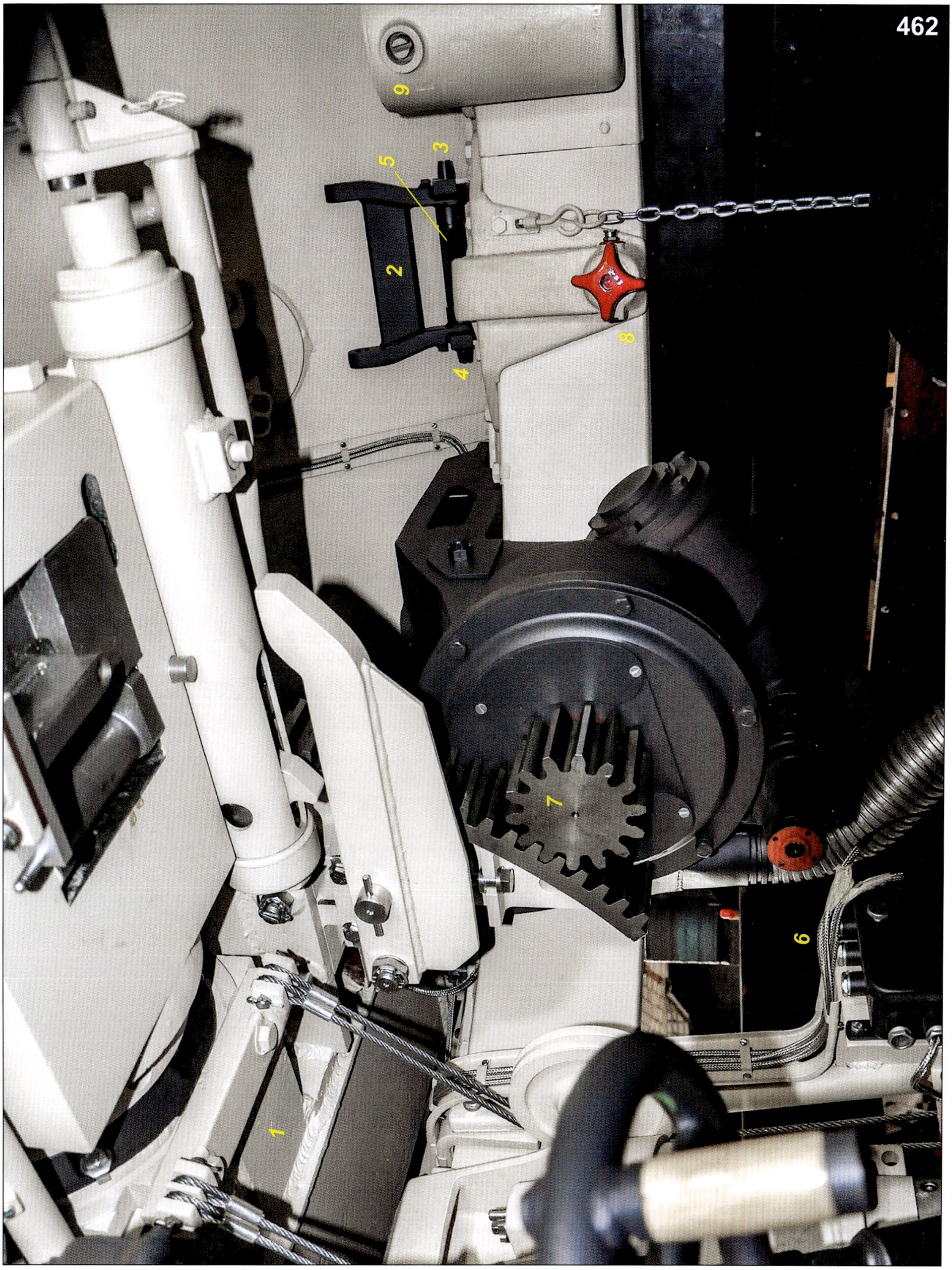

462: This photo, looking at the RHS of the turret via the underside of the main gun breech, shows a number of interesting elements. At ***6*** we can see a number of electrical cables that have been routed in place but are yet not connected to the appropriate connections in the **Kasten Pz. Nr. 5**. At ***7*** we have a clear side view of the meshing of the turret elevation quadrant. At ***8*** we can see the turret traverse lock, **Turmzurrung**, used to lock the turret in place and at ***9*** the configuration of the socket used for the Loaders hand crank for the manual turret traverse mechanism.

463-464: Here we have the spent case basket for the main gun, **Hülsenauffangkasten.** The upper rear edge is bolted to the inside of the turret ring, at ***1***, photo **463**. Spent cases would be ejected from the breech of the gun and would fall into this basket. The cases would then pass through the hinged flaps that are held closed under spring tension, at **2**, photo **464** and into the lower section of the box. The lower box was primarily designed to contain some of the burnt powder gases from the spent cases. A flexible metal hose was connected to the front of the lower box to exhaust these gases out through the turret roof fan.

465: Looking down directly into the spent case basket. The spent rounds would be removed from this box using a large hatch on the RHS, see **2**, photo **463**. At the top of this photo, at ***1***, we see the folding footrest for the Commander, **Klappbare Fußstütze**. This footrest would be lowered to the horizontal position allowing the Commander to stand upon it in order to be able to direct the tank while standing up in the opened cupola.

466

466: A study of the RHS of the breech block of the main gun. Of prime interest is the recoil cylinder in the centre of the photo. The **7.5cm KwK 42** had a normal recoil length of travel of **400mm**. In combat situations, if the main gun was being repeatedly fired, the **Braunark** oil in the cylinder would heat up thus decreasing the oil viscosity. This had the effect of reducing the efficiency of the recoil cylinder being able to brake the recoil and so the length of travel during recoil increased. When the observed length of recoil reached **430mm** all firing of the main gun had to cease to prevent damage to the gun components [23].

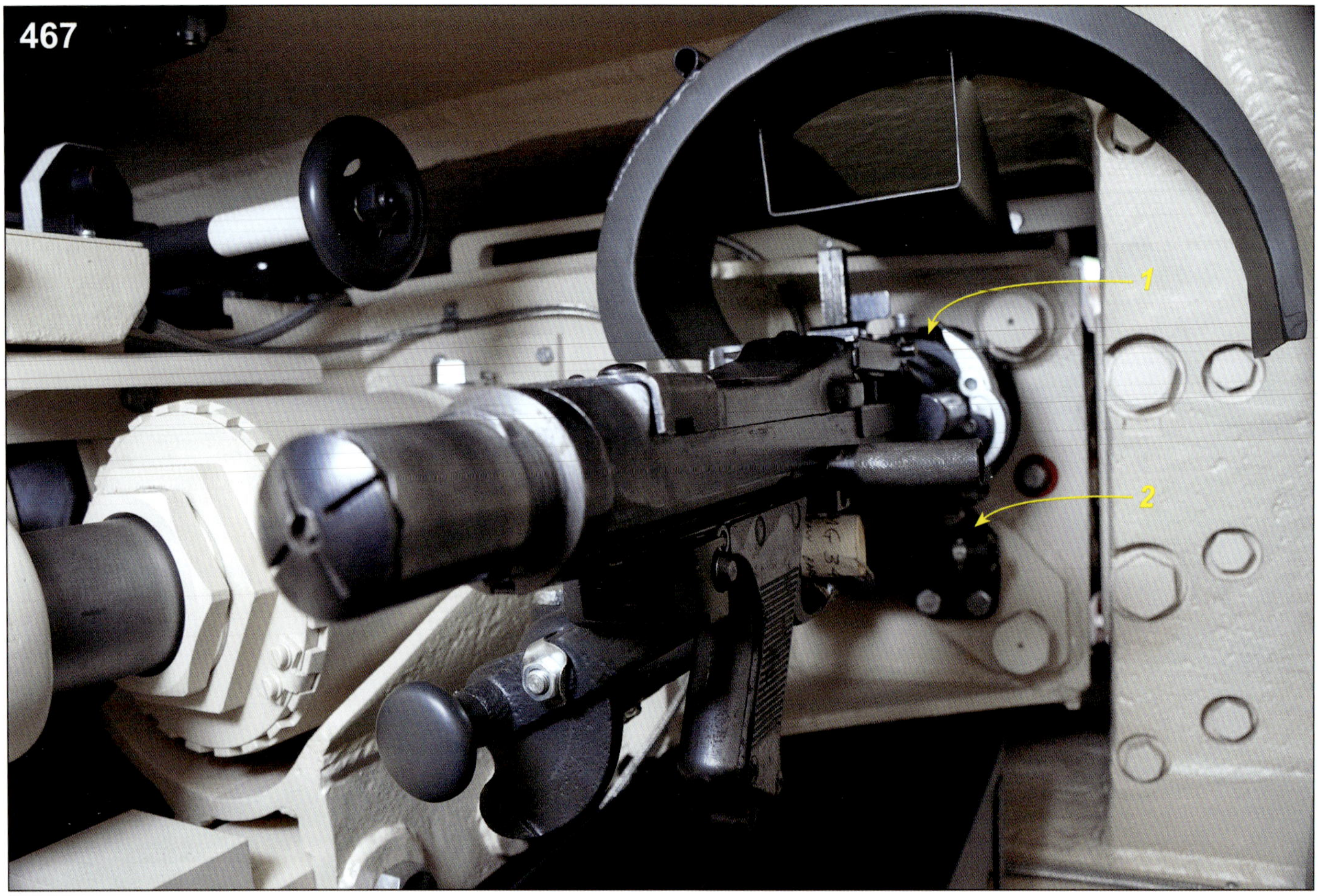

467-468: The coaxial mounted **M.G.34** was in a frame, **MG-Lagerung**, at ***1***, photo **467**, that was bolted to the rear side of the main gun carriage at **2**, photo **467**. This mount could be altered, in terms of degree of weapon presentation (i.e. aligned with the main gun) but it states quite clearly in **D655/1b** that this should only be carried out by a qualified armourer [20].

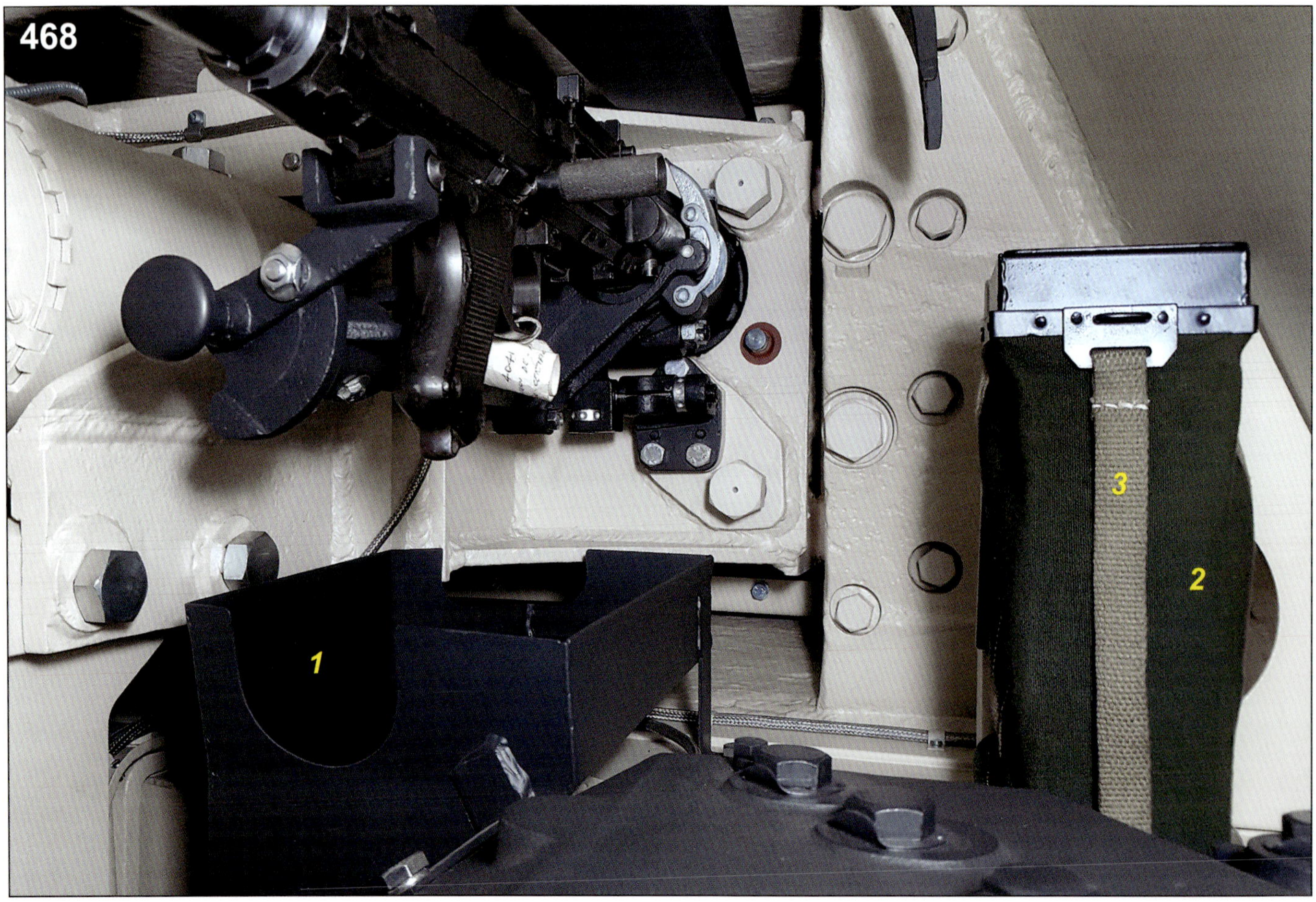

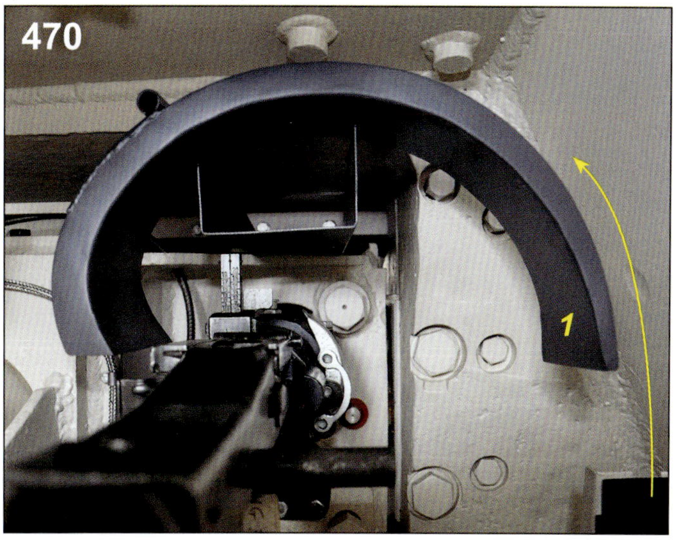

469-470: The **M.G.34** was fed from an ammunition bag, **Gurtsack**, at ***2***, page **180**, photo **468**. Three 50 round cartridge belts were connected together and fed into the **M.G.34** feed plate from the ammunition bag via the slip chute, at ***1***, photo **470**, over the top of the machine gun. The ammunition bags were made from canvas and often had a sown leather base. A canvas strap, at ***3***, page **180**, photo **468**, acted as a carrying handle for each bag.

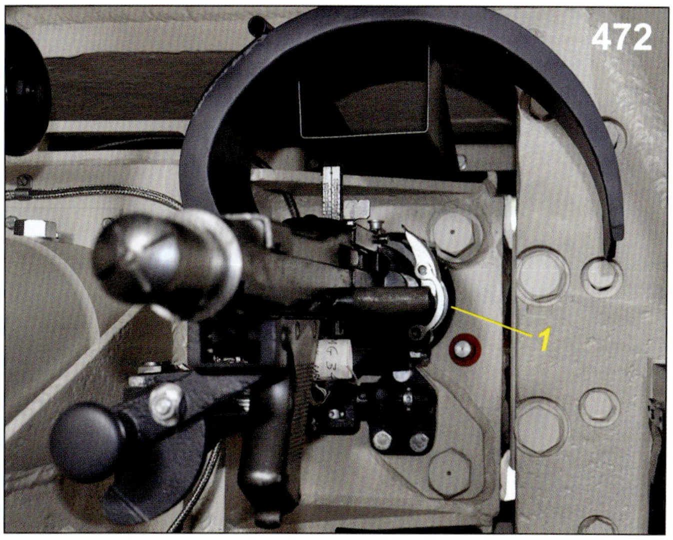

471-472: The front end of the **MG-Lagerung** frame was located in the main gun carriage body and incorporated a sleeve that held an internal compression spring. The compression spring was designed to absorb a proportion of the recoil forces of the machine gun when fired. To emplace the **M.G.34** the machine gun was slid into the frame, barrel first, and was then pulled back until the rear of the gun locked against two forks, at ***1***, photo **471**. The **M.G.34** was then locked into position using the tension clasp at ***1***, photo **472**.

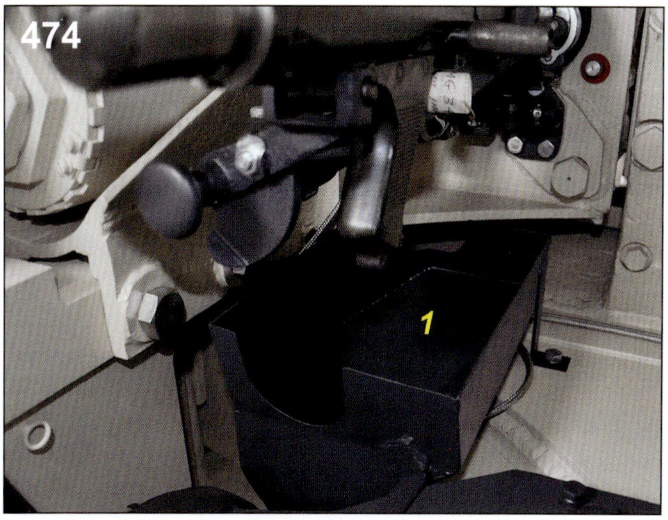

473-474: Here we have a closer view of the tension clasp used to retain the **M.G.34** in the **MG-Lagerung**. The coaxial machine gun was operated by the Gunner using the foot pedal on the turret floor. This foot pedal, page **89**, photo **311**, was connected to the trigger mechanism of the machine gun via a Bowden cable, see ***2***, page **190**, photo **495**. Spent rounds ejected from the **M.G.34** fell down into the hopper, at ***1***, photo **474,** and then down into the spent round drum, at ***2***, page **183**, photo **484**.

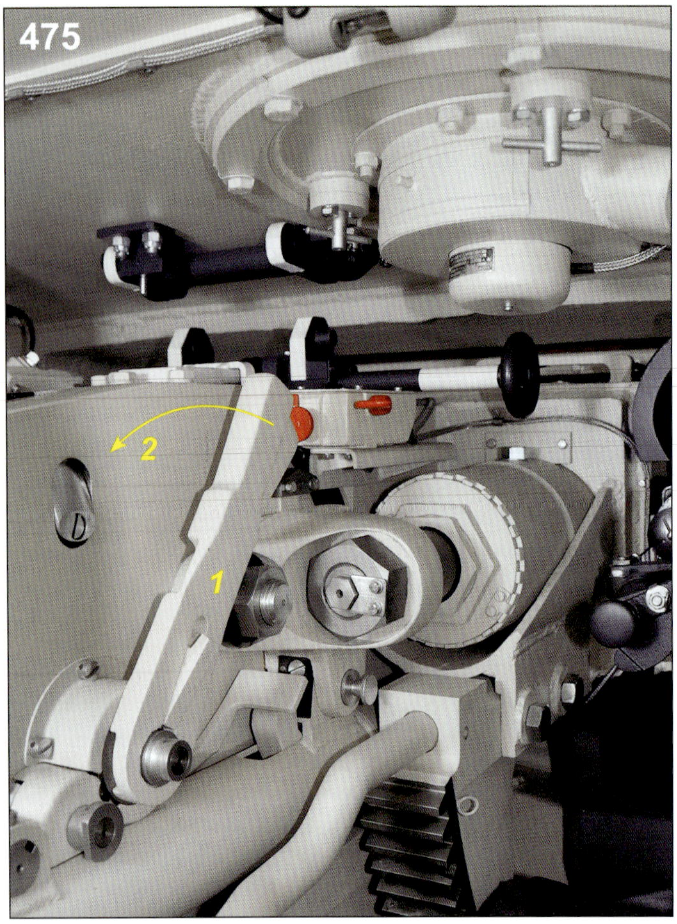

475-476: At ***1***, photo **475**, we see the large handle used for the opening of the breech block. This would be operated by the Loader, when the gun was in the safe position, by pulling the handle back, at ***2***, thus dropping the block down into the open position.

477-478: With the main gun now mounted in the turret the elevation quadrant is now mated to the pinion of the elevation mechanism. The elevation mechanism was operated by the Gunner. The Gunners elevation handwheel, not yet fitted to the tank, was attached to the elevation mechanism via a cardan shaft connected at ***1***, page **188**, photo **491**.

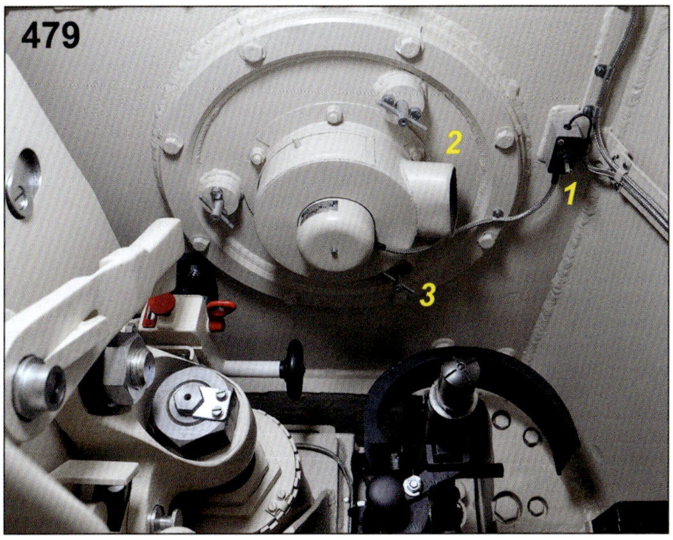

479: The roof mounted exhaust fan, **Lüfter**, was located forward of the Loaders station. The switch for this fan is at ***1***. A flexible metal hose, **Absaugleitung**, ran from the port at ***2***, down the side of the turret to the turret basket floor and into a port in the front of the RHS of the spent shell basket case. This was to help draw gunpowder fumes out the turret from expended rounds.

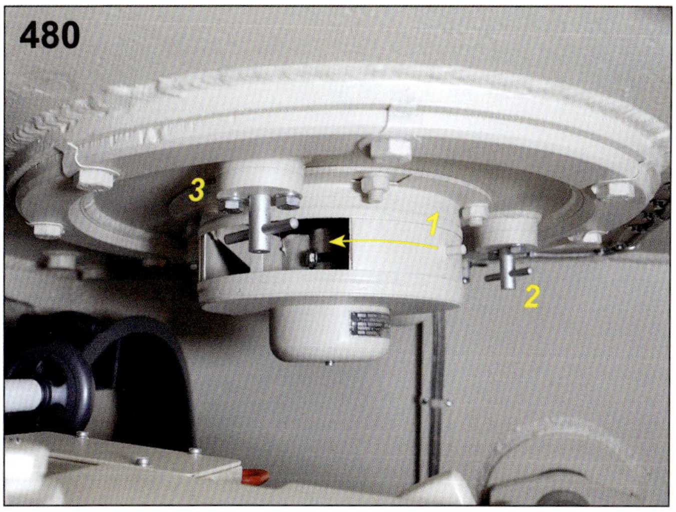

480: The sliding grate when closed, at ***1***, increased the air flow extraction from the spent shell basket case. To make the fan unit airtight the three spigots at ***2***, ***3*** and also ***3*** in photo **479**, would be screwed in with several turns each equally at a time to close the fan vent aperture. Inside the vent aperture is an umbrella shape, with a rubber seal around the edge, that sealed off the hole in the turret roof plate under the external armoured cover.

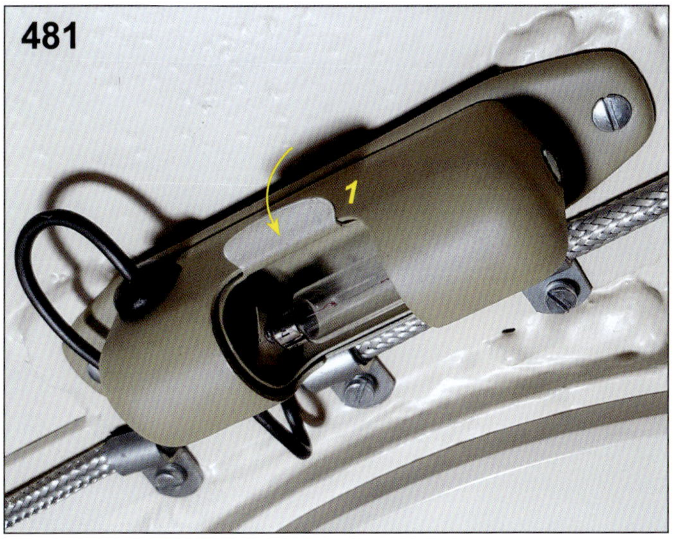

481: A nice study of one of the many crew light units as fitted at various places in the tank. This one is for the Loader and is located to the rear of the roof fan extractor. The amount of light visible could be regulated by movement of the sliding cover, ***1***.

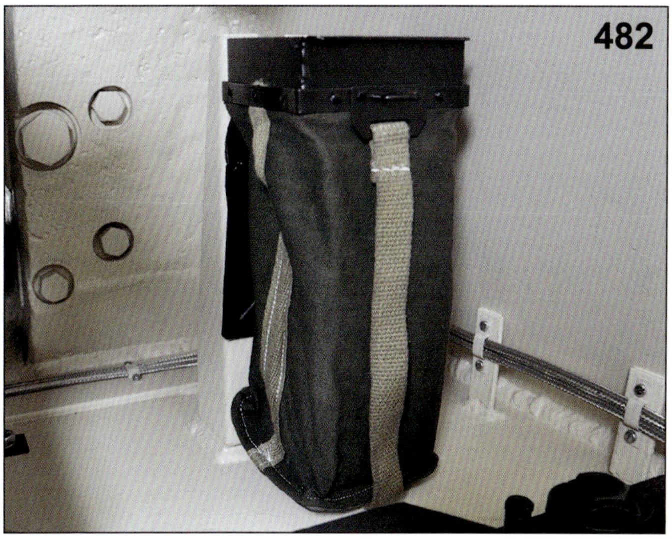

482: The **Gurtsack**, that was located in the front LHS corner of the turret, fed belt ammunition to the coaxially mounted **M.G.34**.

483: The Loaders seat, **Ladeschützensitz**, without the cushion to show the base plate. This seat was not adjustable but could be quickly detached by removing the pin at ***1*** and lifting out the whole seat and support arm. See also ***1***, page **190**, photo **495**.

484: Spent cases from ammunition rounds fired from the **M.G.34** drop down into the sheet metal box, at ***1***, page **180**, photo **468**. These fall through the corrugated metal tubing, at ***1***, into the spent round drum, **Hülsenfänger für M.G.34**, as located on the turret basket floor in front of the Loaders station, at ***2***.

485

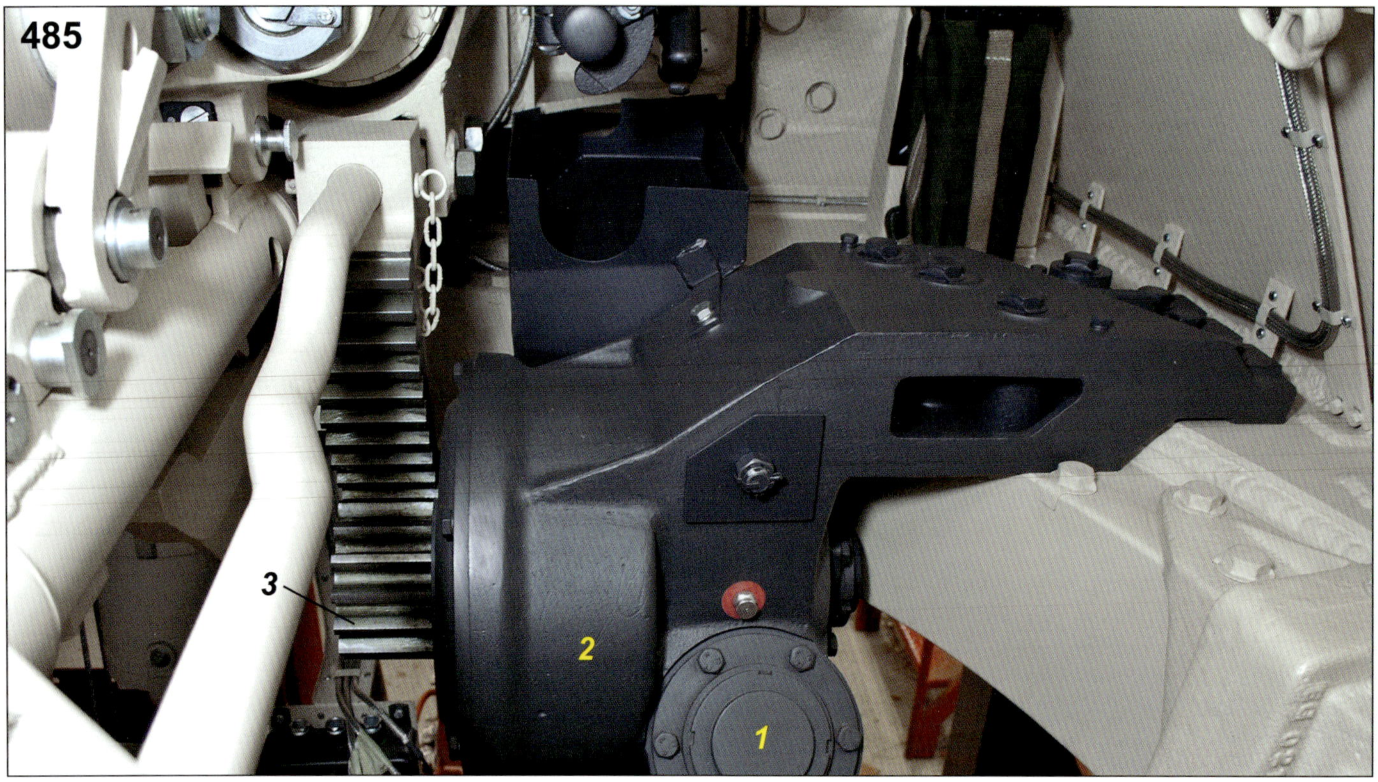

485: The cardan shaft from the Gunners elevation handwheel drives a spur gear connected to a worm gear in the housing at ***1***. This worm gear meshes with a helical gear, via a slip clutch, in the main body at ***2***, to the pinion gear at ***3***. The slip clutch is designed to prevent damage to the elevation mechanism from overwinding of the elevation handwheel by the Gunner. The main gun had an elevation range of **-8°** to **+18°** [23].

486

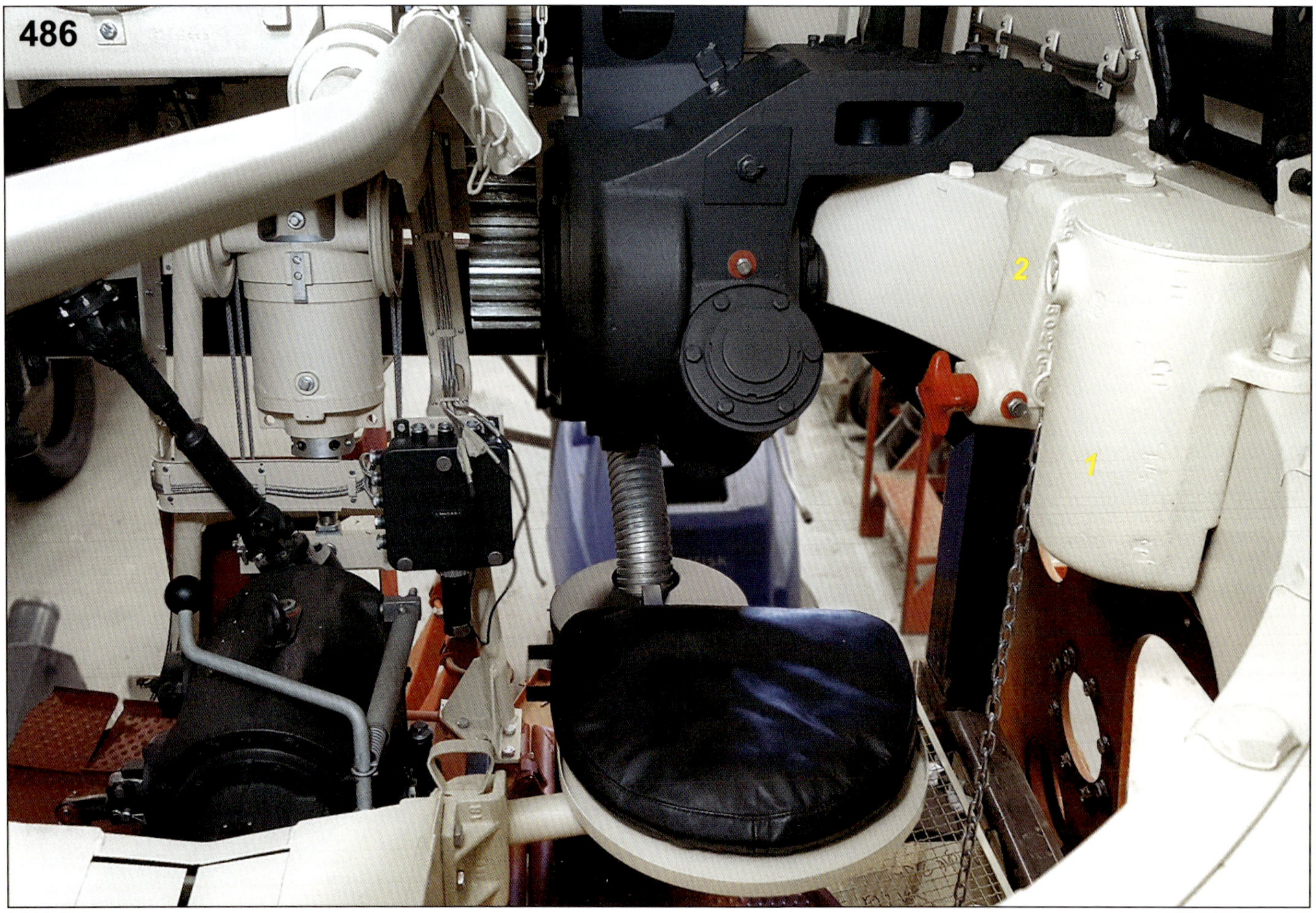

486: Looking down towards the turret basket floor from the Loaders position. Of interest is the manual turret traverse mechanism, **Hilfstrieb zum Turmschwenkwerk**, at ***1***. The loader would insert a hand crank into the socket at ***2***. The crank turned a horizontal shaft with a bevel gear that drove a vertical shaft. At the bottom of this shaft was a spur gear that meshed with the turret ring. This can be clearly seen in the technical illustration, page **204**.

487: Here we have a final view of the RHS upper section of the turret looking forward from the Gunners station. Barring some minor fixtures and fittings the turret is essentially now complete. Again we have to congratulate the team of engineers of the Wheatcroft Collection for the superb quality of their work produced up to this date.

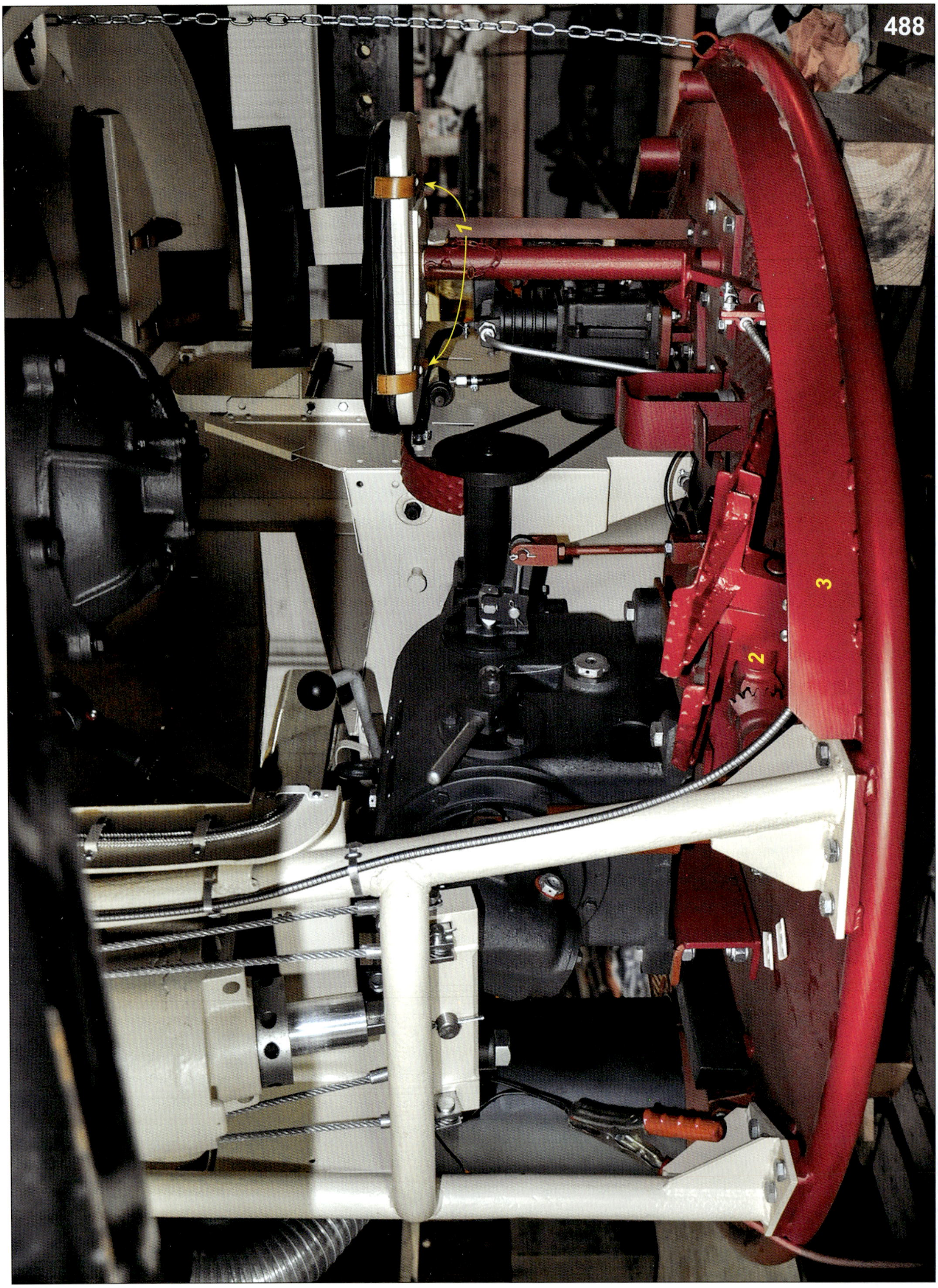

488: Here we have a study of the turret basket floor looking at the Gunners station. The bevel gearing, operated by the foot pedals for the power assisted turret traverse, is seen at ***2***. Note the protective frame at the front LHS quadrant of the turret basket tubular frame, at ***3***. There is no equivalent frame at the front RHS of the turret basket floor.

489-490: Connected to the front turret basket stanchions and at the base of the main gun carriage, at ***1***, page **177**, photo **462**, is the pneumatic equalibrator, **Luftausgleicher**, for the main gun. This equalibrator was designed to alleviate stress on the main gun when being elevated or depressed. Note the cables that also act to restrict free movement of the main gun in the vertical plane. Trojca states the equalibrator was filled with a mixture of air and coolant fluid and was compressed to **~75** atmospheres [23].

491-492: Here we have two views of the RHS of the turret basket floor. The two bevel gears that are driven by the Gunners elevation handwheel, connected at ***1***, photo **491**, are located in the angled housing at the bottom of the main gun elevation mechanism, at ***2***, photo **491**. At ***1***, photo **492**, we can see one of the hinges that allowed the RHS of the turret basket floor to be raised. Note how the spent round **M.G.34** drum sits in a retaining ring welded to the turret basket floor, at ***2***, photo **492**. Obviously when wishing to raise the forward RHS turret basket floor panel this spent round drum would first have to be removed.

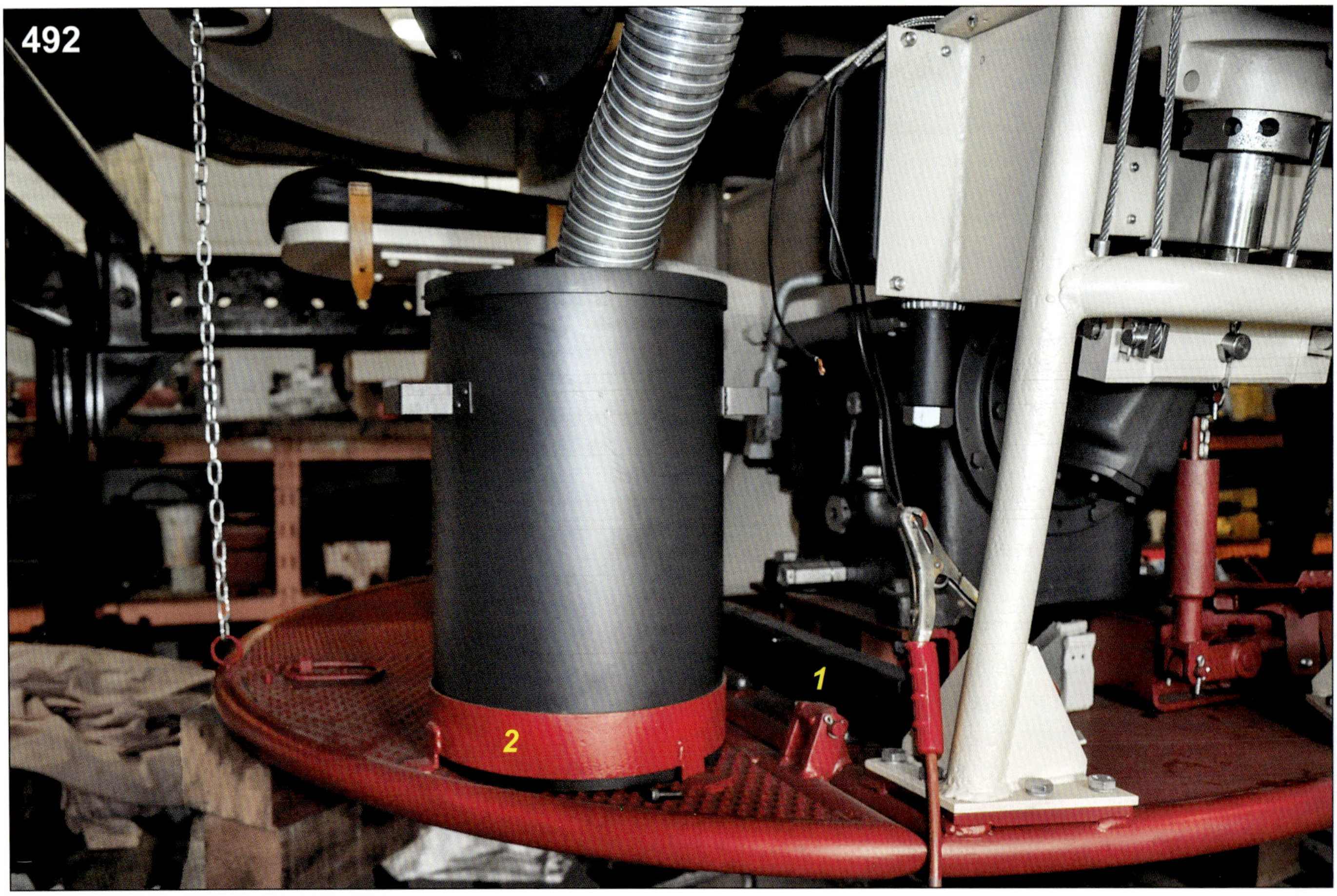

493: A view of the rear side of the main gun spent shell basket. This basket was riveted together from several panels and was bolted to both the turret basket floor and the turret ring. Of interest here is a good view of the Commanders foot step that is held in the folded up position by spring tension, at ***1***.

494: Here we have a clear view of how the pinion gear of the turret traverse mechanism meshes directly with the turret ring gear. The cardan shaft, at ***1***, is connected to the turret traverse take off mechanism for power assisted turret traversal. Note the guard strip, at ***2***, bolted to the underside of the turret ring to prevent any object from being caught in and thus possibly jamming the traverse gearing.

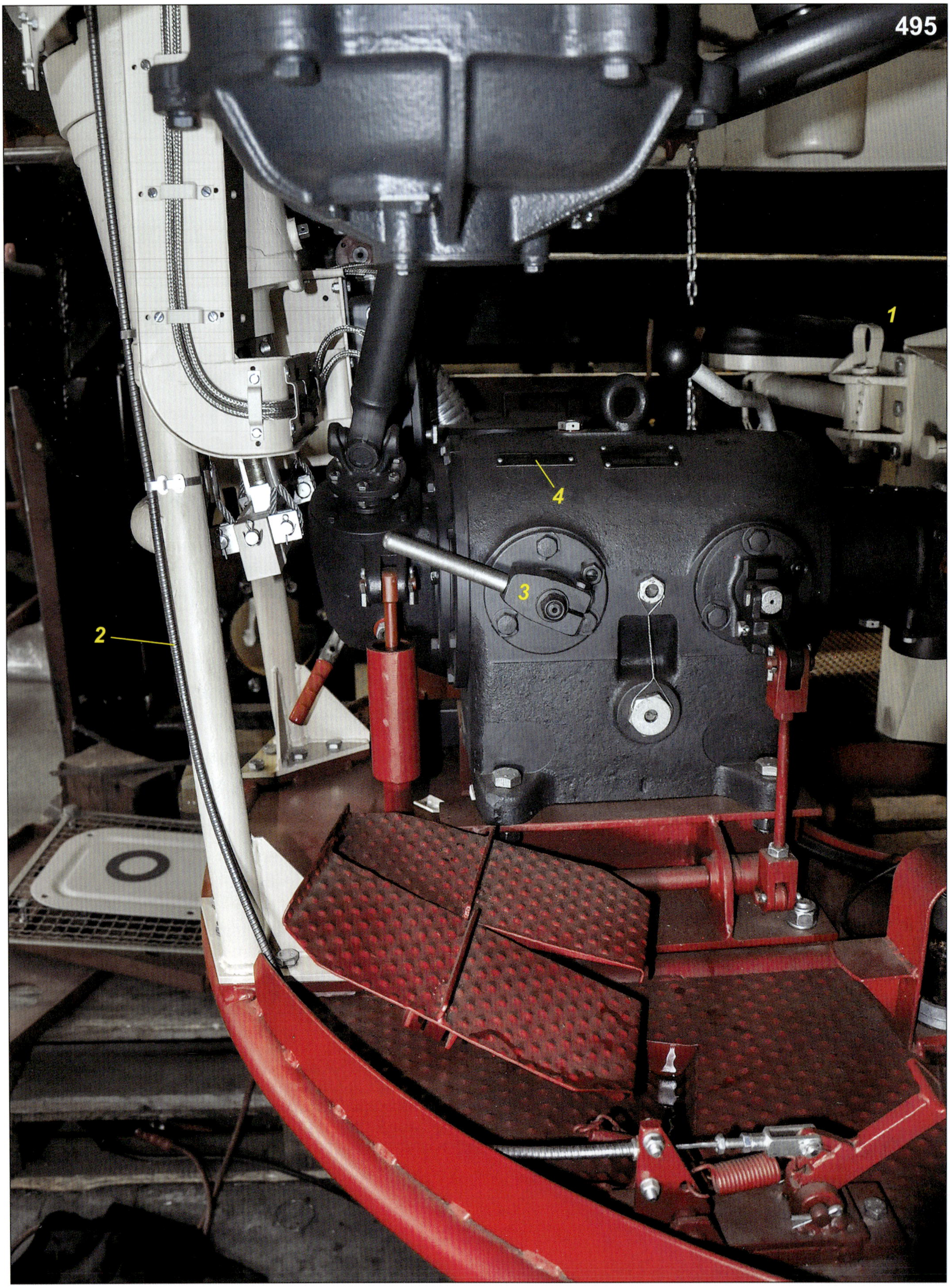

495: A view of the LHS power take off transfer box. The handle, seen at ***3***, was the speed adjustment lever. This was used to increase or decrease the speed of rotation of the turret up to the maximum allowed by the slip clutch in the transfer box. Pushing the lever forward decreased the rotational speed, pulling the lever back increased the speed. This is noted on the data plate at ***4***, **Langsamer <-> Schneller** (**Slow <-> Fast**).

496: The turret basket floor behind the gunners station. When the **M.G.34** was dismounted from the **MG-Lagerung** to be used in the anti-aircraft role, but was not mounted to the **Fliegerbeschuβgerät**, the gun would be stored in the turret. The Bakelite stock of the **M.G.34** would be located in the leather lined receptacle, at ***1***. The barrel of the machine gun would be fitted into a spring clip, still to be manufactured, that was bolted to the turret bearing shield. Note at ***2*** the raised floor plate over the bore evacuator compressor.

Gearbox Installation

Gearbox Installation

These two pages, including both photographs and write up, have been provided with kind permission from Brian Rutter. He describes in some detail the process the restoration engineers had to re-learn in order to be able to both remove and replace the **Zahnradfabrik Friedrichshafen AK 7-200** gearbox.

In the words of Brian:

Here is the basic gist of how to put a gearbox in a Panther.

As the Panther gearbox is mounted in the front of the hull beneath the front glacis plate, it is therefore impossible to lower the gearbox in its horizontal/natural working position into the hull after the removal of the top deck front hatch plate. Also, even if it is turned through 90 degrees whilst horizontal, it still will not fit through the top aperture in the hull roof. The only way to get the gearbox into the hull is to suspend it from its rear end so that it hangs nearly vertically at an angle.

To lower the gearbox into the hull, it first has to have a lifting sub frame attached. This had to be designed/ made so as to give the correct angle for when the gearbox is lowered into the hull allowing clearance between the gearbox and the hull top deck aperture. The lifting ring of the sub frame is located at the rear end of the gearbox.

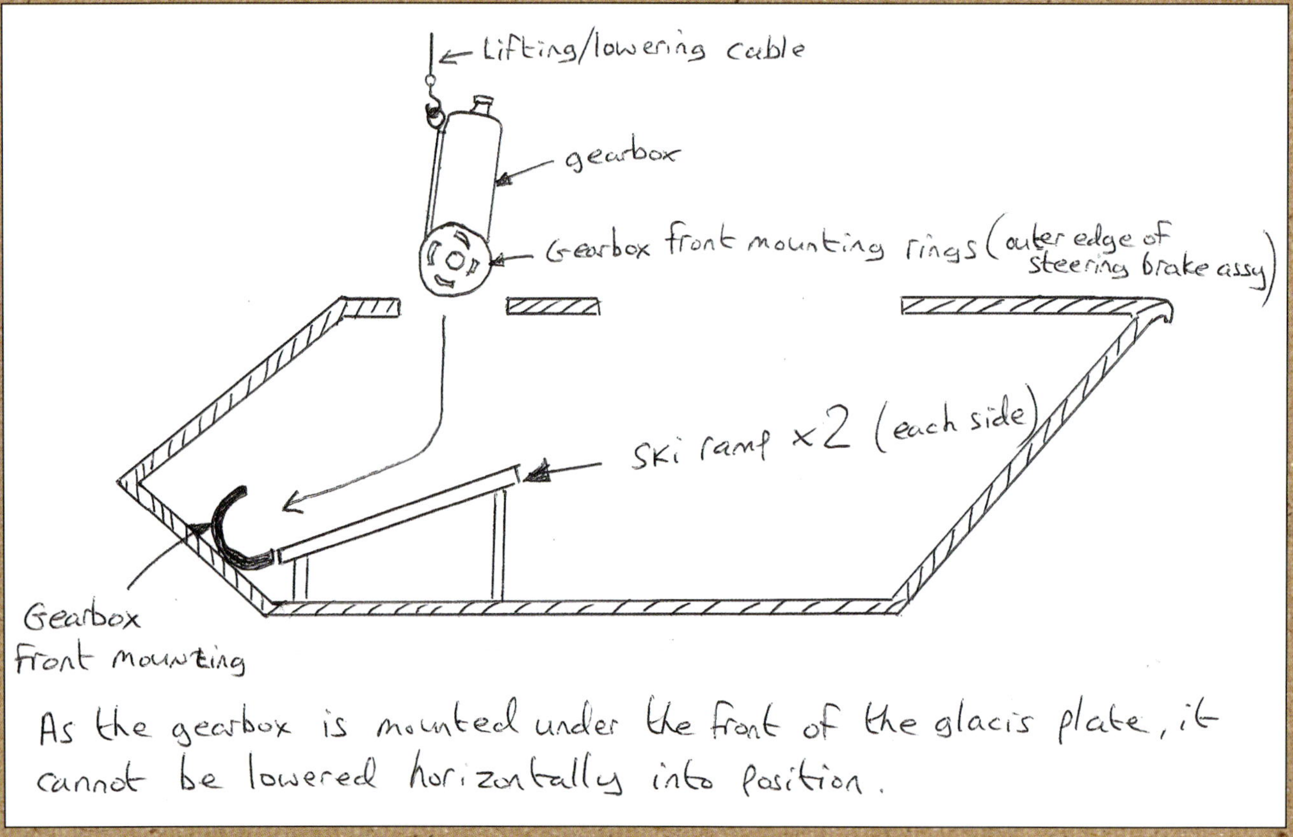

Gearbox Installation

A pair of ski ramps were designed/made and fitted/mounted to the lower bolt holes of the front gearbox mounting. These ski ramps have exactly the same spacing/pitch as the front gearbox mountings. When the gearbox is lowered into the hull, it is then aligned/located onto the ski ramps using the same location lips/rings on it, that hold it into the front mounting in the hull.

As the gearbox is lowered further, (more weight transferred to the ski ramps) gravity then takes the gearbox down the ski ramp into the front of the hull and finally into the front mountings. The gearbox front mountings are then fitted with the gearbox retaining C clamps .

Now that the front of the gearbox is securely retained in the front mountings, the ski ramps can be removed and the rear of the gearbox can be lowered into the rear gearbox mounting and secured. The gearbox can pivot in the front mountings even when secured. This allows for any alignment issues. The lifting sub frame can now be removed from the gearbox.

After the quick release drive shafts and all the brake and driving controls have been re-connected to the gearbox the Radio sub frame assembly can then be re-installed above the gearbox (it is on quick release catches for this purpose). Finally the top deck front hatch plate can be re fitted. To remove the gearbox, the whole procedure is just reversed, using the ski ramps to pull the gearbox up and out with the lifting sub frame.

Zimmerit

Zimmerit was a paste-like coating developed by the German company **Chemische Werke Zimmer & Co (Berlin)**, and was used on mid and late-war German armoured fighting vehicles in order to prevent magnetic mines being attached to the hull. This was applied to the vehicle as a thick putty, patterned, and then hardened with blowtorches. The coating was normally ridged to increase overall thickness, the high points on the pattern increasing the average thickness without adding more weight [22].

The paste was composed of the following:

40% Barium Sulphate – $BaSO_4$
25% Polyvinyl Acetate – PVA (wood glue)
15% pigment (ochre)
10% Zinc Sulphide – ZnS
10% sawdust

Composition

The challenge for restorer Brian Rutter was to recreate the paste with modern commercially available elements, which when painted and then chipped through normal wear and tear, would look the same as the original Zimmerit material.

He achieved this by used a car body filler that had the same natural colour as the original Zimmerit, and then added a specific grade of shot blast grit so as to give the same texture as the original material.

He mixed 5 litre tins of filler with grit at a time (pre-mixed without hardener). When he applied a quantity of new Zimmerit from the tin, he would add only a very small amount of hardener. This gave him a cure time of about 4 hours for application as opposed to the amount recommended by the filler manufacturer, (about 10-15 minutes cure time). This also had the advantage of not discolouring the filler as the hardener was bright red. He used about 20-25 litres of Zimmerit filler on the hull and about 10-15 litres on the turret.

Application

When the tank first arrived at Arnesby there was some original Zimmerit still on the side walls of the hull behind the road wheels. Brian was able to measure the width, pitch and approximate thickness of the application. He applied it by hand and after a little practise, was able to replicate the same pattern as the original Demag style/pattern – according to Brian the trick to this was all in the wrist action!

Accuracy

Given the results, it is quite remarkable that all of this was done quite a few years before we supplied the original war time photos of the actual tank to Brian. There are slight differences in some areas, but overall the Zimmerit is nearly identical to its original appearance 70 years ago.

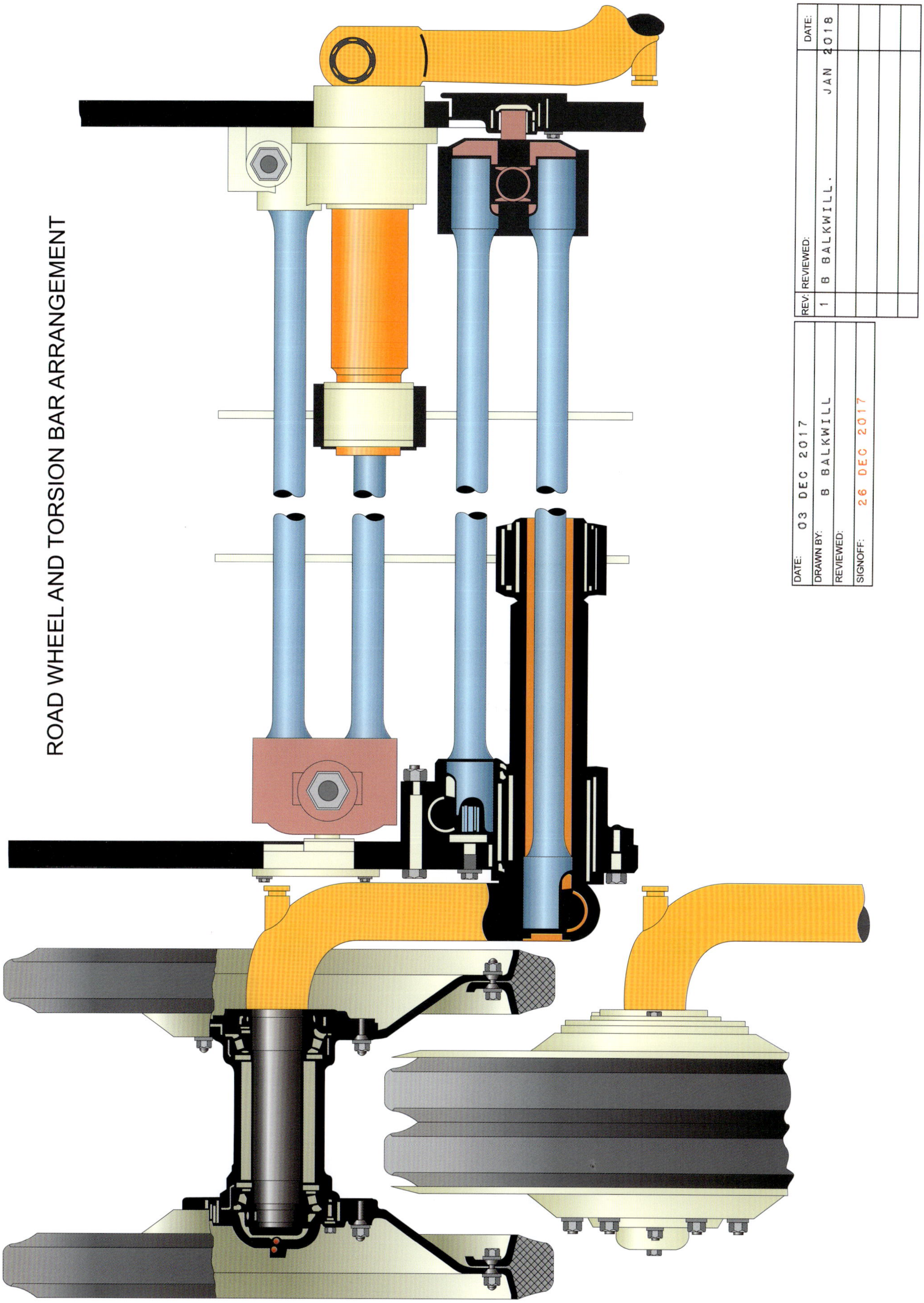
ROAD WHEEL AND TORSION BAR ARRANGEMENT
REV: REVIEWED: DATE:
1 B BALKWILL. JAN 2018
DATE: 03 DEC 2017
DRAWN BY: B BALKWILL
REVIEWED:
SIGNOFF: 26 DEC 2017

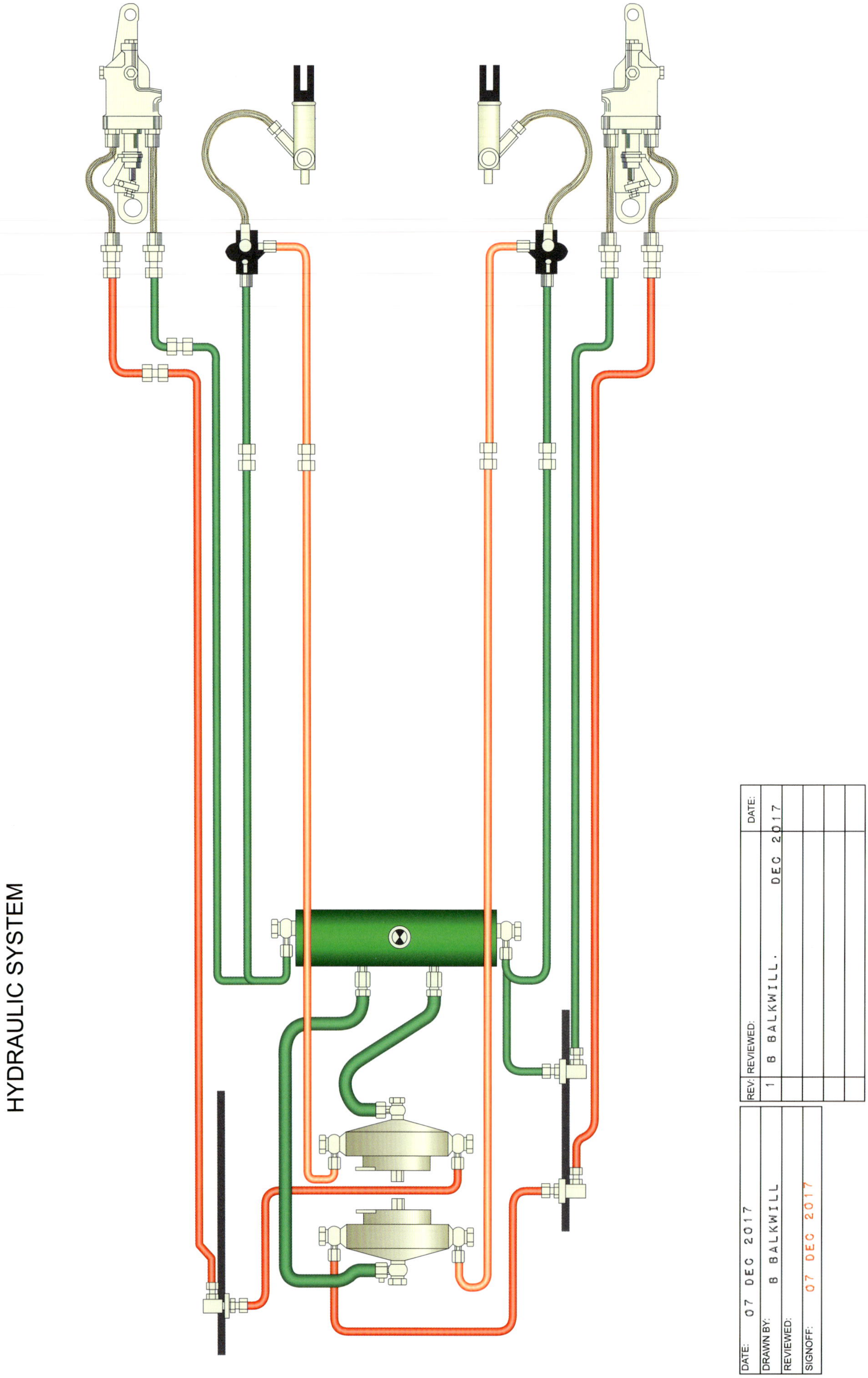
HYDRAULIC SYSTEM
DATE: 07 DEC 2017
DRAWN BY: B BALKWILL
REVIEWED:
SIGNOFF: 07 DEC 2017
REV: REVIEWED: DATE:
1 B BALKWILL. DEC 2017

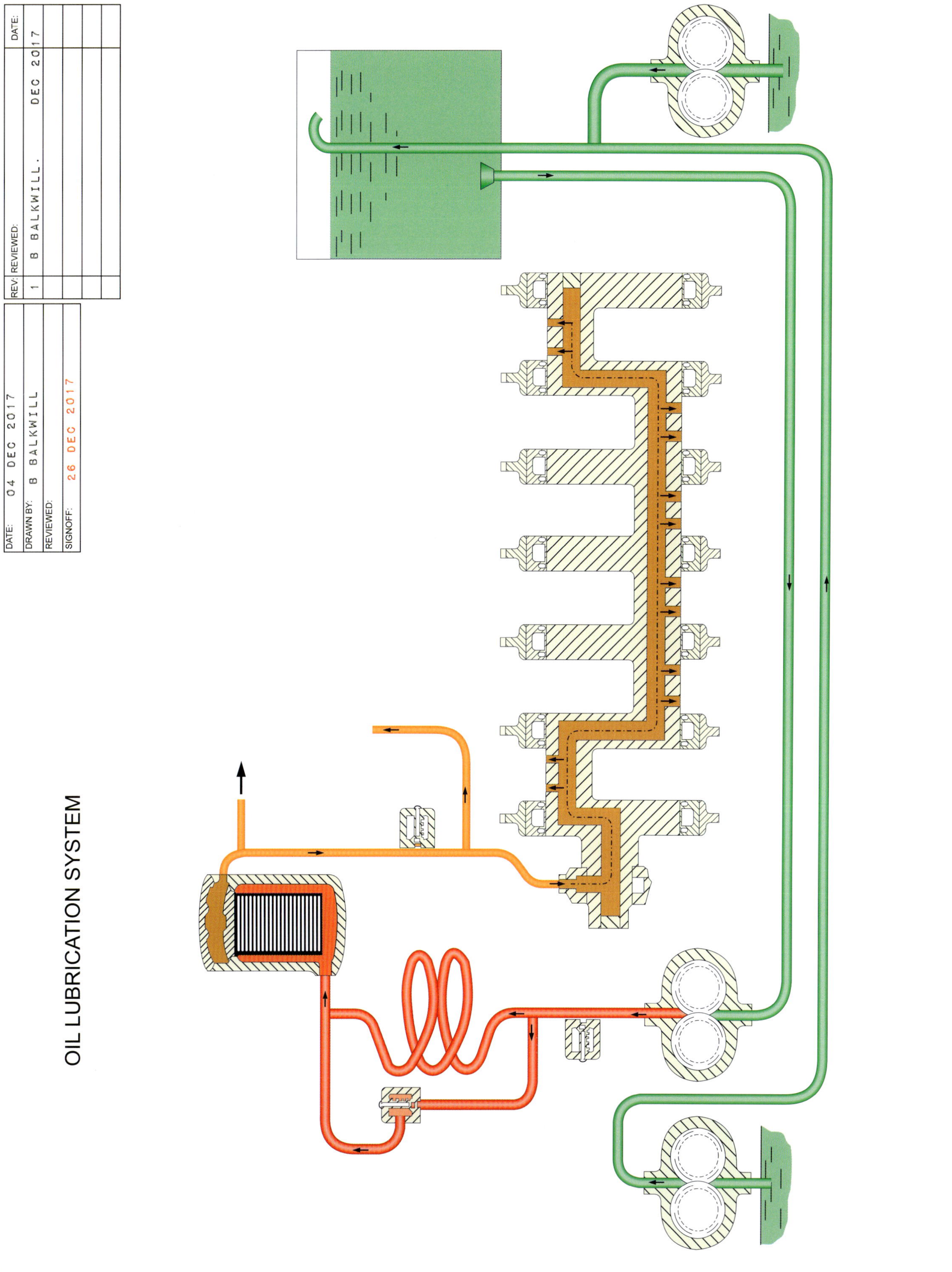
OIL LUBRICATION SYSTEM
DATE: 04 DEC 2017
DRAWN BY: B BALKWILL
REVIEWED:
SIGNOFF: 26 DEC 2017
REV: REVIEWED: DATE:
1 B BALKWILL. DEC 2017

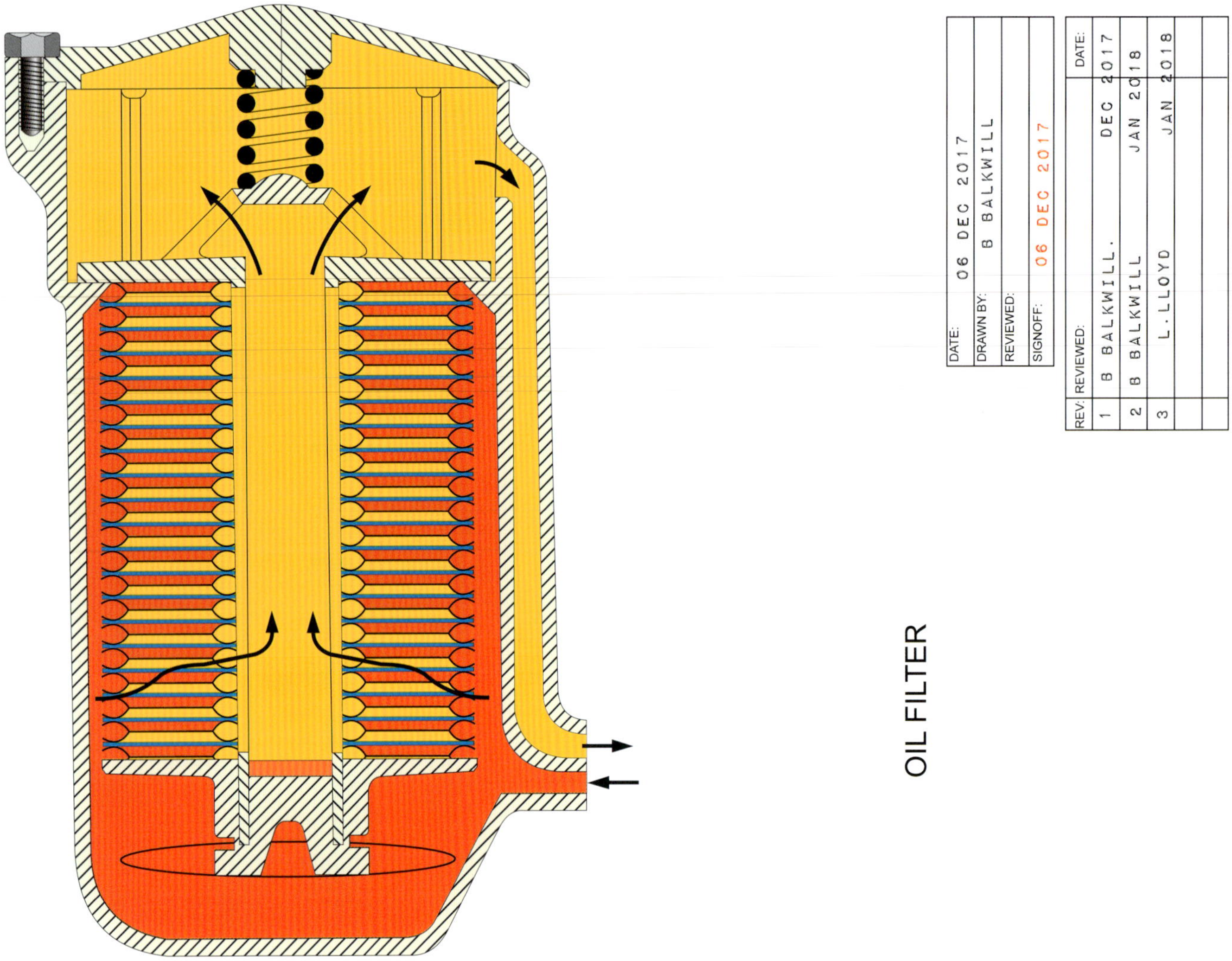
DATE: 06 DEC 2017
DRAWN BY: B BALKWILL
REVIEWED:
SIGNOFF: 06 DEC 2017
REV: REVIEWED: DATE:
1 B BALKWILL. DEC 2017
2 B BALKWILL JAN 2018
3 L.LLOYD JAN 2018
OIL FILTER

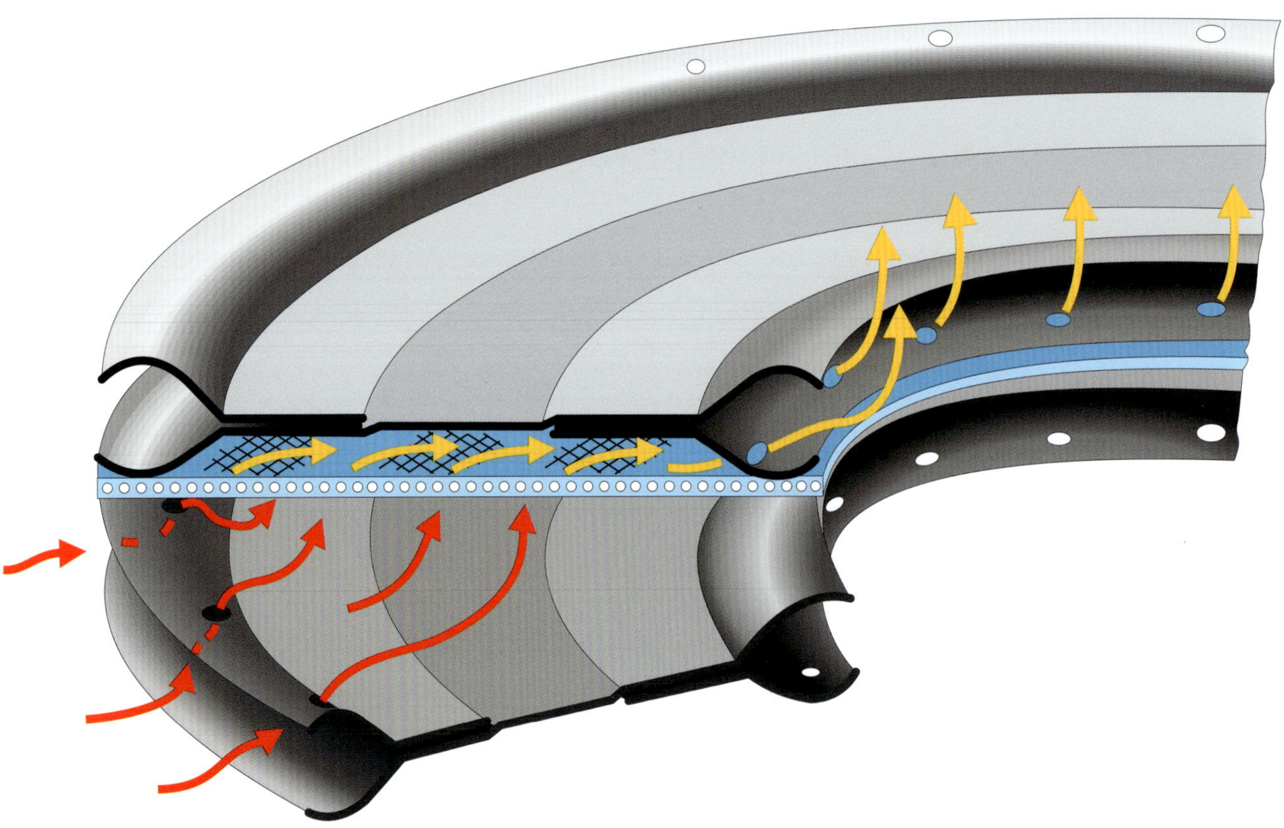

COLD STARTING: **ON**

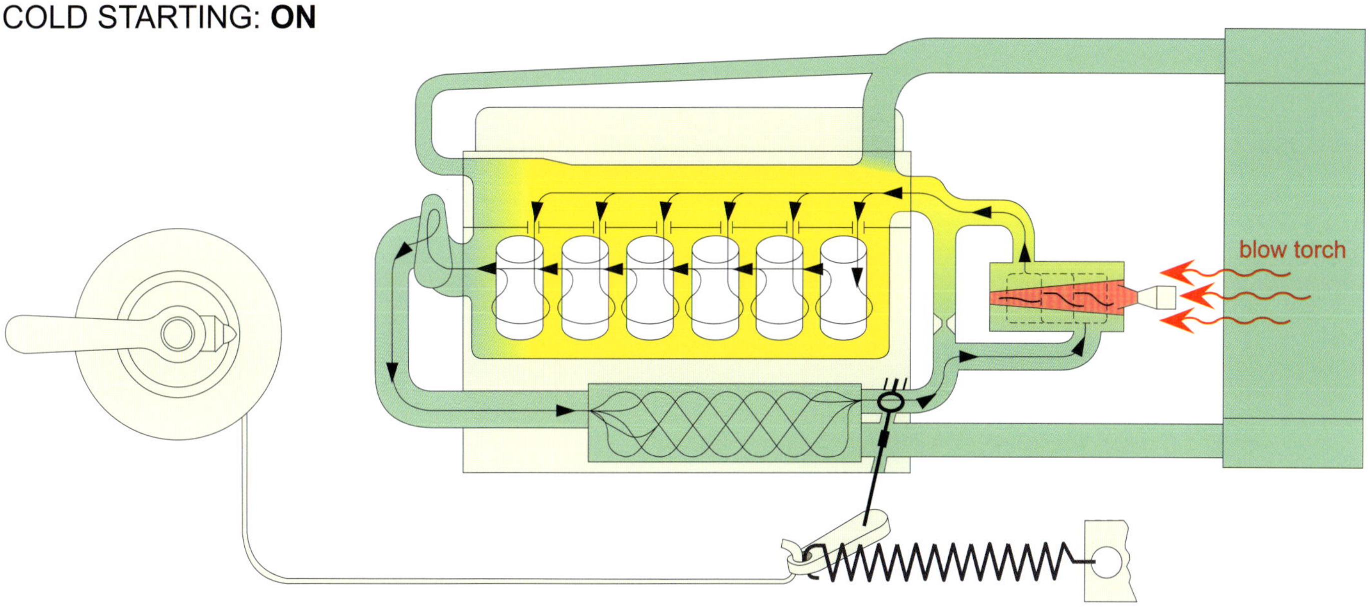

When using the blow torch for cold weather starting the engine is not turned over using the electrical starter. The heating process instead relies on a convection/capillary action to draw coolant around the engine block when the oil cooler bypass valve is operated. This valve cuts off the flow of coolant to the radiators as well as bypassing the flow of coolant through the oil cooler matrix. The principle relies on the fact that hot water rises and cools as it falls, so when the warmed-up coolant in the engine block from the blow torch heat exchanger starts to cool it will fall back through the water pump and down through the oil cooler bypass channel back to the heat exchanger. The whole process continually repeats itself but gradually slows down as the engine block warms until the engine block has warmed up enough to be able to be turned over using the electrical starter.

COLD STARTING: **OFF**

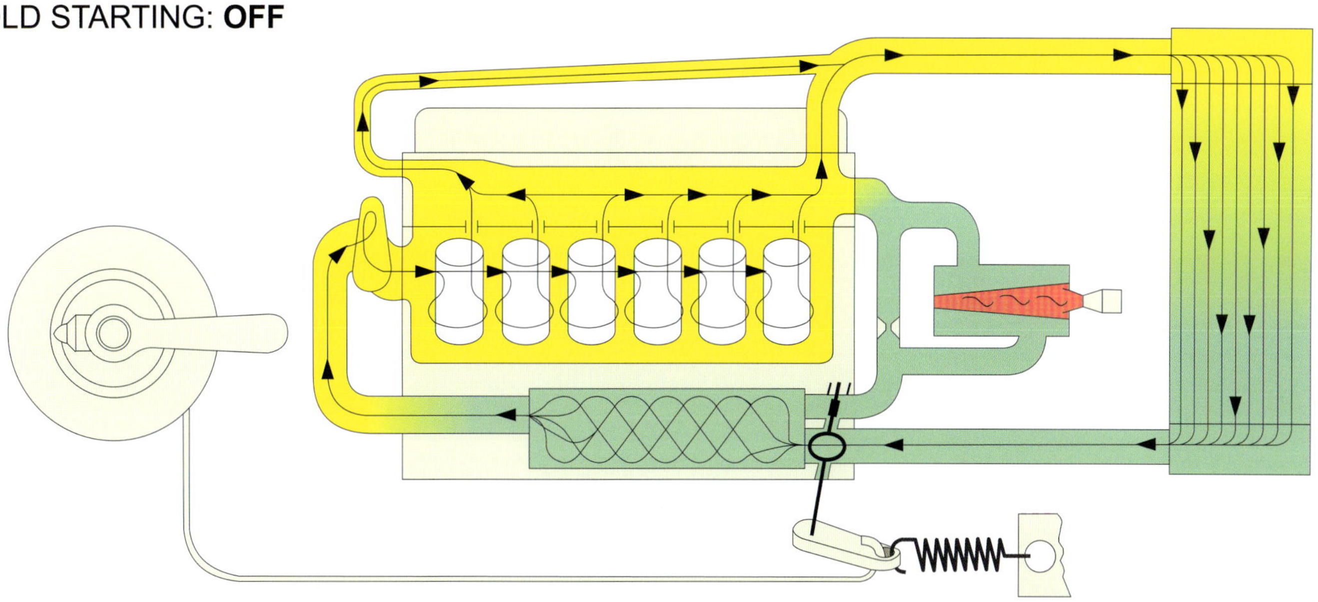

DATE:	05 DEC 2017
DRAWN BY:	B BALKWILL
REVIEWED:	
SIGNOFF:	06 DEC 2017

REV:	REVIEWED:	DATE:
1	B BALKWILL	DEC 2017
2	B. BALKWILL	JAN 2018

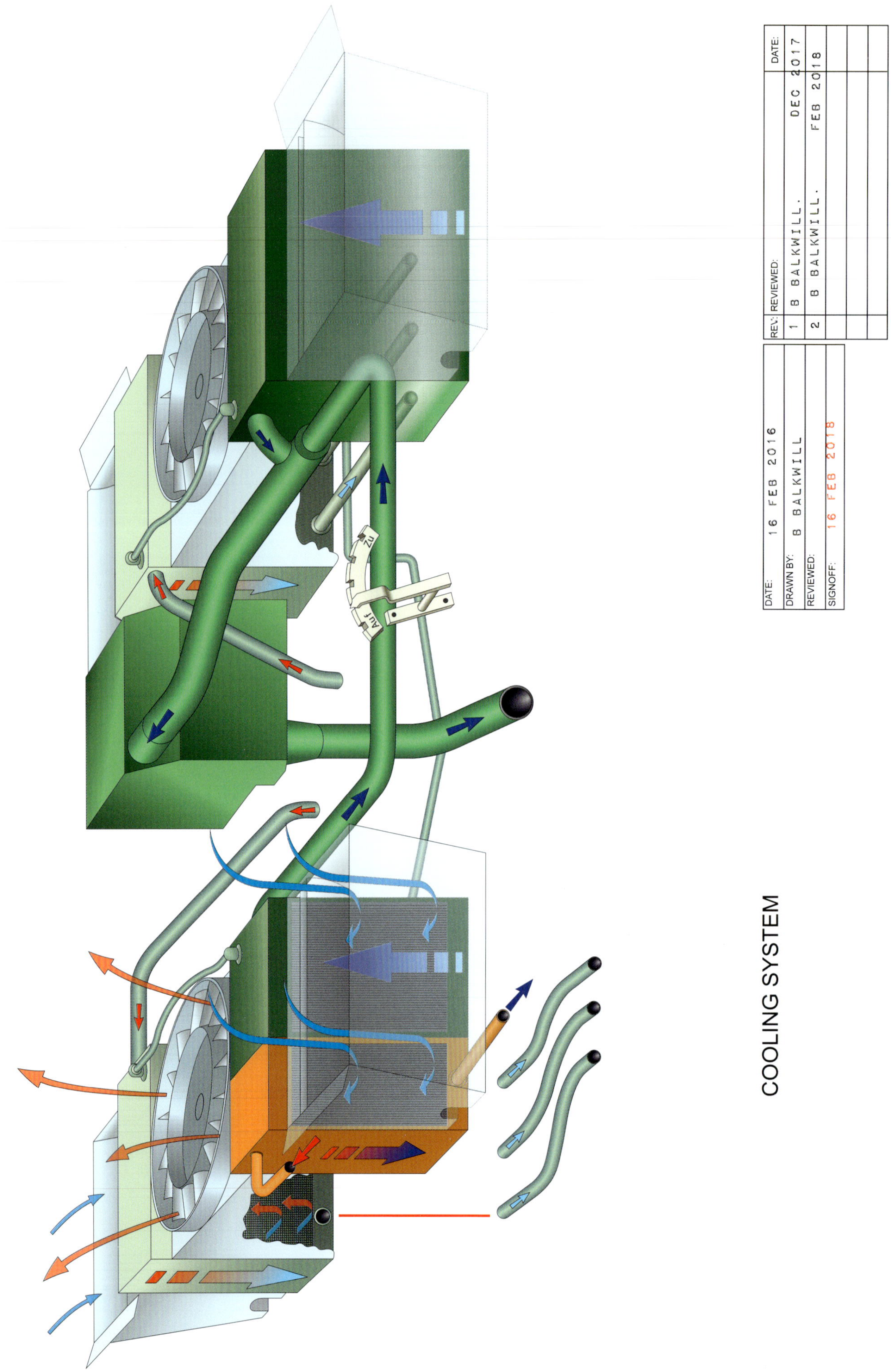
Zu
Auf
DATE: 16 FEB 2016
DRAWN BY: B BALKWILL
REVIEWED:
SIGNOFF: 16 FEB 2018
REV: REVIEWED: DATE:
1 B BALKWILL. DEC 2017
2 B BALKWILL. FEB 2018
COOLING SYSTEM

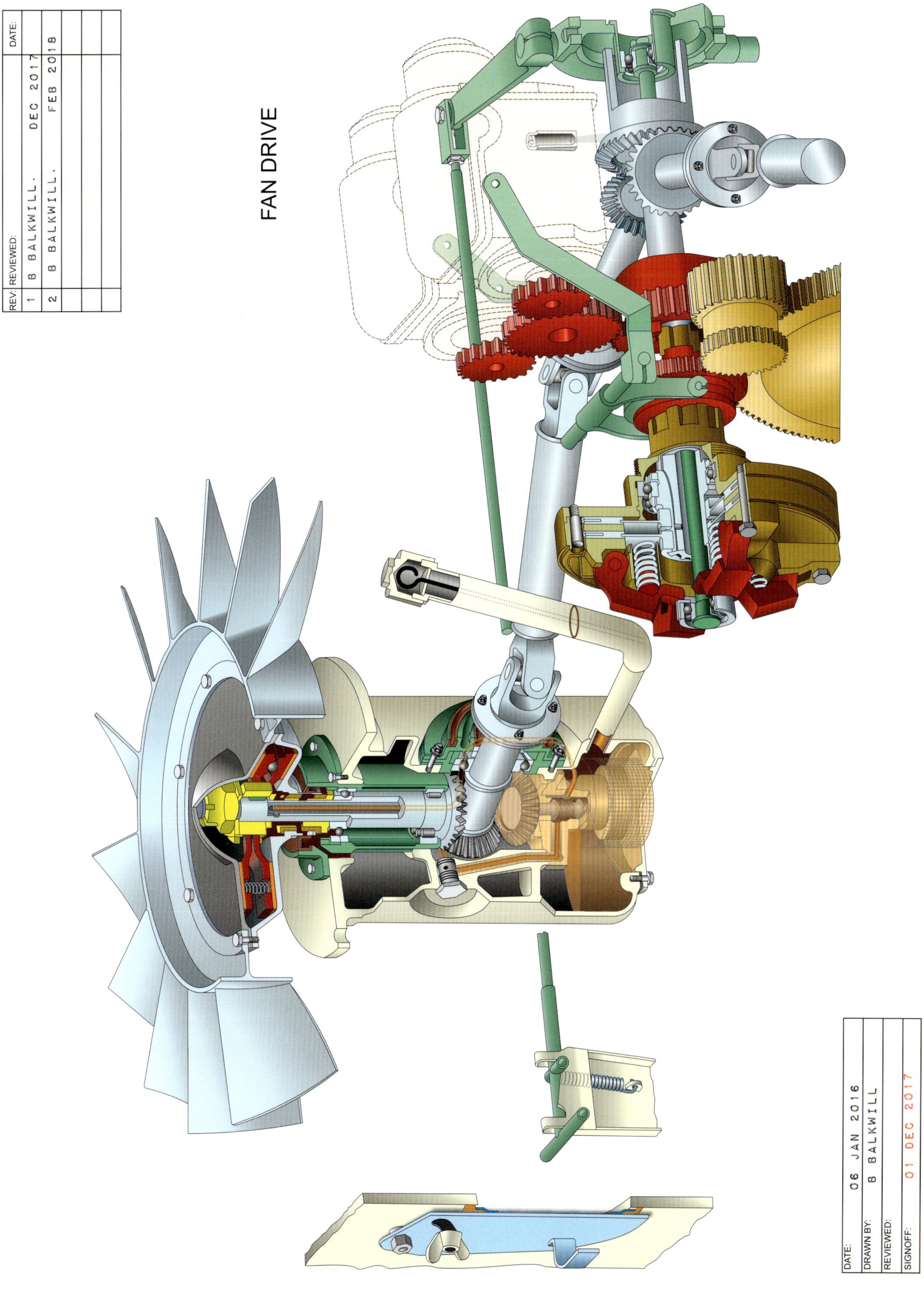
FAN DRIVE
REV: REVIEWED: DATE:
1 B BALKWILL. DEC 2017
2 B BALKWILL. FEB 2018
DATE: 06 JAN 2016
DRAWN BY: B BALKWILL
REVIEWED:
SIGNOFF: 01 DEC 2017

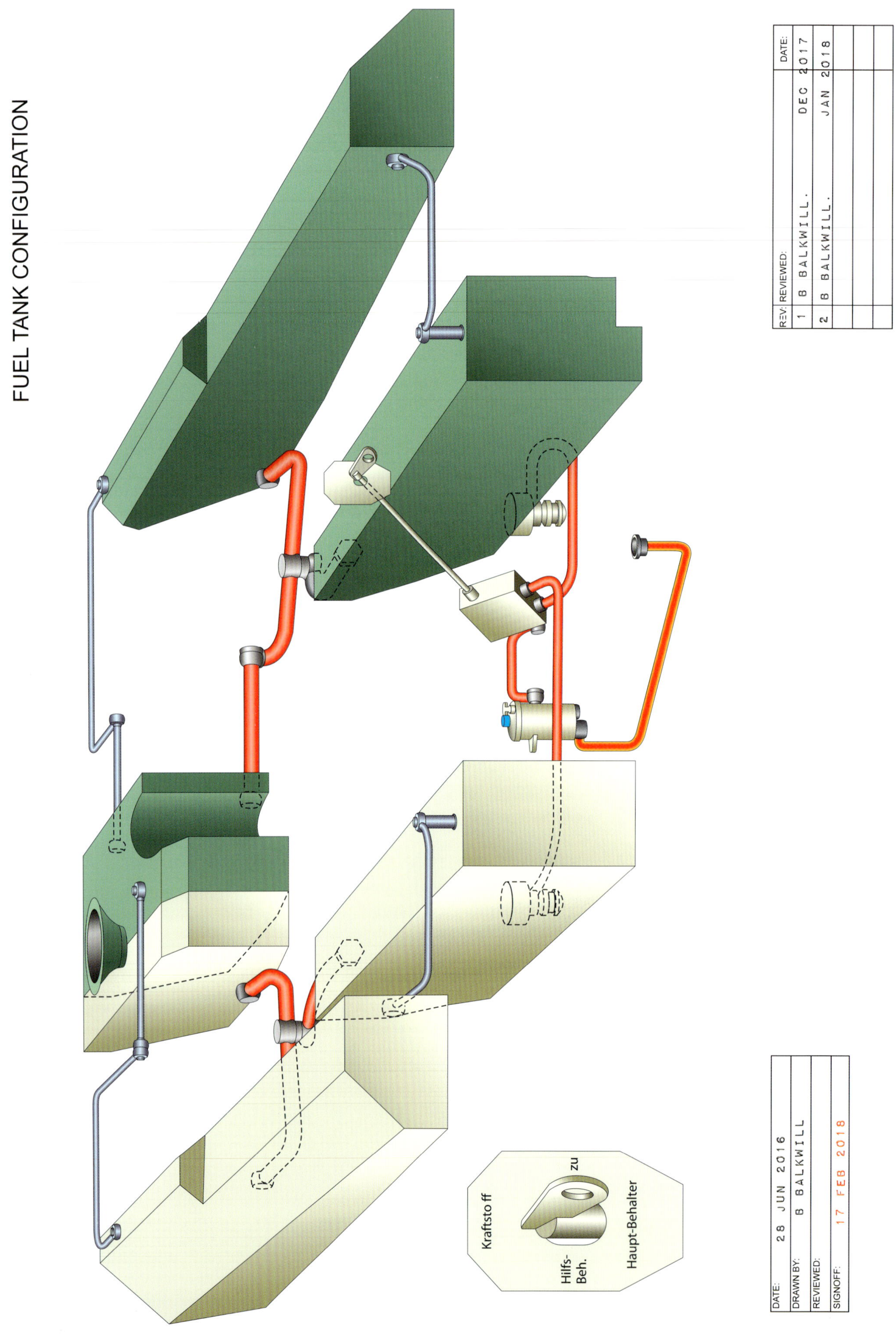
FUEL TANK CONFIGURATION
REV: | REVIEWED: | DATE:
1 | B BALKWILL. | DEC 2017
2 | B BALKWILL. | JAN 2018
Kraftsto ff
zu
Hilfs-
Beh.
Haupt-Behalter
DATE: 28 JUN 2016
DRAWN BY: B BALKWILL
REVIEWED:
SIGNOFF: 17 FEB 2018

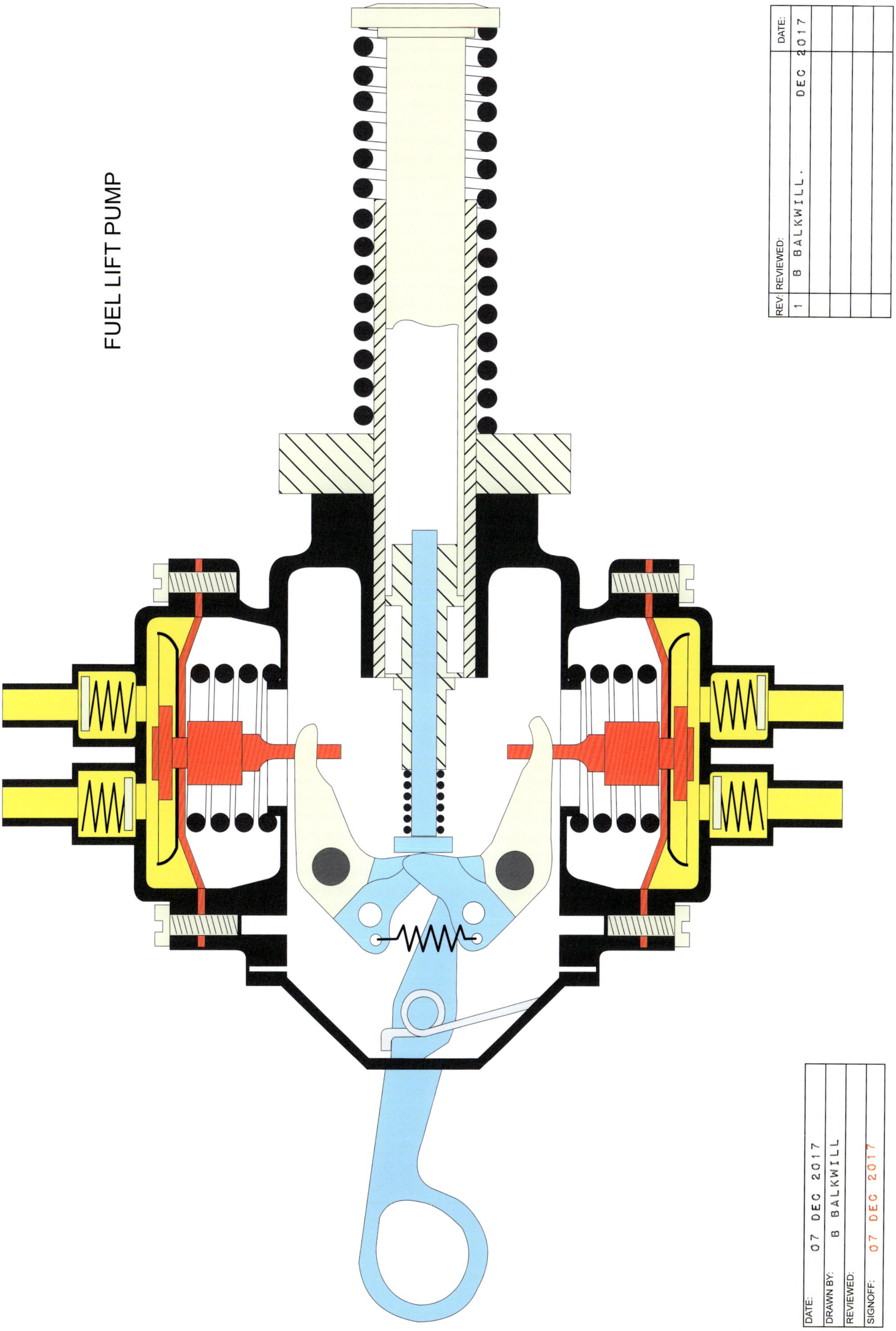
FUEL LIFT PUMP
REV: REVIEWED: DATE:
1 B BALKWILL. DEC 2017
DATE: 07 DEC 2017
DRAWN BY: B BALKWILL
REVIEWED:
SIGNOFF: 07 DEC 2017

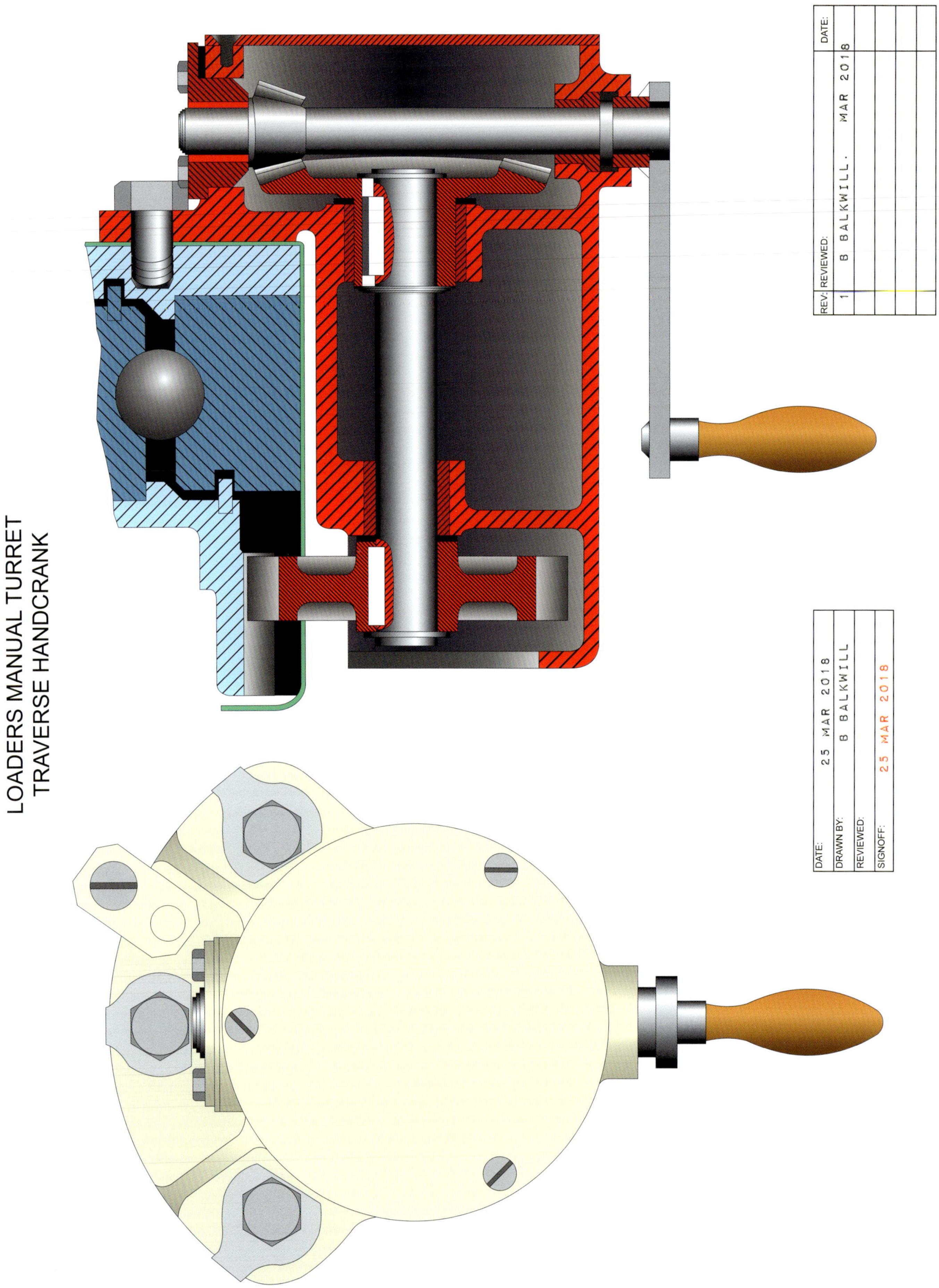
LOADERS MANUAL TURRET
TRAVERSE HANDCRANK
REV: REVIEWED: DATE:
1 B BALKWILL. MAR 2018
DATE: 25 MAR 2018
DRAWN BY: B BALKWILL
REVIEWED:
SIGNOFF: 25 MAR 2018

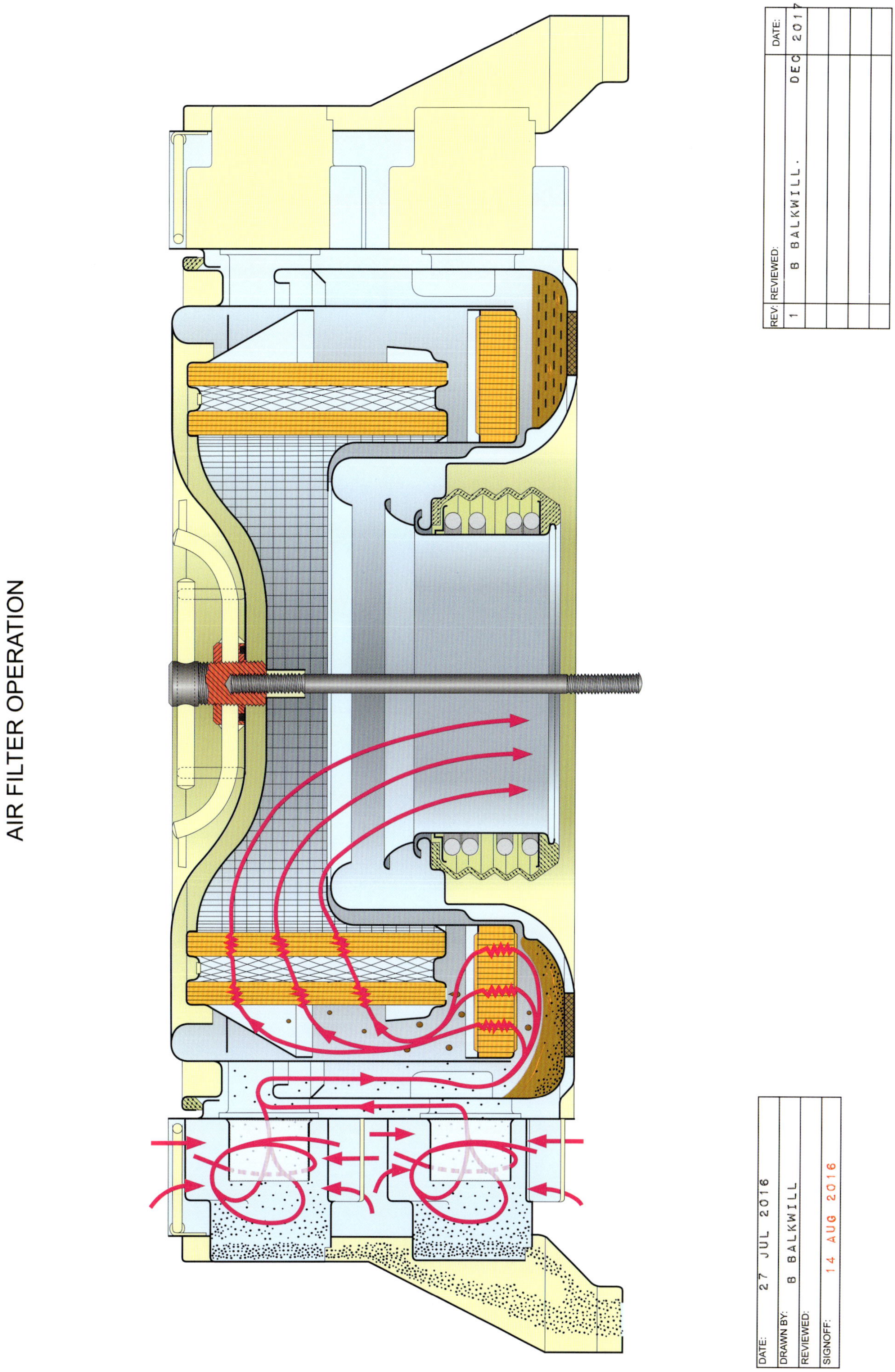
AIR FILTER OPERATION
REV: REVIEWED: DATE:
1 B BALKWILL. DEC 2017
DATE: 27 JUL 2016
DRAWN BY: B BALKWILL
REVIEWED:
SIGNOFF: 14 AUG 2016

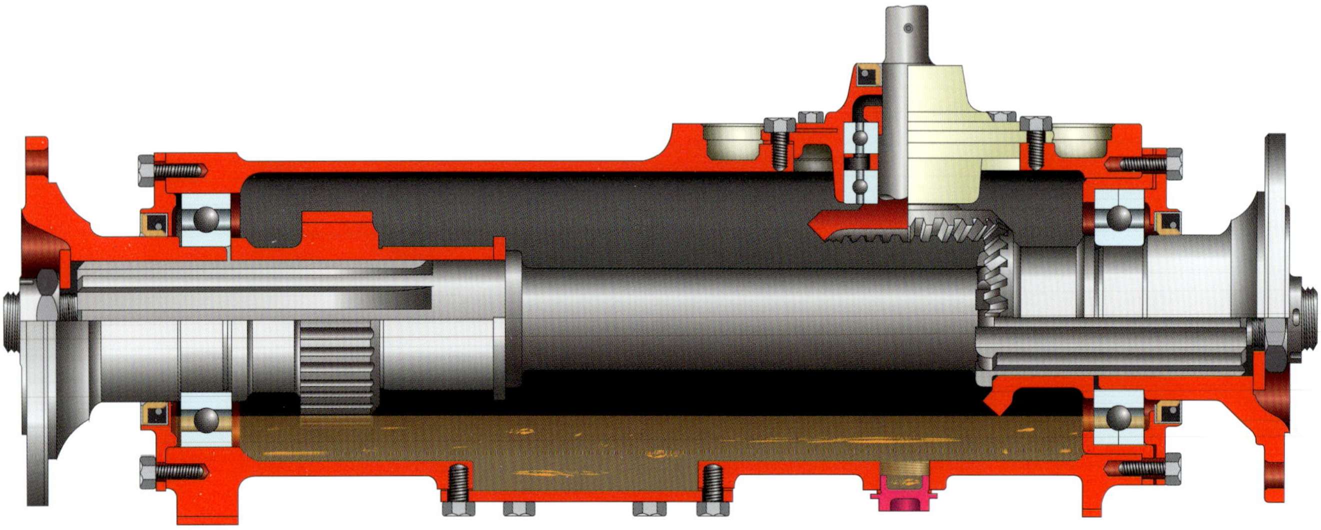

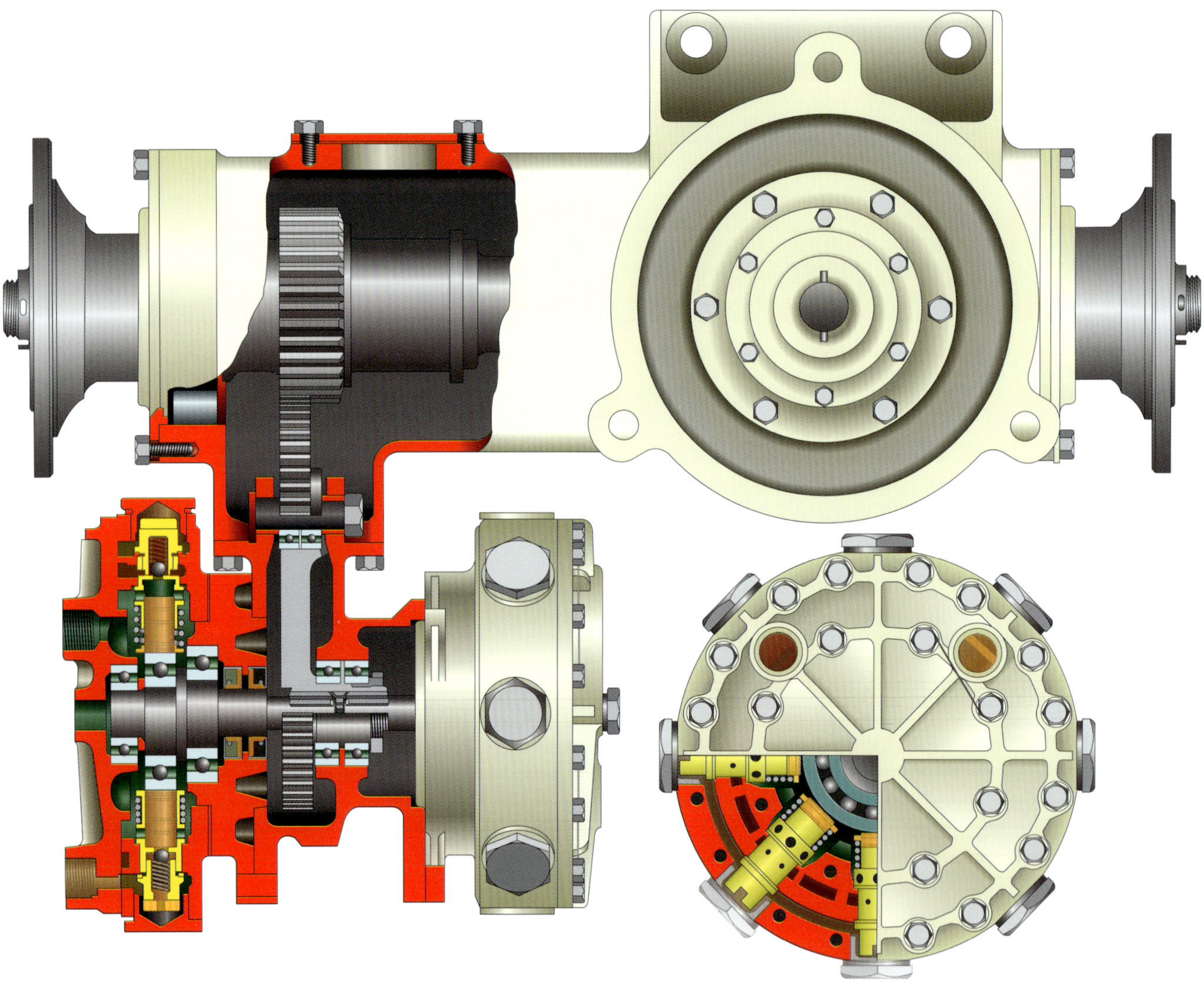

DATE:	13 JUN 2016
DRAWN BY:	B BALKWILL
REVIEWED:	
SIGNOFF:	25 JUN 2016

PTO ASSEMBLY

REV:	REVIEWED:	DATE:
1	B BALKWILL	DEC 2017
2	B. BALKWILL	JAN 2018

Main references used:

[1] **29 July 2013** - email from Martin Block confirming and adding to Paul Hocking data on AHF (Axis History Forum).

[2] **23 December 2010** – email from Vincent Lecourt.

[3] **13 March 2013** – missinglynx.com
http://www.network54.com/Forum/47207/thread/1363183400/Demag+Panther+Ausf+A++Fgst.Nr.+158134

[4] Date unknown (but before **3 April 2015**) – email shown to us by Wheatcroft Collection staff member.

[5] **3rd April 2015** – email from Darren Neely.

[6] **14 October 2017** – email from Fred Blais.

[7] **20 May 2013** – email from Frédéric Deprun.

[8] **20 May 2013** – email from Frédéric Deprun.

[9] **29 July 2013** - email from Martin Block confirming and adding to Paul Hocking data on AHF (Axis History Forum).

[10] **29 July 2013** - email from Martin Block confirming and adding to Paul Hocking data on AHF (Axis History Forum).

[11] **14 December 2017** – email from Dr. Spannocchi.

[12] **Panther Project Volume One - Drivetrain and Hull**; Lee Lloyd, Brian Balkwill & Alasdair Johnston, The Wheatcroft Collection. ISBN 978-0-9556422-0-3 2007.

[13] **Germany's Panther Tank: The Quest for Combat Supremacy**; Thomas L. Jentz, Schiffer Publishing Ltd. ISBN 0-88740-812-5 1995.

[14] **Panther & Its Variants**; Walter J. Spielberger, Schiffer Publishing Ltd. ISBN 0-88740-397-2 1993.

[15] **6 February 2018** - email from Brian Rutter.

[16] **PzKpfw. V Panther 8**; Waldemar Trojca & Wojciech Molski, AJ-Press. ISBN 83-7273-175-X 2006.

[17] **Panzer Tracts No.5-2 Panzerkampfwagen "Panther" Ausfuehrung A**; Thomas L. Jentz & Hilary Louis Doyle, Panzer Tracks. ISBN 0-9744862-1-3 2003.

[18] **Les matériels radio de la Wehrmacht 1935-194**5; Pierre Metsu, Editions Heimdal. ISBN 2-84048-181-2 2004.

[19] **Wireless for Wehrmacht in Detail**; Alois Veselý & František Kořán, Wings & Wheels Publications. ISBN 80-86416-15-1. 2001.

[20] **D655/1b Pz.Kpfw. Ausf. A,D und Abarten Gerätbeschreibung und Bedienungsanweisung zum Fahrgestell**.

[21] **PzKpfw. V Panther 1**; Waldemar Trojca, AJ-Press. ISBN 83-7273-012-X 1999.

[22] **Panther External Appearance & Design Changes**; Roddy Macdougall & Martin Block, Abteilung 502. ISBN 8-436535-579889 2016.

[23] **PzKpfw. V Panther 4**; Waldemar Trojca, AJ-Press. ISBN 83-7273-051-6 2000.

Other references consulted during the course of creating this book:

[24] **Panther In Detail**; Uwe Feist & Bruce Culver, Ryton Publications. 1998.

[25] **Panzer Tracts No.5-1 Panzerkampfwagen "Panther" Ausfuehrung D**; Thomas L. Jentz & Hilary Louis Doyle, Panzer Tracks. ISBN 0-9708407-8-0 2003.

[26] **Panzer Tracts No.5-1 Panzerkampfwagen "Panther" Ausfuehrung G**; Thomas L. Jentz & Hilary Louis Doyle, Panzer Tracks. ISBN 0-9744862-7-2 2004.

[27] **Panther On The Battlefield 2 - Volume 11**; Péter Barnaky, PeKo Publishing Kft. ISBN 978-80072-9-0 2016.

[28] **Operation "Zitadelle" July 1943 The Decisive Battle of World War II**; Franz Kurowski, J.J. Fedorowicz Publishing Inc. ISBN 0-921991-63-0 2003.

[29] **Achtung Panzer No.4 Panther, Jagdpanther & Brummbär**; Hiromu Araki, Koji Ogawa/Dai Nippon Kaiga. ISBN 4-499-22643-0 1994.

[30] **Nurnberg's Panzer Factory A Photographic Study**; Roddy Macdougall & Darren Neely. Panzerwrecks/1010 Printing International Ltd. ISBN 9-781908-032065 2013.

[31] **Panther 2**; Ground Power Special Issue May, '02, Delta Publishing Co. Ltd. ISBN 1-103292-052357 2002.

[32] **Panther 3**; Ground Power Special Issue June, '02, Delta Publishing Co. Ltd. ISBN 1-103292-062356 2002.

[33] **History File N001 Panther Panzerkampfwagen V (SdKfz 171)**; Thomas Anderson, Auriga Publishing International SRL. 2006.

Coming Publications

At the last count the Wheatcroft Collection had seventeen vehicles, in various states of running order or requiring restoration, based on the Medium Tank M4.

medium tank M4

Being one of the most iconic tanks of World War II, and of course in subsequent conflicts later in the 20th Century, we would be remiss if the Research Squad did not take time to address ourselves to the task of documenting the numerous variants of this armoured vehicle as owned by Kevin Wheatcroft.

Our plan is to produce at least two volumes of work on the recording of The Wheatcroft Collections M4 tanks. Recording photographically as previously we will present both exterior and interior details to the highest standard we can achieve...

For up to date news of products from The Research Squad please visit our website at: www.theresearchsquad.com

1

2

Our planned volume, **the shed**, based on the varied range of military and vehicular items as collected by Kevin Wheatcroft over the years, was put on hold as we worked on other more important projects. This volume though we have now essentially completed and will be published in due course...

Please note that all the works in production by The Research Squad are subject to change at very short notice in relation to content and subject material...